Extending OpenStack

Leverage extended OpenStack projects to implement
containerization, deployment, and architecting robust
cloud solutions

Omar Khedher

BIRMINGHAM - MUMBAI

Extending OpenStack

Commissioning Editor: Gebin George
Acquisition Editor: Rahul Nair
Content Development Editor: Abhishek Jadhav
Technical Editor: Swathy Mohan
Copy Editor: Safis Editing, Dipti Mankame
Project Coordinator: Judie Jose
Proofreader: Safis Editing
Indexer: Priyanka Dhadke
Graphics: Tom Scaria
Production Coordinator: Shraddha Falebhai

First published: February 2018

Production reference: 1260218

Published by Packt Publishing Ltd.
Livery Place
35 Livery Street
Birmingham
B3 2PB, UK.

ISBN 978-1-78646-553-5

www.packtpub.com

`mapt.io`

Mapt is an online digital library that gives you full access to over 5,000 books and videos, as well as industry leading tools to help you plan your personal development and advance your career. For more information, please visit our website.

Why subscribe?

- Spend less time learning and more time coding with practical eBooks and Videos from over 4,000 industry professionals

- Improve your learning with Skill Plans built especially for you

- Get a free eBook or video every month

- Mapt is fully searchable

- Copy and paste, print, and bookmark content

PacktPub.com

Did you know that Packt offers eBook versions of every book published, with PDF and ePub files available? You can upgrade to the eBook version at `www.PacktPub.com` and as a print book customer, you are entitled to a discount on the eBook copy. Get in touch with us at `service@packtpub.com` for more details.

At `www.PacktPub.com`, you can also read a collection of free technical articles, sign up for a range of free newsletters, and receive exclusive discounts and offers on Packt books and eBooks.

Contributors

About the author

Omar Khedher is a systems and network engineer. He has been involved in several cloud-related project based on AWS and OpenStack. He spent few years as cloud system engineer with talented teams to architect infrastructure in the public cloud at Fyber in Berlin.

Omar wrote few academic publications for his PhD targeting cloud performance and was the author of *Mastering OpenStack, OpenStack Sahara Essentials* and co-authored the second edition of the *Mastering OpenStack* books by Packt.

I would like to thank immensely my parents and brothers for their encouragement. A special thank goes to Dr. M. Jarraya. A thank you to my dears Belgacem, Andre, Silvio and Caro for the support. Thank you Tamara for the long support and patience. Thank you PacktPub team for the immense dedication. Many thankful words to the OpenStack family.

About the reviewer

Radhakrishnan Ramakrishnan is a DevOps engineer with CloudEnablers Inc, a product-based company targeting on multi-cloud orchestration and multi-cloud governance platforms, located in Chennai, India. He has more than 3 years of experience in Linux server administration, OpenStack Cloud administration, and Hadoop cluster administration in various distributions, such as Apache Hadoop, Hortonworks Data Platform, and the Cloudera distribution of Hadoop. His areas of interest are reading books, listening to music, and gardening.

> *I would like to thank my family, friends, employers and employees for their continued support.*

Packt is searching for authors like you

If you're interested in becoming an author for Packt, please visit `authors.packtpub.com` and apply today. We have worked with thousands of developers and tech professionals, just like you, to help them share their insight with the global tech community. You can make a general application, apply for a specific hot topic that we are recruiting an author for, or submit your own idea.

Table of Contents

Preface

OpenStack is a very popular cloud computing platform that has enabled several organizations to successfully implement their Infrastructure as a Service (IaaS) platforms in the last few years. This book will guide you through new features of the latest OpenStack releases and how to bring them into production straight away in an agile way.

It starts by showing you how to expand your current OpenStack setup and approach your next OpenStack Data Center generation deployment. You will discover how to extend your storage and network capacity, and also take advantage of containerization technology, such as Docker and Kubernetes in OpenStack. In addition, it is an opportunity to explore the power of big data as a service implemented in OpenStack by integrating the Sahara project. This book will teach you how to build Hadoop clusters and launch jobs in a very simple way. Then, it will dedicate time to automating and deploying applications on top of OpenStack. You will discover how to create and publish your own application in simple steps using the novel application catalog service in OpenStack code named Murano. The final part of the book will shed the light on the identity service and will go through a consolidated authentication setup using Keystone. The book will be enclosed by leveraging the right tool to conduct and extend benchmarking performances tests against an operating OpenStack environment using the Rally platform. By the end of this book, you will be ready to enter the next phase of OpenStack success by extending and customizing your private cloud based on your requirements.

Who this book is for

This book is for system administrators, cloud architects, and developers who have experience working with OpenStack and are ready to step up and extend its functionalities. A good knowledge of the basic OpenStack components is required. In addition, familiarity with Linux boxes and a good understanding of network and virtualization jargon is required.

What this book covers

Chapter 1, *Inflating the OpenStack Setup*, describes installing OpenStack from a basic setup model and introduces an expanded OpenStack layout.

Chapter 2, *Massively Scaling Computing Power*, explores the ways to scale the computing availability in a large infrastructure.

Chapter 3, *Enlarging the OpenStack Storage Capabilities*, itemizes the different storage options available in OpenStack and custom plugins.

Chapter 4, *Harnessing the Power of the OpenStack Network Service*, extends the usage of the OpenStack network service.

Chapter 5, *Containerizing in OpenStack*, integrates the Magnum project in OpenStack and itemize its workflow.

Chapter 6, *Managing Big Data in OpenStack*, extends the private cloud setup by covering the big data world and elastic data processing in OpenStack using the Sahara project.

Chapter 7, *Evolving Self-Cloud Ready Applications in OpenStack*, teaches you how to automate deploying applications on top of OpenStack using Murano project.

Chapter 8, *Extending the Applications Catalog Service*, explores the power of Murano plugins by creating customized ones.

Chapter 9, *Consolidating the OpenStack Authentication*, introduces the reader to the new implementation of Keystone in OpenStack and the federated identity concept.

Chapter 10, *Boosting the Extended Cloud Universe*, increases the availability and performance of the OpenStack infrastructure at scale.

To get the most out of this book

The book assumes a moderate level of the Linux operating system and being familiar with the OpenStack ecosystem. A good knowledge and understanding of networking and virtualization technology is required. Having an experience with containerization will help to move faster through the chapters of the book.
Few examples have been written in Python and YAML that would require a basic knowledge on both languages but not necessary.

The installation of the OpenStack environment can be performed at any environment with available resources. The lab environment in this book uses the following software and tools:

- Operating system: CentOS 7 or Ubuntu 14.04
- OpenStack: Mitaka and later releases
- VirtualBox 5.0 or newer
- Vagrant 2.0.1 or newer
- Ansible server 2.4 or newer
- Python 2.7

The OpenStack installation will require the following hardware specifications:

- A host machine with CPU hardware virtualization support
- 8 CPU cores
- 16 GB RAM
- 60 GB free disk space

Feel free to use any tool for the test environment such as Oracle's VirtualBox, Vagrant, or VMware workstation. Many chapters implement a new OpenStack deployment to target the objectives of each one in a fresh installed environment. Feel free to re-deploy OpenStack with different releases across each lab. Make sure that you target the right release with the supported projects. This page can be a good reference to compare different OpenStack releases: https://releases.openstack.org/.

At the time of writing this book, several packages are being developed for new releases. Some old versions might go to end of life. This does not cover the operating system version or system management tools. It is recommended to check the latest version for each package that might not be available anymore based on the provided links throughout this book.

Download the example code files

You can download the example code files for this book from your account at www.packtpub.com. If you purchased this book elsewhere, you can visit www.packtpub.com/support and register to have the files emailed directly to you.

You can download the code files by following these steps:

1. Log in or register at www.packtpub.com.
2. Select the **SUPPORT** tab.
3. Click on **Code Downloads & Errata**.
4. Enter the name of the book in the **Search** box and follow the onscreen instructions.

Once the file is downloaded, please make sure that you unzip or extract the folder using the latest version of:

- WinRAR/7-Zip for Windows
- Zipeg/iZip/UnRarX for Mac
- 7-Zip/PeaZip for Linux

The code bundle for the book is also hosted on GitHub at **https://github.com/PacktPublishing/Extending-OpenStack**. In case there's an update to the code, it will be updated on the existing GitHub repository.

We also have other code bundles from our rich catalog of books and videos available at https://github.com/PacktPublishing/. Check them out!

Download the color images

We also provide a PDF file that has color images of the screenshots/diagrams used in this book. You can download it from https://www.packtpub.com/sites/default/files/downloads/ExtendingOpenStack_ColorImages.pdf.

Conventions used

There are a number of text conventions used throughout this book.

CodeInText: Indicates code words in text, database table names, folder names, filenames, file extensions, pathnames, dummy URLs, user input, and Twitter handles. Here is an example: "Install the nova-docker plugin."

A block of code is set as follows:

```
...
[xenapi]
xenapi_connection_url=http://
xenapi_connection_username=
xenapi_connection_password=
...
```

When we wish to draw your attention to a particular part of a code block, the relevant lines or items are set in bold:

```
[DEFAULT]
compute_driver = xenapi.XenAPIDriver
...
```

Any command-line input or output is written as follows:

```
# git add -A
# git commit -a -m "Add Test Compute Node 02"
```

Bold: Indicates a new term, an important word, or words that you see onscreen. For example, words in menus or dialog boxes appear in the text like this. Here is an example: "Create the first **Node Group Template** for Spark slave node."

Warnings or important notes appear like this.

Tips and tricks appear like this.

Get in touch

Feedback from our readers is always welcome.

General feedback: Email feedback@packtpub.com and mention the book title in the subject of your message. If you have questions about any aspect of this book, please email us at questions@packtpub.com.

Errata: Although we have taken every care to ensure the accuracy of our content, mistakes do happen. If you have found a mistake in this book, we would be grateful if you would report this to us. Please visit www.packtpub.com/submit-errata, selecting your book, clicking on the Errata Submission Form link, and entering the details.

Piracy: If you come across any illegal copies of our works in any form on the Internet, we would be grateful if you would provide us with the location address or website name. Please contact us at copyright@packtpub.com with a link to the material.

If you are interested in becoming an author: If there is a topic that you have expertise in and you are interested in either writing or contributing to a book, please visit authors.packtpub.com.

Reviews

Please leave a review. Once you have read and used this book, why not leave a review on the site that you purchased it from? Potential readers can then see and use your unbiased opinion to make purchase decisions, we at Packt can understand what you think about our products, and our authors can see your feedback on their book. Thank you!

For more information about Packt, please visit packtpub.com.

1
Inflating the OpenStack Setup

"The past resembles the future more than one drop of water resembles another."

-Ibn Khaldoun

Nowadays, OpenStack has become a very mature cloud computing software solution, more so than it ever was before. It is a unique project because of its tremendous growth in setup and development. Now, thanks to OpenStack, it has become possible to build your own cloud in a cheaper, more elegant, and more flexible way. The official OpenStack website, `https://www.openstack.org/` defines the reason for using such a great solution:

> *OpenStack software controls large pools of compute, storage, and networking resources throughout a data center, managed through a dashboard or through the OpenStack API. OpenStack works with popular enterprise and open source technologies making it ideal for heterogeneous infrastructure.*

By looking at the roadmaps of OpenStack's development over the past few years, several open source projects have been incubated under the umbrella of OpenStack, such as big data, databases, security, and containerization technology, and the list is still growing. In each new OpenStack release, a new project becomes more mature and better integrated in the cloud platform. This creates more opportunities to expand the **cloud universe** functionalities and grow your new next generation data center.

In this chapter, we will cover the following topics:

- Briefly parsing the OpenStack components and the innovation areas
- Implementing a first architectural design of OpenStack private cloud
- Checking the latest tools and processes to build a production-ready OpenStack environment

- Discussing the needs to adopt the **Infrastructure as Code** (**IaC**) concept for successful OpenStack management and implementation
- Exploring new opportunities to enlarge the OpenStack setup by tackling the cloud setup in both a test and a production environment using Ansible

Revisiting the OpenStack ecosystem

OpenStack has been designed to be deployed on a loosely coupled architectural layout. By defining each component of its ecosystem to run independently, it becomes possible to distribute each service among dedicated machines to achieve redundancy. As defined, the base services that constitute the core components in OpenStack are compute, network, and storage services. Based on this, the OpenStack community takes advantage of the base services and the design approach of the cloud software, and keeps developing and joining new open source projects to the OpenStack ecosystem. A variety of new **X-As-A-Service** projects appear with nearly every OpenStack release.

Getting up to speed with expanding the private cloud setup involves getting to grips core OpenStack services and terms. The following table shows the main projects in OpenStack in its early releases with their corresponding code names:

Code name	Service	Description
Nova	Compute	Manages instance resources and operations
Glance	Image	Manages instance disk images and their snapshots
Swift	Object storage	Manages access to object storage level through REST API
Cinder	Block storage	Manages volumes for instances
Neutron	Network	Manages network resources to instances
Keystone	Identity	Manages authentication and authorization for users and services
Horizon	Dashboard	Exposes a graphical user interface to manage an OpenStack environment

Of course, the evolution of the OpenStack ecosystem has kept growing to cover more projects and include more services. Since October 2013 (the date of Havana's release), the OpenStack community has shifted to enlarge the services provided by OpenStack within an exhaustive list. The following table shows the extended services of OpenStack (Mitaka release) at the time of writing:

Code name	Service	Description
Ceilometer	Telemetry	Provides monitoring of resource usage
Heat	Orchestration	Manages the collection of resources as single unit using template files
Trove	Database	**Database as a Service (DBaaS)** component
Sahara	**Elastic Data Processing (EDP)**	Quickly provisions the Hadoop cluster to run an EDP job against it
Ironic	Bare-metal	Provisions bare metal machines
Zaqar	Messaging service	Enables notification and messaging services
Manilla	Shared filesystems	Provides shared **File system As A Service (FSaaS)**, allowing to mount one shared filesystem across several instances
Designate	Domain name service	Offers DNS services
Barbican	Key management	Provides key management service capabilities, such as keys, certificates, and binary data
Murano	Application catalog	Exposes an application catalog allowing the publishing of cloud-ready applications
Magnum	Containers	Introduces **Container as a Service (CaaS)** in OpenStack
Congress	Governance	Maintains compliance for enterprise policies

At the official OpenStack website, you can find a very informative page project-navigator that shows the maturity and adoption statistics for each OpenStack project and the age in years in which it has been in development. You can find this website at `https://www.openstack.org/software/project-navigator`.

Ultimately, if you want to expand your OpenStack environment to provide more **X-As-A-Service** user experience, you may need to revisit the core ecosystem first. This will enable you to pinpoint how the new service will be exposed to the end user and predict any change that needs more attention regarding the load and resources usage.

Grasping a first layout

Let's rekindle the flame and implement a basic architectural design. You probably have a running OpenStack environment where you have installed its different pieces across multiple and dedicated server roles. The architectural design of the OpenStack software itself gives you more flexibility to build your own private cloud. As mentioned in the first section, the loosely coupled design makes it easier to decide how to run services on nodes in your data center. Depending on how big it is, your hardware choices, or third-party vendor dependencies, OpenStack has been built so that it can't suffer from *vendor lock-in*. This makes it imperative that we do not stick to any specific design pattern or any vendor requirements.

The following figure shows a basic conceptual design for OpenStack deployment in a data center:

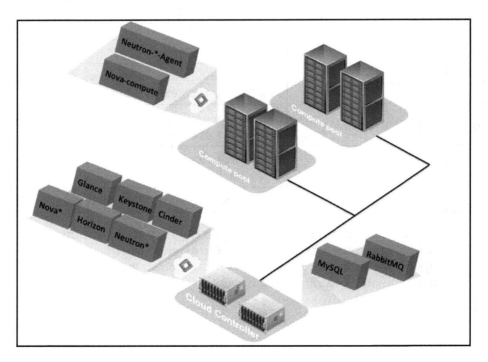

Postulating the OpenStack setup

OpenStack, as a distributed system, is designed to facilitate the designing of your private cloud. As summed up in the previous section, many components can run across different fleets of nodes. When it comes to a large infrastructure, the OpenStack setup can scale to more than one location, forming multisite environments that are geographically dispersed. In order to manage large-scale infrastructure with OpenStack, it becomes crucial to find a promising approach that makes any deployment, change, or update of the underlying infrastructure more consistent and easy to operate.

A very new and promising approach that will transform the way of managing IT infrastructures is IaC. Covering the challenges and principles of such model could fill an entire book. In the next section, we will cover how we will deploy our OpenStack environment on a large scale by adopting such an approach.

Treating OpenStack as code

The Infrastructure as Code concept provides several best practices and patterns that will help us achieve remarkable results for the portfolio of systems within an organization. Without going deeply into details of this concept, the following points show us the advantages of using IaC for our OpenStack deployment:

- It automates the deployment of all OpenStack components through dozens of nodes with less effort, time, cost, and with more reliability
- It audits the OpenStack environment with every change and update
- It defines the desired state of the OpenStack infrastructure
- The system recovers faster from failures by reproducing systems easily from unexpected changes during OpenStack deployment
- It improves the robustness of OpenStack's infrastructure
- It keeps services available and consistent

In order to take advantage of the mentioned benefits of the concept of IaC, OpenStack environment components can be transformed to a defined role. Each role describes one or more specific elements of the OpenStack infrastructure and details how they should be configured.

Such roles can be written in a **configuration definition file**, which is a generic term to describe a role of a service or server. Nowadays, many tools have been developed for this purpose such as Chef, Puppet, and Ansible and have a better system management experience. The continuous growth of the OpenStack ecosystem was a result of the support and dedication of several giant and medium enterprises around the globe. This interest to provide a unique cloud software solution was not limited only to the OpenStack code source but also the contribution to automate its deployment. This covers the development of ready-production artifacts to manage and operate an OpenStack environment through system management tools. That includes Chef cookbooks, Ansible playbooks, and Puppet manifests.

Growing the OpenStack infrastructure

The ultimate goal of the Infrastructure as Code approach is to improve the confidence of the systems running in production. In addition, this can be coupled with infrastructure growth. Expanding the OpenStack layout, for example, cannot be achieved without taking into account an agile approach that keeps its different components across the data center running without interruption. Moreover, adding new components or integrating a new service into the OpenStack ecosystem setup will result in a design change. New components should talk to existing ones with few new resource requirements. This challenge can be delegated to a **Version Control System** (**VCS**). Whatever changes are made, keeping the OpenStack setup self-descriptive in VCS through definition files and scripts will define the desired state of the private cloud. This avoids any process that would end up *reinventing the wheel*; while it needs only to expand and correlate code describing the existing OpenStack setup.

To ensure that the OpenStack infrastructure resists changes as the code that describes it grows, a very agile way must exist to emphasize system configuration changes. This can be inspired by software development practices. This enables us to apply modern software development tools to deploy and extend an OpenStack infrastructure, for example. At this stage, a DevOps movement has appeared that brings software developers and operators together to collaborate. Of course, exploiting the new modern approach and its derived practices and ideas will bring beneficial results when growing or upgrading your OpenStack private cloud environment.

The next diagram resumes a simplistic shape of a standard change management life cycle for the deployment infrastructure code of OpenStack:

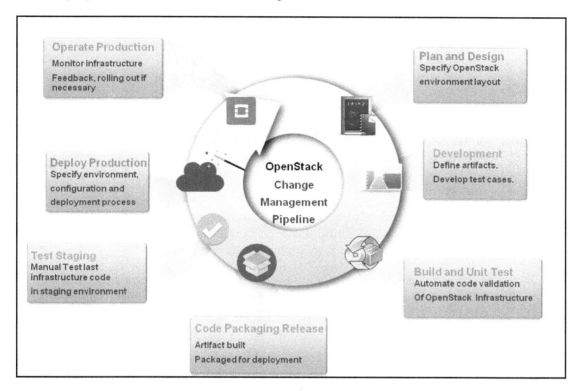

The different stages can be discussed as follows:

- **Plan and design**: The very early stage of planning the general layout of the OpenStack infrastructure and the related components that are willing to install, integrate, and deploy them.

- **Development stage**: This involves running tests for the latest versions of the infrastructure file definitions. In general, local tools, such as **Vagrant** and other virtualized local test environments, are used to test the changed files and commit them to a VCS.
- **Build and unit test stage**: Once a change is committed to VCS, a phase of code validation will be managed by a **Continuous Integration (CI)** system. It will run several activities or jobs by checking the syntax, code compilation, and unit tests.

 CI is an innovative practice that enables us to rapidly and effectively identify any defected code at an early stage. Jenkins and TeamCity are two of the most famous CI tools used by most software development enterprises. Such tools offer an automated test build of the software code, which provides fast feedback about its correctness at every commit of change.

- **Code packaging and release**: The CI tool should give a green light to process the changes. In this stage, the build has been done successfully and the configuration artifact will be packaged to be available for later phases.

 During a classic application job build, one or more files are generated that will be uploaded to the configuration repository. A configuration artifact can be versioned and portable, but it must be consistent.

- **Test staging**: At this stage, several tests should be executed on similar production environments. The most effective infrastructure code test runs on multiple stages. For example, you should start with a first test stage for one OpenStack service on its own. Then, you should propagate the first test with the second one by integrating other OpenStack components.
- **Deploy to production**: That applies in the final stage where the modeled changes that have been tested will be applied with zero downtime. Some great release techniques can be engaged at this stage, such as **Blue-Green** deployment.

The Blue-Green deployment technique ensures near zero downtime and reduces the risk of disturbing a running production environment when applying changes. During the change, two identical production environments are running. The live one is named *Blue*, and the idle one is named *Green*. A complete switch to Green environment will happen only when it was deployed and fully tested with the necessary checks and requirements. In the case of an unexpected issue in the live environment, it is still possible to rapidly roll out the last change by switching to the first Blue environment (the previous infrastructure version).

- **Operate in production**: This is the very last stage where it proves the degree of consistency of the last changes in a running production environment. It should also be possible to roll the changes out quickly and easily.

Deploying OpenStack

Integrating new services, updating, or upgrading some or all of the OpenStack components are all critical operational tasks. Such moments raise the need for the usage of software engineering practices. As mentioned in the previous section, applying such practices with Infrastructure as Code will help you deliver a high-quality code infrastructure. The end result will enable you to deploy a fully automated, robust, and continuous deliverable OpenStack environment.

To tweak the installation of a complete and extensible OpenStack environment, we need to start deploying a first test environment. As was promised in the beginning of this chapter, we will use a system management tool that will help us not only to deploy our first OpenStack layout rapidly, but also to carry feedback from testing results, such as unit testing.

Chef, Puppet, SaltStack, and many other system management tools are great tools that can do the job. You will probably have used one or more of them. Ansible will be chosen for this section and the upcoming sections as the system management tool for end-to-end OpenStack deployment and management.

Ansible in a nutshell

According to the new trend of cloud infrastructure developers, every operational task must be capable of automation. Many system management tools offer automation capabilities and have been extended to cover more advanced features, such as emulating parts of a given system for a fast file definition validation. Of course, every infrastructure tool must show its capability of making an easy-to-use, realistic full test and deployment. Compared to Chef or Puppet, for example, Ansible could be reckoned to be the *simplest* form of IT orchestration and automation tool. This is because Ansible does not require any agent or daemon to be running on the managed host or instance. It simply needs a Secure Shell connection, and then all it needs to do is copy the Ansible modules to the managed hosts and execute them, and that is it!

By the virtue of its simplicity, agentless architecture, deploying and expanding a large OpenStack infrastructure becomes much less complicated. Ansible uses **playbooks** to modularize its definition configuration files written in the YAML markup format.

As with Chef or Puppet, configuration files in Ansible are organized in a specific definition layered hierarchy, as follows:

- **Playbook**: A Playbook can be seen as a high level code of the system deployment. The code instructs which host or group of hosts will be assigned to which role. It encapsulates a few specific parameters to enable Ansible run user as *root* for example.
- **Role**: A role represents the intended logical function of a host or group of hosts. The role file exposes tasks and customized functions to configure and deploy a service in one or a fleet of hosts.

When transforming the OpenStack infrastructure into code and then roles, a good practice to adopt when creating roles is to break down the OpenStack services into individual roles per Playbook. Each role will describe a specific OpenStack component or service that makes it reusable and decreases attempts to change the code.

- **Module**: Another good reason that proves the simplicity of Ansible is the usage of modules. Basically, a module comes with a predefined encapsulated code that is ready to run against a target host. Running a module many times against a host will take effect only when a change is explicitly made. Besides the current modules available at http://docs.ansible.com/ansible/latest/modules_by_category.html, you can always create and customize your own modules in other languages.

- **Variable**: Defining variables in Ansible is straightforward from Playbooks, Modules, or Roles. When dealing with OpenStack deployment, defining, and setting variable placeholders must be done with care for a safe, dynamic change of the system's attributes.

- **Facts**: Another interesting part of the Ansible workflow is the gathering of the facts of the target system when executing a playbook against it. The information about the system, such as network configuration, operating system, and other low-level details, will be saved in a variable named `facts`. By default, Ansible captures the target system details unless you explicitly disable this in the Playbook.

- **Inventory**: Ansible will need a list of hosts to run the coded playbooks against. This is where the inventory comes for a collection of nodes defined by their IP addresses, hostnames, or **Fully Qualified Domain Name** (**FQDN**). The inventory list is an **INI** formatted file named simply *hosts*, and is located by default in the Ansible server under the /etc/ansible/ directory. Ansible comes with two different approaches to gathering different hosts inventory. These are described as follows:
  - **Static inventory**: This elaborates the inventory list manually in a single defined host or into groups.
  - **Dynamic inventory**: When it comes to a large number of nodes in a production OpenStack setup, Ansible offers a better way to handle this situation. It is possible to create an inventory script collector and invoke it to pull host information at runtime.

A very useful example to automate the inventory list of a given OpenStack environment can be found at `http://docs.ansible.com/ansible/latest/intro_dynamic_inventory.html#example-openstack-external-inventory-script`.

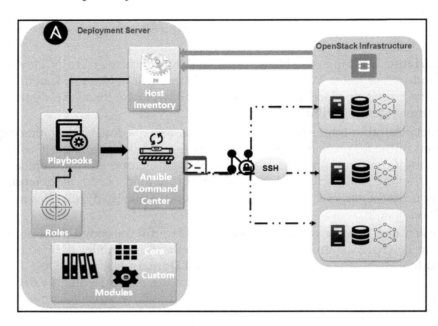

Testing the OpenStack environment

As a result of inheriting an agile method to build a consistent production environment, we will need to start by building the basic code blocks of the OpenStack infrastructure in a separate test environment. This means that testing a new introduced feature, for example, should take place continuously. A new feature, fixed plugin version, or an updated new specific OpenStack package is considered a change. These should first be tested in a similar production environment and in an automated way. To speed up the building and extending of an OpenStack production setup, we will need a test environment.

Prerequisites for the test environment

The OpenStack test environment will involve the setup of the deployment machine, the Ansible deployment server, and the target hosts, which are the different OpenStack nodes that Ansible will run its playbooks against.

To speed up a simple installation approach, in this section, we will use a very promising OpenStack project named **OpenStack-Ansible (OSA)**. Rackspace Private Cloud Software has initiated this project and has been officially integrated with the support of the OpenStack community. It aims to deploy an OpenStack private cloud by the means of Ansible Playbooks. OSA was released to run an OpenStack environment for production-ready deployment.

 OSA is an OpenStack project initiated by Rackspace to install and deploy OpenStack environment through Ansible Playbooks. The OpenStack services environment run based on **LXC** containers to isolate components and services running in a node. Formerly, the OSA project was named `os-ansible-deployment` on **Stackforge** before it moved to join the OpenStack open source community tent. The official website of the OSA project can be found at GitHub at: `https://github.com/openstack/openstack-ansible`.

In addition, the OSA project could run in **All-In-One** (**AIO**) mode. It takes advantage of Linux containerization technology, **Linux Container** (**LXC**), so different infrastructures and OpenStack services will run isolated in different containers, but on the same machine.

 LXC is a way to isolate processes from others on a Linux system. Linux containers share the same Linux kernel and any other resources running on it. LXC is a very lightweight virtualization technology; its lightness is achieved by rapidly packaging a runtime environment into a self-contained image. To read more about the container, refer to the LXC official website, `https://linuxcontainers.org/lxc/introduction/`.

Conceptually, this approach would somewhat resolve the trade-off of the time consumed for code testing, in our case playbooks, and the delivery speed of the complete suite and consistent OpenStack environment.

Setting up the Ansible environment

In this section, we will need to ensure that we have the proper hardware requirements to set up a complete development environment for testing the OpenStack infrastructure code, as the follows:

- **Cloud controller**:

    - **Memory**: At least 3 GB RAM
    - **Processor**: At least 2 CPUs 64-bit x86
    - **Disk space**: At least 30 GB free disk space

- **Network**: At least 2 NICs

- **Compute node**:
    - **Memory**: At least 4 GB RAM
    - **Processor**: At least 4 CPUs 64-bit x86
    - **Disk space**: At least 40 GB free disk space
    - **Network**: At least 2 NICs
- **Ansible deployment host**:
    - **Memory**: At least 1 GB RAM
    - **Processor**: At least 1 CPUs 64-bit x86
    - **Disk space**: At least 10 GB free disk space
    - **Network**: At least 1 NIC

OSA also requires the following software versions for all machines:

- Ubuntu LTS 14.04 LTS or later
- Linux kernel version 3.10.0.34—generic or later
- Python support 2.7 or later
- Network Time Protocol client installed
- Secure Shell server and client for Ansible to run

 At the time of writing this book, OSA is still being heavily developed to support RedHat, CentOS, and Gentoo Linux versions.

Another key testing tool for a successful automated test is the usage of virtualization technology. Instead of running the OSA installation in a bare metal machine, we can install any hypervisor on top of it and be able to harness more tests in an isolated environment. For this purpose, we will use VirtualBox to create the required virtual machines and couple it with Vagrant to build a reproducible development environment.

Setting up all the required networks in our test environment might be confusing. To mimic a real production setup, many virtual network interfaces should exist per virtual machine.

For the sake of simplicity, we will use two network interfaces per cloud controller and compute node as physical interfaces as follows:

- **eth0**: This is connected to LXC internal virtual network. It is dedicated to Ansible deployment and to SSH to the containers per each virtual machine. It also allows you to download packages from the internet.
- **eth1**: This enables internal communication between different OpenStack components, including compute, networking, and infrastructure services.

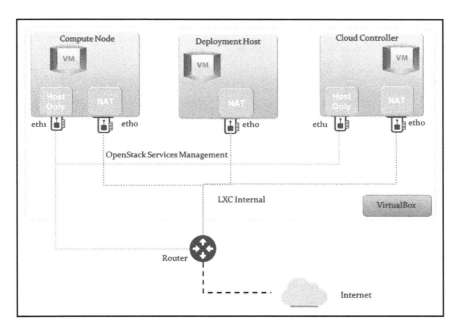

Make sure you enable internal communication for each virtual machine by setting each adapter device in VirtualBox to **Allow All**, as follows:

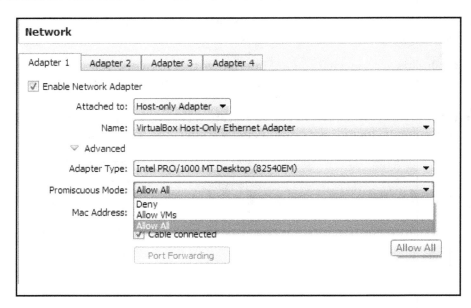

The next section will guide us through a complete setup of our test environment using Ansible.

Running the OSA installation

The next wizard will guide you through a simple OpenStack setup in a local virtualized environment. As described in the previous section, we will distribute different service roles for each virtual machine. Note that a test environment should reflect a logical design of a proper production setup. In this example, several services have been encapsulated into a single node while this approach should be refined more. As a start, and for the sake of simplicity, the common services of OpenStack and the infrastructure will be distributed as follows:

- **Cloud controller**: This will run most of the OpenStack services, including computing services (excluding the hypervisor computing service, **nova-compute**), object and block storage, image, identity, dashboard, and network services. In addition, common shared infrastructure services will be installed in the same host, including database, message queueing, and load balancing services.

- **Compute node**: It will simply run the compute service **nova-compute** and network agents.
- **Ansible deployment host**: This will store the OSA playbook's repository and Ansible daemons.

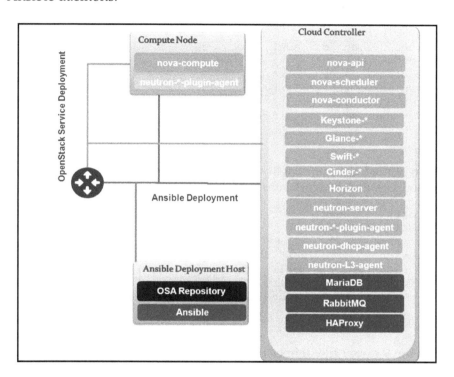

Automating the operating system installation saves a lot of time, and eventually, the usage of Vagrant empowers the automation of tests. When getting more involved in extending the code of the OpenStack infrastructure, automating tests using local virtualized infrastructure might catch problems quickly. For the rest of the setup, we will rely on the Vagrant file that defines the nodes in our OpenStack environment. Let's start by defining the Ansible Deployment Host.

To start with, create a new Vagrant file named `Vagrantfile`:

```
Vagrant.configure(2) do |config|
   config.vm.box = "ubuntu/trusty64"
```

First, we define the operating system version that will be used for the whole deployment test environment. As we discussed previously, the Linux flavor selected for OSA is Ubuntu.

The next chunk of the Vagrant file defines the Ansible Deployment host that is assigned as a adh variable as well as the hostname:

```
# Ansible Deployment Host
config.vm.define :adh do |adh|
  adh.vm.hostname= "adh"
  adh.vm.provider "virtualbox" do |vb|
        vb.customize ["modifyvm", :id, "--memory", "1024"]
        vb.customize ["modifyvm", :id, "--cpus", "2"]
        vb.customize ["modifyvm", :id, "--nicpromic2", "allow-all"]
      end
end
```

The next section of the Vagrant file will define the Cloud Controller node name, its customized resources, and network setup:

```
# Cloud Controller Host
config.vm.define :cc do |cc|
  cc.vm.hostname= "cc"
  cc.vm.provider "virtualbox" do |vb|
        vb.customize ["modifyvm", :id, "--memory", "3072"]
        vb.customize ["modifyvm", :id, "--cpus", "3"]
          vb.customize ["modifyvm", :id, "--nicpromic2", "allow-all"]
      end
end
```

The last part of the Vagrant file defines the Compute Node name, its customized resources, and network setup:

```
# Compute Node
config.vm.define :cn do |cn|
  cn.vm.hostname= "cn"
  cn.vm.provider "virtualbox" do |vb|
        vb.customize ["modifyvm", :id, "--memory", "4096"]
        vb.customize ["modifyvm", :id, "--cpus", "4"]
          vb.customize ["modifyvm", :id, "--nicpromic2", "allow-all"]
      end
end
end
```

It is recommended to run the Vagrant file part by part. This will help us diagnose any configuration issue or syntax error during the vagrant run. To do this, it is possible to comment the Cloud Controller and Compute Node code blocks in the Vagrant file:

1. We can start by running the first Ansible Deployment Host block and running the following command line:

   ```
   # vagrant up
   ```

   This will download the Ubuntu image and create a new virtual machine named adh.

2. The first virtual machine should be up and running with the Ubuntu image installed:

   ```
   # vagrant ssh
   ```

3. Next step requires you to download and install the required utilities as mentioned in the previous section, including the Git, NTP, and SSH packages as follows:

   ```
   ubuntu@adh: $ sudo apt-get install aptitude build-essential git ntp
   ntpdate openssh-server python-dev sudo
   ```

4. We will use the latest stable master branch of the OSA repository:

   ```
   ubuntu@adh: $ git clone
   https://github.com/openstack/openstack-ansible.git /opt/openstack-
   ansible
   ```

   To use a previous OpenStack release, instruct your Git command line to clone the openstack-ansible repository from the desired branch of the OpenStack release code name:
   ```
   $ git clone -b stable/OS_RELEASE
   https://github.com/openstack/openstack-ansible.git
   ```
   /opt/openstackansible where OS_RELEASE refers to the OpenStack release name. Please note that openstack-ansible repository does not include all the previous OpenStack releases and keeps at maximum the four latest releases.

5. A file located at `/etc/openstack_deploy/openstack_user_config.yml` will need to tweak it a bit in order to reflect the customized environment setup described previously. We will need to specify the network IP ranges and nodes that will be running services attached to their interfaces:
    1. First, specify that CIDRs will be used for our OpenStack test environment:

    ```
    ---
    cidr_networks:
      management: 172.16.0.0/16
      tunnel: 172.29.240.0/22

    used_ips:
      - 172.16.0.101,172.16.0.107
      - 172.29.240.101,172.29.240.107
    ```

The **tunnel** network defined in the `cidr_networks` stanza defines a tunneled network using VXLAN by tenant or project in OpenStack.

    2. We can add a new section to specify where the common infrastructure services, such as the database and messaging queue, will be running. For the sake of simplicity, they will run on the same Cloud Controller node, as follows:

    ```
    # Shared infrastructure parts
    shared-infra_hosts:
      controller-01:
        ip: 172.16.0.101
    ```

    3. The next part will instruct Ansible to run the rest of the OpenStack services and APIs in the Cloud Controller machine as follows:

    ```
    # OpenStack infrastructure parts
    os-infra_hosts:
      controller-01:
        ip: 172.16.0.101
    ```

4. Optionally, network and storage services can run on the same Cloud Controller node as follows:

```
# OpenStack Storage infrastructure parts
storage-infra_hosts:
   controller-01:
      ip: 172.16.0.101
# OpenStack Network Hosts
network_hosts:
   controller-01:
      ip: 172.16.0.101
```

5. Add the following section to instruct Ansible to use the Compute Node to run the `nova-compute` service:

```
# Compute Hosts
compute_hosts:
   compute-01:
      ip: 172.16.0.104
```

6. The last part of our initial configuration setup for the test environment will include specifying where to wrap the OpenStack cluster behind the load balancer. For this purpose, HAProxy will be used and installed in the Cloud Controller node, as follows:

```
haproxy_hosts:
   haproxy:
      ip: 172.16.0.101
```

6. Next, we can edit another simple file that describes specific OpenStack configuration options located at `/et/openstack_deploy/user_variables.yml`. For now, we will need to configure Nova to use qemu as a virtualization type. We can also adjust the allocation ratio for both RAM and CPU, as follows:

```
--------
## Nova options
nova_virt_type: qemu
nova_cpu_allocation_ratio: 2.0
nova_ram_allocation_ratio: 1.0
--------
```

7. The final configuration file that we need to edit is /etc/openstack-deploy/user_secrets.yml. This is where root users passphrases for services such as database and compute will be stored once they are created in Keystone. The following script will enable us to generate a random passphrase and store for later use in future setup:

```
# scripts/pw-token-gen.py --file /etc/openstack-deploy/user_secrets.yml
```

```
Creating backup file [ /opt/openstack-ansible/etc/openstack_deploy/user_secrets.yml.tar ]
Operation Complete, [ /opt/openstack-ansible/etc/openstack_deploy/user_secrets.yml ] is ready
```

8. Now we have our development machine in place with the required preconfigured files. We can continue running the rest of the vagrant file to prepare the Cloud Controller and Compute Node hosts. To do this, uncomment the Cloud Controller and Compute Node and run the following command line:

```
# vagrant up
```

9. The OSA exposes a bootstrap script that allows you to download the right version of Ansible and generate a wrapper openstack-ansible script that will load the OpenStack user variable:

```
# scripts/bootstrap-ansible.sh
```

```
- executing: git clone https://git.openstack.org/openstack/openstack-ansibl
- executing: git archive --prefix=repo_build/ --output=/tmp/tmpR3aLx3.tar a
- extracting repo_build to /etc/ansible/roles/repo_build
- repo_build was installed successfully
- dependency pip_install is already installed, skipping.
- dependency apt_package_pinning is already installed, skipping.
- dependency galera_client is already installed, skipping.
- executing: git clone https://git.openstack.org/openstack/openstack-ansibl
- executing: git archive --prefix=repo_server/ --output=/tmp/tmptmjiap.tar
- extracting repo_server to /etc/ansible/roles/repo_server
- repo_server was installed successfully
```

10. Once completed successfully, the `openstack-ansible` script will be used to run the playbooks. The first run will install and configure the containers in the mentioned nodes described in `/etc/openstack_deploy/openstack_user_config.yml`. The first playbook will be running is `setup-hosts.yml`, located under `/opt/deploy-openstack/playbooks`:

    ```
    # openstack-ansible setup-hosts.yml
    ```

    ```
    TASK: bootstrap-host : Install required packages ---------------------- 954.66s
    TASK: pip_install : Get Modern PIP ------------------------------------- 17.68s
    TASK: bootstrap-host : Start the network interfaces -------------------- 9.68s
    TASK: bootstrap-host : Update apt-cache -------------------------------- 4.47s
    TASK: bootstrap-host : Format the Swift files -------------------------- 3.99s
    TASK: pip_install : Install pip packages ------------------------------- 3.83s
    TASK: setup ------------------------------------------------------------ 2.62s
    TASK: pip_install : Install PIP ---------------------------------------- 2.00s
    TASK: pip_install : Create pip config directory ----------------------- 1.69s
    TASK: bootstrap-host : Determine the fastest available OpenStack-Infra wheel mirror --- 1.58s
    + popd
    /opt/openstack-ansible
    ```

    This will identify the target hosts, validate network configurations, and create loopback volumes for use per LXC container.

11. The next playbook run should instruct Ansible to install HAProxy in the Cloud Controller node by running `haproxy-install.yml`:

    ```
    # openstack-ansible haproxy-install.sh
    ```

12. If the previous step has been completed with no failure, it means that Ansible did not face any connectivity issue to reach the nodes. Then, we can easily proceed to run the next playbook that will configure LXC containers to install common OpenStack services, such as database and messaging queue services. By default, Galera and RabbitMQ will be installed. OSA provides a playbook named `setup-infrastructure.yml` to make this happen, as follows:

    ```
    # openstack-ansible setup-infratructure.yml
    ```

13. The next step will configure LXC containers and install the OpenStack core services across the Cloud Controller and Compute Node as follows. The playbook to run is named `setup-openstack.yml`:

```
# openstack-ansible setup-openstack.yml
```

14. Once completed, it is possible to list all the service containers using the following command line from the Ansible Deployment Host:

```
# lxc-ls --fancy
```

```
                                          STATE    AUTOSTART GROUPS              IPV4
aodh_container-70cdf33d                   RUNNING 1         onboot, openstack 10.255.255.171,
ceilometer_api_container-16fe9226         RUNNING 1         onboot, openstack 10.255.255.189,
ceilometer_collector_container-72ab041c   RUNNING 1         onboot, openstack 10.255.255.209,
cinder_api_container-cd15f0d2             RUNNING 1         onboot, openstack 10.255.255.41,
cinder_scheduler_container-489fc683       RUNNING 1         onboot, openstack 10.255.255.132,
galera_container-1930b1a0                 RUNNING 1         onboot, openstack 10.255.255.66,
glance_container-33f98508                 RUNNING 1         onboot, openstack 10.255.255.190,
gnocchi_container-386eb4bc                RUNNING 1         onboot, openstack 10.255.255.40,
heat_apis_container-a9372f6a              RUNNING 1         onboot, openstack 10.255.255.143,
heat_engine_container-99b8aab1            RUNNING 1         onboot, openstack 10.255.255.108,
horizon_container-dcb08a11                RUNNING 1         onboot, openstack 10.255.255.188,
keystone_container-db00df62               RUNNING 1         onboot, openstack 10.255.255.133,
memcached_container-592df24c              RUNNING 1         onboot, openstack 10.255.255.147,
neutron_agents_container-729a602f         RUNNING 1         onboot, openstack 10.255.255.202,
neutron_server_container-1ba99d59         RUNNING 1         onboot, openstack 10.255.255.231,
nova_api_metadata_container-d772dc9d      RUNNING 1         onboot, openstack 10.255.255.219,
nova_api_os_compute_container-38a80900    RUNNING 1         onboot, openstack 10.255.255.154,
nova_cert_container-64420c97              RUNNING 1         onboot, openstack 10.255.255.236,
nova_conductor_container-68ce1148         RUNNING 1         onboot, openstack 10.255.255.210,
nova_console_container-552f6a20           RUNNING 1         onboot, openstack 10.255.255.5, 1
nova_scheduler_container-a4606380         RUNNING 1         onboot, openstack 10.255.255.146,
rabbit_mq_container-d8b9ac65              RUNNING 1         onboot, openstack 10.255.255.233,
repo_container-aa32c35e                   RUNNING 1         onboot, openstack 10.255.255.230,
rsyslog_container-59f5f9d8                RUNNING 1         onboot, openstack 10.255.255.136,
swift_proxy_container-88f11481            RUNNING 1         onboot, openstack 10.255.255.225,
utility_container-55723a11                RUNNING 1         onboot, openstack 10.255.255.138,
```

15. From the previous output, identify the container prefixed as `utility_container-XXX`. This is a particular container that includes the OpenStack client command lines. Use the `lxc-attach` tool to connect the Cloud Controller utility container as follows:

```
# lxc-attach --name cc_utility_container-55723a11
----
* Documentation: https://help.ubuntu.com/
Last login: Mon Sep 12 22:56:33 2016 from 172.29.236.100
root@utility-container-55723a11:~#
```

16. Now propagate the OpenStack credentials in the environment and also use the generated username/password for admin to access the Horizon dashboard:

```
root@utility-container-55723a11:~# cat openrc
root@utility-container-55723a11:~# source openrc
```

```
# COMMON OPENSTACK ENVS
export OS_ENDPOINT_TYPE=internalURL
export OS_INTERFACE=internalURL
export OS_USERNAME=admin
export OS_PASSWORD=c157e74cfe1fdae08663ef7b1350552ed5bb970ed6bc
export OS_PROJECT_NAME=admin
export OS_TENANT_NAME=admin
export OS_AUTH_URL=http://172.29.236.100:5000/v3
```

17. Run a test OpenStack API query to check the availability of services. For example, we can check the status of the network service as follows:

```
root@utility-container-55723a11:~# openstack service show neutron
```

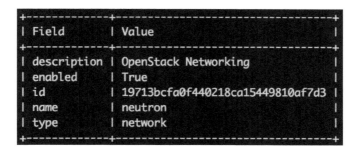

```
+-------------+----------------------------------+
| Field       | Value                            |
+-------------+----------------------------------+
| description | OpenStack Networking             |
| enabled     | True                             |
| id          | 19713bcfa0f440218ca15449810af7d3 |
| name        | neutron                          |
| type        | network                          |
+-------------+----------------------------------+
```

18. Another setup validation of our test environment is to check the type of virtualization that has been configured in the compute container. To do so, point to the `nova-api-os-compute-container-XXXX` container and check the `libvirt` stanza in the `/etc/nova/nova.conf` file:

```
[libvirt]
....
use_virtio_for_bridges = True
cpu_mode = host-model
  virt_type = qemu
....
```

19. You can always connect to the OpenStack dashboard by pointing the browser to the Cloud Controller's exposed IP address. The username and password reside in the environment file `openrc`:

The `lxc-*` tool provides several commands with great features. A good practice when a container does not function properly because of file corruption, for example, a simple step that will just destroy and recreate it again by running the problematic playbook service. You can use the following command line to stop a container:
```
# lxc-stop --name <container-name>
```
To completely destroy a container, use the following command line:
```
# lxc-destroy --name <container-name>
```
, this will destroy a container.

Production OpenStack environment

Before starting to deploy our infrastructure code in the production environment, several important points must be considered:

- The infrastructure code should be fully tested in both test and staging (preproduction) environments.
- Any new service that will extend the OpenStack layout should go through a change management pipeline.
- Make sure that the base production setup is 100% consistent. Fragile components should not exist
- The OpenStack services production setup should be seen as Ansible modules. When you are adding a new module for further service extension, it should be designed integrally and tested independently.
- Design for failure. OpenStack is well architected to keep its components highly available.

In this section, we will go through a sample production layout. The first deployment will bring the basic OpenStack services up and running. Bear in mind that the first design layout should be extensible and managed from the system management tool.

The sample diagram layout shown in the first section of this chapter can be extended, and eventually more services can be forked across different nodes.

As the OpenStack production environment must provide redundancy and service extensibility, Ansible Playbooks have been designed for that purpose.

The following diagram illustrates an extended layout of the production environment, which defines the following hosts:

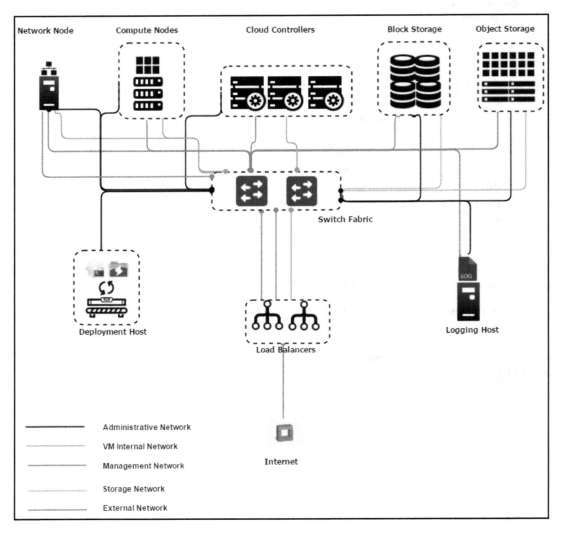

- **Cloud Controllers**: These running the following OpenStack management services:
    - Keystone-* APIs
    - Glance-* APIs
    - Nova-* APIs

- Cinder-* APIs
- Neutron-server
- Swift proxy
- Horizon

Optionally, the cloud controller could run a common service infrastructure as follows:

- RabbitMQ
- MySQL Galera database

 Messaging queue and database services could run in separate clusters for better service isolation and redundancy.

- **Compute Nodes**: These run the following hypervisor machines:
  - Nova-compute
  - Neutron--plugin-agent
- **Logging host**: Logs generated by OpenStack services need to be shipped and filtered for fast troubleshooting tasks. Log host will run a full logging stack including the following:
  - ElasticSearch
  - Logstash
  - Rsyslog
  - Kibana
- **Network node(s)**: This will run the following Neutron agents:
  - L2 agent
  - L3 agent
  - DHCP agent
- **Block storage node(s)**: This will host block storage volumes, along with installed LVM, and run the following OpenStack services:
  - Cinder-volume
  - Cinder-scheduler
- **Object storage node(s)**: Optionally, a dedicated storage blob device can run the following object storage service:
  - Swift-* API

- **Load balancer node(s)**: This runs the following services:
  - HAProxy
  - Keepalived

 If you are running a different load balancer other than HAProxy, make sure you consider a new configuration layout for the Ansible Playbook running the HAProxy installation.

- **Deployment host**: This will run the following services:
  - Ansible service and repository
  - Razor PXE boot server

From a network perspective, a production setup might differ slightly from a staging environment because of the network device's high cost. On the other hand, it is essential to design an OpenStack production setup that is as close to this ideal as possible, in a pre production environment even if you have to consolidate different networks in the same logical interface. For this reason, designing a network layout differs depending on the cost and performance of the hardware devices that can be used. The previous diagram depicts a network layout suitable to support and integrate new OpenStack services. It would be easy to extend it at scale.

The different network segments are as follows:

- **Administrative network**: Dedicated network to run Ansible and PXE boot installer.
- **VM internal network**: This is a private network between virtual machines and the L3 network, providing routing to the external network and floating IPs backward to the virtual machines.
- **Management network**: This consists of OpenStack services communication, including infrastructure services, such as databases queries and queue messaging traffic.
- **Storage network**: This isolates storage traffic using a virtual LAN through switch for both block and object storage clusters.
- **External network**: This faces the public internet, providing external connectivity to instances. It exposes virtual IPs for load balancers used to connect internal OpenStack services APIs.

At this level, a successful run of the playbooks will be achieved when the following criteria are met:

- A network is configured correctly
- Target machines are reachable by Ansible
- Required packages are installed per target host
- The `/etc/openstack_deploy/openstack_user_config.yml` file will just need to be adjusted based on the networking IP configuration. The basic physical environment parameters that will be customized are as follows:
    - `cidr_networks`
        - `management`
        - `tunnel`
        - `storage`
    - `used_ips`
    - `global_overrides`: `internal_lb_vip_address` and `external_lb_vip_address`
    - `shared-infra_hosts`
    - `os-infra_hosts`
    - `storage-infra-hosts`
    - `identity_hosts`
    - `compute_hosts`
    - `storage_hosts`
    - `network_hosts`
    - `repo-infra_hosts`
    - `log_hosts`
    - `haproxy_hosts`

In addition, the `/etc/openstack_deploy/user_variables.yml` file can be adjusted to use `kvm` as a virtualization type for the Compute Nodes. The previous layout can be extended more with additional components using Ansible playbooks.

Summary

In this chapter, we briefly introduced the use case of adopting the IaC approach in our OpenStack private cloud deployment. At a very high level, we covered some important topics regarding the new trend of approaching a robust private cloud environment in no time. For this purpose, we started by designing a sample layout from the basic building blocks of OpenStack. We also introduced Ansible as our automation and system management tool for OpenStack. Of course, Chef, Puppet, or Salt are capable of automating such an installation, so feel free to use any software you feel more familiar with. Using Ansible, we took advantage of Ansible-OpenStack playbooks, which we were able to use rapidly to provision a minimal OpenStack environment in simple LXC containers. Finally, we set the first design blocks of our production environment.

In the first chapter, you should have learned a key topic about how you drive your private OpenStack cloud environment to be treated as code. Bear in mind that this approach will open the curtains for your private cloud to add more functionalities and features without the pain of manual configuration or service downtime. The journey will continue to extend what we designed and enlarge the computing power of the current environment, which will be covered in the next chapter.

2
Massively Scaling Computing Power

"Only two things are infinite, the universe and human stupidity, and I'm not sure about the former."

–Albert Einstein

There is always a reason to enlarge your private OpenStack cloud environment—successful deployment. Preparing a layout design that's ready to grow on demand is quite challenging. For this reason, OpenStack has been designed to grow seamlessly. Procurement of additional resources as needed should be straightforward. That is where *capacity planning management* best practices come into play. It is essential to ensure that any request to the OpenStack resource pools should be served without limitation. On the other hand, from an infrastructure perspective, the available hardware that runs an OpenStack private cloud will always have capacity limits including computing, networking, and storage resources. Taking into account the latter consideration, we will look at the fundamental building blocks of OpenStack (compute service) in detail and push the limits of computing power in your private cloud. In this chapter, we will cover the following points:

- Discussing the compute service in detail and adding a new compute node using Ansible
- Listing and configuring supported hypervisors in OpenStack, including Docker and Xen

- Defining new approaches on how to scale the compute service by leveraging a few OpenStack terminologies regarding compute cluster segregation
- Learning the mechanism of scheduling and weighing in OpenStack to boost the compute workload

Decomposing the compute power

The compute service in Nova is considered to be the core component of OpenStack. Understanding how to scale out the workload among several identical compute nodes might require to briefly revisit the building blocks of Nova:

- **nova-compute**: This runs on the compute node as described in Chapter 1, *Inflating the OpenStack Setup*. It is responsible for communicating with the hypervisors. Nova-compute interacts with each hypervisor by means of drivers. It creates compute resources by picking up requests from the message queue.
- **nova-scheduler**: This runs on the cloud controller as described in Chapter 1, *Inflating the OpenStack Setup*. It is responsible for finding the right placement (physical server) of the initiated request to create a VM. The request will be left in the message queue along with additional information regarding the server information where the nova-compute service will create the compute resource.
- **nova-api**: This runs on the cloud controller as described in Chapter 1, *Inflating the OpenStack Setup*. It is responsible for handling API calls from other services through the messaging queue service.
- **nova-conductor**: This runs on the cloud controller as described in Chapter 1, *Inflating the OpenStack Setup*. It is responsible for managing access to the database for read/write operations for security and data coherence reasons.
- **nova-consoleauth**: This runs on the cloud controller as described in Chapter 1, *Inflating the OpenStack Setup*. It is responsible for providing authentication to the VNC console by the means of the VNC protocol.
- **Metadata service**: Optionally, this can run on the compute node as described in Chapter 1, *Inflating the OpenStack Setup*. It is responsible for booting a virtual machine with a custom configuration that will be consumed by the compute service.

Bear in mind that other Nova services have not been cited, including nova-volume and nova-network. These Nova services will not be used, and are replaced in our setup by Cinder, for persistent storage on our virtual machines, and Neutron, for instance networking. Additionally, other non-mandatory Nova services, such as `nova-serialproxy` and `euca-tools`, are not covered in this chapter. The nova-cells service will be discussed in the later parts of this chapter.

The following diagram illustrates an overview of the different components forming the OpenStack compute service:

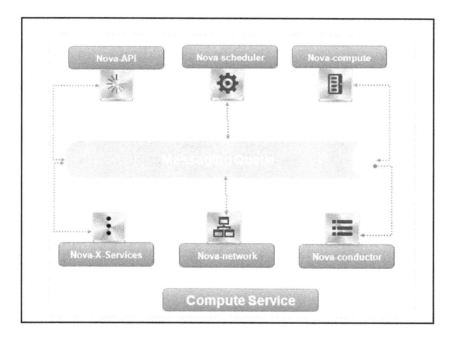

Empowering the compute service

In this section, we will add a new compute host to our first initial OpenStack environment using Ansible. The new compute node will have similar hardware requirements to the first compute node, as follows:

- **Memory**: At least 4 GB RAM
- **Processor**: At least 4 64-bit x86 CPUs

- **Disk space**: At least 40 GB free disk space
- **Network**: At least two NICs

The following excerpt will be added to the `vagrant` file in our test environment:

```
...
# Compute Node
config.vm.define :cn02 do |cn02|
  cn02.vm.hostname= "cn02"
  cn02.vm.provider "virtualbox" do |vb|
          vb.customize ["modifyvm", :id, "--memory", "4096"]
          vb.customize ["modifyvm", :id, "--cpus", "4"]
              vb.customize ["modifyvm", :id, "--nicpromic2",
"allow-all"]
          end
  end
end
```

The following steps will instruct the Ansible deployment host to add the new compute node to the pool as follows:

1. Configure the target host to be reachable by ADH (an LXC-internal network). Make sure that you have properly configured the networking setup in VirtualBox. This can be applied by just running `vagrant` as follows:

    `# vagrant up`

    The `vagrant` file will launch a new virtual machine by installing the operating system within its required virtual hardware configuration.

2. Before we start to deploy the new compute node, we will need to first go through the Ansible configuration files discussed in Chapter 1, *Inflating the OpenStack Setup*. The following stanza will be added to the `/etc/openstack_deploy/openstack_user_config.yml` file to instruct Ansible to use the second compute node and run the `nova-compute` service:

    ```
    # Compute Hosts
    compute_hosts:
    ...
      compute-02:
        ip: 172.16.0.105
    ```

3. The last change can be committed to `git` as follows:

    `# git add -A`
    `# git commit -a -m "Add Test Compute Node 02"`

4. Now we have a new host added to the list of compute nodes, we can start the deployment by running Ansible playbooks from ADH as follows:

```
# cd /opt/openstack-ansible/playbooks
# openstack-ansible setup-hosts.yml --limit compute-02
```

 The `--limit` option will only run the new updates described in the Ansible playbooks, configuration files. Using it will keep the infrastructure intact by only executing the latest version of the playbook scoped code.

5. Updating the infrastructure using Ansible can be performed as follows:

```
# openstack-ansible os-nova-install.yml --skip-tags nova-key-
distribute --limit compute-02
```

This will reduce the task of deploying the whole OpenStack infrastructure to install only a new compute node. Additionally, it is essential to point out that using the `--skip-tags` flag is needed since the new keys in the additional compute nodes will not be initially collected for nova SSH authentication. As per using a `--limit` flag in the `openstack-ansible` command line, adding a new host to the host list can be performed as follows:

```
# openstack-ansible setup-hosts --limit NEW_HOST_NAME
```

6. The next step is straightforward we will instruct Ansible to install the `nova-compute` service using the `os-nova-install.yml` playbook:

```
# openstack-ansible os-nova-install.yml --tags nova-key-
create,nova-key-distribute
```

To list all tags defined for OpenStack, use the following command line under the playbook directory:

```
# openstack-ansible openstack-setup.yml -list-tags
```

7. As mentioned in our initial test environment layout depicted in `Chapter 1`, *Inflating the OpenStack Setup*, a compute node will require us to run a Neutron agent. The following command line will run the Neutron agent playbook in the deployment host as follows:

```
# openstack-ansible os-neutron-install.yml --limit compute-02
```

To ensure that the `nova public key` attribute has been successfully created, run the `setup-openstack.yml` playbook on all hosts.

Varying the compute flavor

One of the key successes of OpenStack is its exposure to other hypervisor vendors—**no vendor lock-in**. As virtualization platforms have continued to evolve over the last decade, cloud providers have faced a major challenge regarding how to unlock their opportunities to keep growing. OpenStack makes it possible to support and integrate more virtualization technologies at pace—more freedom of choice. Extending your private OpenStack cloud should not only be limited to bringing more power to the compute fleet, but also enabling flexibility across supported virtualization platforms. At the time of writing, OpenStack supports the following hypervisor technologies:

- **Kernel-based Virtual Machine** (KVM) (libvirt)
- QEMU
- LXC
- XenServer
- VMware
- Docker
- Hyper-V

An exhaustive list of the supported hypervisors in OpenStack can be found at `http://docs.openstack.org/developer/nova/support-matrix.html`. The matrix is being updated to fix bugs and test new features for each hypervisor.

Since we have run QEMU in our test environment, and we have briefly seen how to configure it to use KVM in Chapter 1, *Inflating the OpenStack Setup*, we will discuss in the next few sections how your initial OpenStack private cloud can be extended by supporting other hypervisor types.

Meeting Docker

If you are not familiar with Docker, then we could examine it briefly. Basically, the term Docker falls into the same containerization technology paradigm. Unlike Linux containers, Docker is a great software that has the following qualities:

- It isolates a containers workload within the same infrastructure or machine (shared resources)
- It is much lighter and faster in running applications on shared compute resources
- It allows a direct interaction with the underlying driver devices
- It can be installed and run on bare metal machines
- It enables saving, rolling back, and creating snapshots of the state of containers
- It provides a new level of image portability by committing and sharing images for later use

> To read more about Docker, more information can be found at www.docker.com.

Out of the box, Docker helps enterprises to build intuitive microservice applications. Although Docker is not intended to replace virtual machines, it can be considered as an excellent tool for software and application packaging, and it brilliantly enforces the immutable infrastructure pattern.

> Immutable infrastructure is a disposable environment that relies on the consistency of its component deployment. Unlike mutable infrastructure, every component can be replaced at every deployment without affecting the production pipeline. This requires a fully automated runtime environment that is inspired by programming patterns such as **Continuous Integration (CI)** and **Continuous Delivery (CD)**.

Docker is still emerging as a successful tool, especially for cloud environments. As OpenStack kept enlarging its virtualization platform support list, Docker has been recently added to the list of supported hypervisors. OpenStack exposes a new node driver, `docker.DockerDriver`, it contacts the Docker registry holding images and uploads them to Glance. New spawned instances will be running Docker engine to run containers. Note that any internal communication between a Docker virtual driver and a Docker agent is performed using HTTP API calls, as shown in the following diagram:

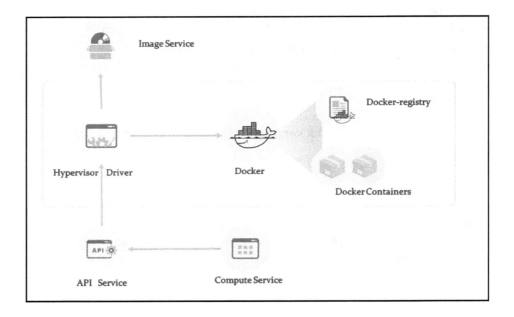

Joining Docker

The next section will guide you through a standard setup to add a third compute node in our test environment. The latter host will run `nova-compute` within configured Docker as a hypervisor. It will also run Neutron agent. The third compute node will have similar hardware requirements to the first and second compute nodes as follows:

- **Memory**: At least 4 GB RAM
- **Processor**: At least 4 64-bit x86 CPUs
- **Disk space**: At least 40 GB free disk space
- **Network**: At least two NICs

The following excerpt will be added to the `vagrant` file in our test environment:

```
...
# Compute Node Docker
config.vm.define :cn03 do |cn03|
  cn03.vm.hostname= "cn03"
  cn03.vm.provider "virtualbox" do |vb|
          vb.customize ["modifyvm", :id, "--memory", "4096"]
          vb.customize ["modifyvm", :id, "--cpus", "4"]
            vb.customize ["modifyvm", :id, "--nicpromic2",
"allow-all"]
        end
  end
```

The next steps will instruct the Ansible deployment host to add the new compute node to the pool as follows:

1. Configure the target host to be reachable by the ADH (the LXC-internal network). This can be applied by just running `vagrant` as follows:

   # vagrant up

   The `vagrant` file will launch a new virtual machine by installing the operating system within its required virtual hardware configuration.

2. Once the new virtual machine is up and running, we can start installing Docker on it. After establishing an SSH session to the `cn03` host, make sure that you install the prerequisites packages for Docker installation as follows:

   $ sudo apt-get update

4. Next, add a new entry to the `apt` sources file for the Ubuntu operating system:

   $ sudo vim /etc/apt/sources.lisd.d/docker.list
   deb https://apt.dockerproject.org/repo ubuntu-trusty main

5. Install the Docker engine after updating the source `apt` packages as follows:

   $ sudo apt-get update
   $ sudo apt-get install docker-engine

6. Docker should be installed and ready to run:

   $ sudo service docker start

7. Install the `nova-docker` plugin:

```
$ git clone -b stable/mitaka
https://github.com/openstack/nova-docker
$ cd src/novadocker/
$ python setup.py install
```

8. By now, we have a compute node running Docker ready to go. Before we start to deploy the new compute node, we will first need to go through the Ansible configuration files discussed in Chapter 1, *Inflating the OpenStack Setup*. The following stanza will be added to the `/etc/openstack_deploy/openstack_user_config.yml` file to instruct Ansible to use the third compute node and run the `nova-compute` service:

```
# Compute Hosts
compute_hosts:
...
  compute-03:
    ip: 172.16.0.106
```

9. We can edit another simple file that describes specific OpenStack configuration options located at `/et/openstack_deploy/user_variables.yml`. For now, we will need to configure Nova to use Docker as a virtualization type:

```
--------
## Nova options
nova_virt_type: docker
```

10. The last change can be committed to `git` as follows:

```
# git add -A
# git commit -a -m "Add Compute Node 03 for Docker Support"
```

11. Now that we have a new host added to the list of compute nodes, we can start the deployment by running Ansible playbooks from the ADH as follows:

```
# cd /opt/openstack-ansible/playbooks
# openstack-ansible setup-hosts.yml --limit compute-03
```

12. Updating the infrastructure using Ansible can be performed as follows:

```
# openstack-ansible os-nova-install.yml --skip-tags nova-key-
distribute --limit compute-03
```

13. The next step is straightforward we will instruct Ansible to install the `nova-compute` service using the `os-nova-install.yml` playbook:

```
# openstack-ansible os-nova-install.yml --tags nova-key-
create,nova-key-distribute
```

14. The following command line will run the Neutron agent playbook in the deployment host as follows:

```
# openstack-ansible os-neutron-install.yml --limit compute-03
```

15. Make sure that `compute-03` has been configured to support the Docker driver by checking the `/etc/nova/nova.conf` file:

```
[DEFAULT]
compute_driver = novadocker.virt.docker.DockerDriver
...
```

16. Create a `rootwrap` configuration for `nova-docker`. This can be created by copying a Docker `filters` file from the `nova-docker` package to the `rootwrap.d` folder in the compute node:

```
# cp nova-docker/etc/nova/rootwrap.d/docker.filters \
/etc/nova/rootwrap.d/
```

17. On the `compute-03` host, add the `nova` user to the `docker` user group so Nova and Docker can communicate locally :

```
# usermod -aG docker nova
```

18. In order to pick up the latest changes performed on the Nova service, restart the compute service as follows:

```
# service openstack-nova-compute restart
```

Meeting Xen

Xen has joined the list of hypervisors supported by the Nova project since the earliest releases of OpenStack. Unlike other virtual machine monitoring technologies, Xen uses different ways of managing virtual machines. From an architectural perspective, there are a number of key features for using Xen hypervisor technology, such as the following:

- It can evolve a paravirtualization technique that requires a slight modification to the guest operating systems to support Xen. Using paravirtualization technology, the Xen hypervisor could reach a high performance compared to other virtualization techniques.
- Virtual machines and hardware devices are managed by management domain **Domain 0 (Dom0)**. This is considered to be the first domain that runs after Xen boot.

 In some documentation, Domain 0 can be noted as a **privileged domains**.

- It is based on a micro kernel design.
- It supports both virtualization techniques—**Hardware Virtual Machine (HVM)** and **Paravirtualized Virtual Machine (PVM)**.

 To read more about the Xen hypervisor, check the official wiki website out at https://wiki.xenproject.org/wiki/Main_Page.

Xen can be a great choice of hypervisor under OpenStack. However, the Xen hypervisor design might appear quite complex and would need to have a basic understanding of the different terms standing behind it. Underpinning Xen technology finds the different tool stacks that expose an API and specific tools as follows:

- **Xen Lightweight (XL):** This is the default Xen tool stack that is shipped along with Xen when it is installed.

 Formerly, XEND was designed as the default toolstack of Xen; it has deprecated since the Xen 4.1 release.

- **Xen libvirt**: This is the generalized Xen tool stack. Xen can be managed by libvirt by the means of the libvirt Xen driver.
- **Xen Cloud Platform (XCP)**: This is the combination of the Xen project and the Xen API. The development of XCP is intended to facilitate the management and control of the virtualization layer by including additional functionalities compared to the default Xen tool stack. XCP is an XenServer open source version targeting a cloud platform solution. It exposes a suite of features that are well integrated in the OpenStack platform.
- **XenServer (commercial product)**: This is a Citrix property product based on Xen. It is an XCP distribution, but it leverages more advanced features.

A brief comparison of features between XCP and XenServer (different commercial flavors) can be found at `https://wiki.xenproject.org/wiki/Archive/XCP/XenServer_Feature_Matrix`.

As OpenStack supports the Xen hypervisor, it is possible to choose between the different Xen projects and tool stacks cited previously. Based on the Nova integration design layout, the following diagram illustrates how a compute service in OpenStack would connect to different Xen hypervisor distributions:

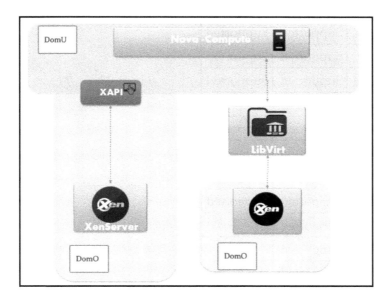

The previous diagram might give you a rough idea on how the nova-compute service runs on the Xen Domain U type. This design is intended to separate the OpenStack compute node domain and Dom0 for better isolation. At the time of writing, a few additional features have been added to the Xen hypervisor for OpenStack support. The next table gives a general overview of the novelty hypervisor support for both libvirt Xen and XenServer:

Features by resource	libvirt Xen	XenServer
Instance operations		
Launch	Supported	Supported
Suspend	Supported	Supported
Shutdown	Supported	Supported
Reboot	Supported	Supported
Rescue	Supported	Supported
Resize	Supported	Supported
Live migration	Supported	Supported
Evacuate		
Status	Supported	Supported
Pause	Supported	Supported
Resume	Supported	Supported
Restore	Supported	Supported
Volume operations		
Support	Supported	Supported
Attach	Supported	Supported
Detach	Supported	-
Snapshot	Supported	Supported
Swap	Supported	-
Fiber channel	Supported	-
iSCSI	Supported	Supported
Network operations		
Security groups	Supported	Supported

Flat	Supported	Supported
VLAN	Supported	Supported

Joining Xen

The next step will guide you through a standard setup to add a fourth compute node in our test environment. The latter host will run `nova-compute` service supporting XenServer hypervisor features with an installed Neutron agent service. The new compute node will have similar hardware requirements to the previous installed compute nodes in the test environment, as follows:

- **Memory**: At least 4 GB RAM
- **Processor**: At least 4 64-bit x86 CPUs
- **Disk space**: At least 40 GB free disk space
- **Network**: At least two NICs

The following excerpt will be added to the `vagrant` file in our test environment:

```
...
# Compute Node XenServer
config.vm.define :cn04 do |cn04|
  cn04.vm.hostname= "cn04"
  cn04.vm.provider "virtualbox" do |vb|
        vb.customize ["modifyvm", :id, "--memory", "4096"]
        vb.customize ["modifyvm", :id, "--cpus", "4"]
            vb.customize ["modifyvm", :id, "--nicpromic2", "allow-
all"]
        end
    end
    end
```

The next steps will instruct the Ansible deployment host to add the new compute node to the pool as follows:

1. Configure the target host to be reachable by ADH (the LXC-internal network). This can be applied by just running `vagrant` as follows:

   ```
   # vagrant up
   ```

   This will launch a new virtual machine by installing the operating system within its required virtual hardware configuration.

2. Once the new virtual machine is up and running, we can start installing XenServer on it. After establishing an SSH session to the `cn04` host, make sure that you install the prerequisite packages for XenServer installation, including `pip`, as follows:

```
$ wget https://bootstrap.pypa.io/get-pip.py
$ python get-pip.py
```

3. Next, we will need to install the Xen hypervisor in the new machine:

```
$ sudo apt-get update
$ sudo apt-get install xen-hypervisor-4.4-amd64
```

4. Check if Xen is properly working by issuing the following command:

```
$ sudo xl info
<SNAPSHOT: Version and Domain0>
```

5. So far, XenServer is up and running. The next step requires us to adjust our Ansible playbooks and modify the `/etc/openstack_deploy/openstack_user_config.yml` as discussed in `Chapter 1`, *Inflating the OpenStack Setup*. The fourth compute node will be added so that Ansible will point to it to install the compute service and run the `nova-compute` service:

```
# Compute Hosts
compute_hosts:
...
  compute-04:
    ip: 172.16.0.107
```

6. We can edit another simple file that describes specific OpenStack configuration options located at `/et/openstack_deploy/user_variables.yml`. For now, we will need to configure Nova to use Xen as a virtualization type:

```
--------
## Nova options
nova_virt_type: xen
```

7. The last change can be committed to `git` as follows:

```
# git add -A
# git commit -a -m "Add Compute Node 04 for Xen Support "
```

8. Now that we have a new host added to the list of compute nodes, we can start the deployment by running Ansible playbooks from ADH as follows:

```
# cd /opt/openstack-ansible/playbooks
# openstack-ansible setup-hosts.yml -limit compute-04
```

9. Updating the infrastructure using Ansible can be performed as follows:

```
# openstack-ansible os-nova-install.yml --skip-tags nova-key-distribute --limit compute-04
```

10. The next step is straightforward: We will instruct Ansible to install the nova-compute service using the os-nova-install.yml playbook:

```
# openstack-ansible os-nova-install.yml --tags nova-key-create,nova-key-distribute
```

11. The following command will run the Neutron agent playbook in the deployment host as follows:

```
# openstack-ansible os-neutron-install.yml --limit compute-04
```

12. The new compute node should include the Xen driver in the /etc/nova/nova.conf file:

```
[DEFAULT]
compute_driver = xenapi.XenAPIDriver
...
```

13. Make sure that the following stanza exists in the Nova configuration file:

```
...
[xenserver]
connection_url=http://
connection_username=
connection_password=
vif_driver=nova.virt.xenapi.vif.XenAPIOpenVswitchDriver
...
```

14. Additionally, the L2 Neutron agent can be configured to support Xen. This can be adjusted in the Neutron wrapper file, `/etc/neutron/rootwrap.conf`:

```
...
[xenapi]
xenapi_connection_url=http://
xenapi_connection_username=
xenapi_connection_password=
...
```

15. The final step of the Xen hypervisor integration in OpenStack is to restart the compute service and the network service agent as follows:

```
# service openstack-nova-compute restart
# service neutron-openvswitch-agent restart
```

16. Download and test a CirrOS guest image to `glance`:

```
# wget
http://ca.downloads.xensource.com/OpenStack/cirros-0.3.4-x86_64-dis
k.vhd.tgz
# glance image-create --name xen_cirros_pp --container-format ovf -
-disk-format vhd --property vm_mode=xen --visibility public --file
cirros-0.3.4-x86_64-disk.vhd.tgz
```

17. Launch a new instance from the new compute node:

```
# nova boot --image xen_cirros_pp --flavor m1.nano --poll cirros
```

18. You can check the virtual machines managed by Xen using the `virsh` command as follows:

```
# virsh -c xen: list
Id    Name                          State
------------------------------------------------------------
1     instance-000001               running
```

Check out the latest supported hypervisor drivers from the OpenStack marketplace website
at `https://www.openstack.org/marketplace/drivers/`.

Segregating the compute resources

What about letting your OpenStack cloud environment go beyond its limits? This can be the right moment to revisit the design of your private cloud when it grows in size. Most importantly, an operational team should be aware that the offered service should keep functioning continuously. To become more efficient as the user's resource base grows, one should pinpoint more specifically the worker blocks of the cloud—compute nodes. Again, OpenStack comes with great concepts that would help to massively scale your compute power. This is where the art of **segregation** comes. Segregation in OpenStack can be classified into two main umbrellas:

- **Infrastructure segregation**: This involves logical grouping based on conceptual and physical capabilities. Typically, it defines a specific number of clusters organized to scale horizontally.
- **Workload segregation**: This defines the optimal location from which to run a given workload based on the compute host power capabilities.

Reasoning for infrastructure segregation

Segregating resources is a beneficial strategy that has inspired many techniques to divide a variety of workloads in your cloud so that they are running in a dedicated suite of compute resources. Many factors might require us to use segregation in OpenStack, such as network latency, hardware capabilities, hypervisor types, or hardware preferences. The OpenStack Nova project offers a broad number of logical approaches to segregate compute resources, including the following:

- Cells
- Host aggregates
- Regions
- **Availability zones (AZ)**

Let's dive deeper in each of the mentioned terms and open the curtains for a wide, massive, and scalable OpenStack infrastructure.

Defining regions

A region can be considered as an independent, full deployment of OpenStack services. It might include its own running network, storage, API endpoints, and compute resources. Nova services can be fully installed in more than one region. At this high level, an OpenStack environment can scale its compute power in a multi-region setup by leveraging more compute and Nova API endpoints. The following diagram exposes a possible multi-region Nova setup for OpenStack. The key benefit of this design is to simplify the compute advertisement endpoints across all regions by sharing the same identity service. That would help operators to consolidate all authentications calls through one interface, shown as follows:

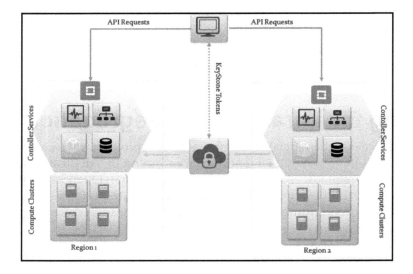

Practically, a given user can choose in which region its virtual machine should run. Regions can be defined and managed using the `keystone` command. The following command will create a new region called `Region AF-Nord`:

```
# keystone endpoint-create --region "Region AF-Nord"
```

Defining AZ

Diving a bit deeper, a given region can group one or more AZs. It simply defines a logical grouping of compute nodes. At a more granular level, a user can specify which AZ will host his/her instance(s). The blessing of such a conceptual segregation model is in its simple usage.

There is no need for any additional installation of any services, it just grabs and gathers the Nova services installed and running in a given region. Moreover, the modification and changes of the grouping can be adjusted on the fly. You will realize the enormous advantages of using the AZs when designing for a fault cloud environment. Relying on one group of compute nodes sharing the same physical infrastructure is risky and might lead to an out of service situation when the main switch connecting them goes down for some reason.

 Bear in mind that AZs are not limited to Nova services. A block storage service (such as Cinder) also supports AZ grouping options.

A user can choose to boot an instance based on specific factors, such as the following:

- Power supply
- Network latency
- Storage backend type
- Country location
- Data center placement
- Rack ID

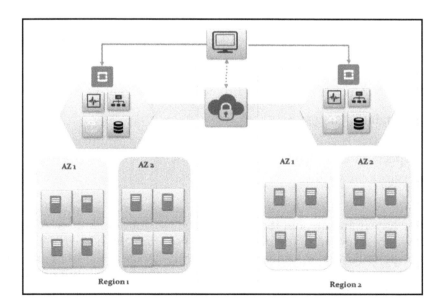

Using the `nova` command, it is possible to explicitly specify the target AZ called `AZ-1`:

```
# nova boot --flavor m2.large --image centos --availability-zone "AZ-1"
```

As the AZs are being created, the `nova` command enables us to check which host is running which service. The following example illustrates the presence of two AZs called `internal` and `AZ-1`. The cloud controller machine (`CC01`) is running on an internal AZ, while AZ-1 will be grouping compute nodes, including, for example, `CN01`, as follows:

```
# nova availability-zone-list
+----------------------+------------------------------------------+
| Name                 | Status                                   |
+----------------------+------------------------------------------+
| internal             | available                                |
|  |- CC01             |                                          |
|  |  |- nova-conductor   | enabled :-) 2016-09-26T23:19:25.000000 |
|  |  |- nova-consoleauth | enabled :-) 2016-09-26T23:19:21.000000 |
|  |  |- nova-scheduler   | enabled :-) 2016-09-26T23:19:21.000000 |
|  |  |- nova-cert        | enabled :-) 2016-09-26T23:19:25.000000 |
| AZ-1                 | available                                |
|  |- CN01             |                                          |
|  |  |- nova-compute     | enabled :-) 2016-09-26T23:19:20.000000 |
+----------------------+------------------------------------------+
```

Defining host aggregate

So far, there might be a slight confusion between **AZ** and **host aggregate** terminologies. Using host aggregate, it is possible to group compute nodes based on granular specifications and hardware profile categories. The latter criteria is defined on metadata, which describes each compute node, including information regarding the following:

- Disk and data storage type
- Network speed
- CPU speed and frequency
- Hypervisor capabilities

To avoid any confusion between AZ and host aggregate, keep in mind that end users will not explicitly use any aggregate, but it can be defined by cloud operators. A newly created host aggregate will be exposed to the public as a flavor from Nova's perspective, from which users can spawn virtual machines and implicitly choose the host aggregate. Additionally, a compute node can belong to several host aggregates, but not too many AZs.

Another slight difference is in the common grouping choices—logical groupings with host aggregate are considered based on more granular, common-host capabilities and hardware profiles. The following multi-region OpenStack infrastructure example uses three different host aggregates that could be defined based on some special characters, ordered as follows:

- **Host aggregate 1**: Groups compute nodes spread over three different AZs within two different regions. The cloud operator noted that the machines in Group 1 have fast and optimized disk types that support SSD.
- **Host aggregate 2**: Groups compute nodes spread over two different AZs, but within the same region. The cloud operator noted that machines in Group 2 are supported by CPU hardware within GPU architecture.
- **Host aggregate 3**: Groups compute nodes located in **Region 2** within the same AZ. The cloud operator noted that machines in Group 3 are connected through a fast, underlining network hardware and will be dedicated to a high-performance network:

The following diagram illustrates a sample host aggregation layout across different regions and AZs in an OpenStack private cloud environment:

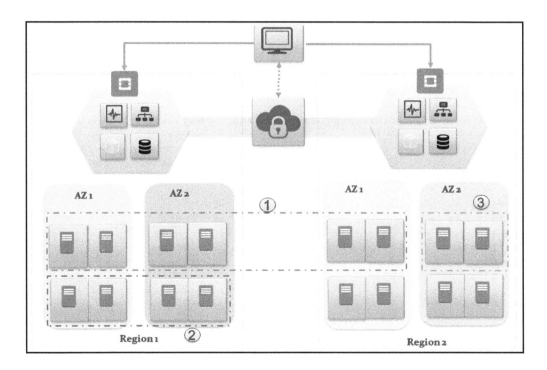

It should also be noted that the order of configuration is quite important. Host aggregates must first be defined and then applied to a given AZ. The following example will create a host aggregate as follows:

```
# nova aggregate-create agg-AZ-1 AZ-1
+----+----------+-------------------+-------+-------------------------+
| Id | Name     | Availability Zone | Hosts | Metadata                |
+----+----------+-------------------+-------+-------------------------+
| 1  | agg-AZ-1 | AZ-1              |       |'availability_zone=AZ-1' |
+----+----------+-------------------+-------+-------------------------+
```

To add a compute node named CN_47 to a created host aggregate, use the following nova command:

```
# nova aggregate-add-host CN_47 1
Host CN_47 has been successfully added for aggregate 1
+----+----------+-------------------+---------+------------------------+
| Id | Name     | Availability Zone | Hosts   | Metadata               |
+----+----------+-------------------+---------+------------------------+
| 1  | agg-AZ-1 | AZ-1              | 'CN_47' | 'availability_zone=AZ- |
                                                                    1' |
+----+----------+-------------------+---------+------------------------+
```

Optionally, using a nova command, it is possible to extend the list of metadata for a given host aggregate. The following example will tag the created host aggregate as SSD enabled within supported GPU support hardware:

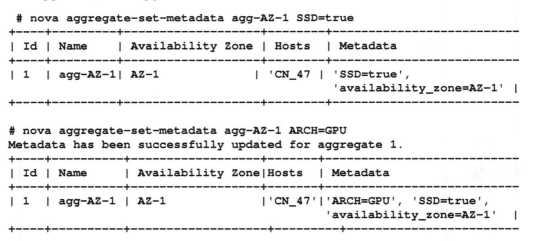

```
# nova aggregate-set-metadata agg-AZ-1 SSD=true
+----+----------+-------------------+---------+----------------------------
| Id | Name     | Availability Zone | Hosts   | Metadata
+----+----------+-------------------+---------+----------------------------
| 1  | agg-AZ-1 | AZ-1              | 'CN_47  | 'SSD=true',
                                                'availability_zone=AZ-1' |
+----+----------+-------------------+---------+----------------------------
```

```
# nova aggregate-set-metadata agg-AZ-1 ARCH=GPU
Metadata has been successfully updated for aggregate 1.
+----+----------+------------------+-------+----------------------------
| Id | Name     | Availability Zone|Hosts  | Metadata
+----+----------+------------------+-------+----------------------------
| 1  | agg-AZ-1 | AZ-1             |'CN_47'|'ARCH=GPU', 'SSD=true',
                                            'availability_zone=AZ-1'  |
+----+----------+------------------+-------+----------------------------
```

Defining your own image templates and Nova flavors will depend on which way your hardware data center has been portioned and ordered in terms of capabilities and performance. Defining a particular flavor to the end user must be calculated in advance by checking in how many instances a compute node could host in both best and worst cases. This must also include RAM and CPU over-commitment values. For example, we can create a new metadata tag called `special` that will be applied to the `agg-AZ-1` host aggregate:

```
# nova aggregate-set-metadata agg-AZ-1 special=true
Metadata has been successfully updated for aggregate 1.
+----+----------+-------------------+---------+------------------------
| Id | Name     | Availability Zone | Hosts   | Metadata
+----+----------+-------------------+---------+------------------------
| 1  | agg-AZ-1 | AZ-1              | 'CN_47' | 'ARCH=GPU', 'SSD=true',
                                             | 'availability_zone=AZ-
                                                 1', | 'special=true'

+----+----------+-------------------+---------+------------------------
```

We will add a new flavor that will be associated only to the host aggregates tagged as `special=true` in their metadata, which in our example is `agg-AZ-1`. This can be done as follows:

```
# nova flavor-create --is-public true c4.special 99 8096 100 8
+----+------------+-----------+------+-----------+------+-------+----------+
| ID | Name       | Memory_MB | Disk | Ephemeral | Swap | VCPUs | Is_Public
|
+----+------------+-----------+------+-----------+------+-------+----------+
| 99 | c4.special | 8096      | 100  | 0         |      | 8     | True
+----+------------+-----------+------+-----------+------+-------+----------+
# nova flavor-key 99 set special=true
# nova flavor-show 99
+----------------------------+---------------------+
| Property                   | Value               |
+----------------------------+---------------------+
| OS-FLV-DISABLED:disabled   | False               |
| OS-FLV-EXT-DATA:ephemeral  | 0                   |
| disk                       | 100                 |
| extra_specs                | {"special": "true"} |
| id                         | 99                  |
| name                       | c4.special          |
| os-flavor-access:is_public | True                |
| ram                        | 8096                |
| rxtx_factor                | 1.0                 |
| swap                       |                     |
| vcpus                      | 8                   |
+----------------------------+---------------------+
```

The usage of host aggregates and AZs is quite broad. Depending on how cloud operators classify the different entities that keep running their own data centers, combining both of them nicely would generate a vast, scalable, and reliable OpenStack cloud environment.

Defining cells

The concept of the cell was introduced to add another scalability layer, more specifically on top of Nova services. When designed to scale our compute infrastructure horizontally, this might add more load to the shared infrastructure services, such as message queues and databases. Although the latter common service can be clustered and designed for fault tolerance, performance degradation is still possible. As hundreds of compute nodes submit requests and API calls to message queues and databases, expanding the compute fleet power might result in a bottleneck at this level. To simplify this concept, each compute endpoint will be maintained individually. Each endpoint will be considered as a child cell derived from a parent cell. Note that the parent cell will run its own message queue and compute service API. A pertinent update within the latest OpenStack releases (from the Juno release), a newly introduced Nova service `nova-cells` will be required to be running in each cell. As with the child cell, each one will be running its own messaging queue and database service. Since it is logically an independent compute stack, each cell will be running its own `nova-conductor`, `nova-scheduler`, and `nova-compute` services per compute host. Logically, this forms a tree structure, as illustrated in the following figure:

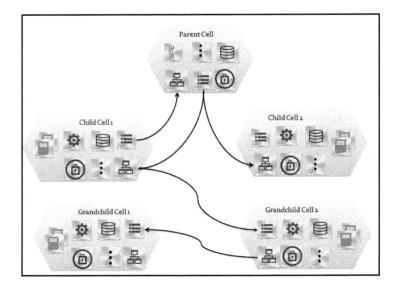

Basically, the new `nova-cells` service will be handling all the API calls and requests between different cells across the same OpenStack environment by the means of RPC calls. It also selects on which cell an instance will be running. To enable cell functionality, download and install the `openstack-nova-cells` package:

```
# apt-get install openstack-nova-cells
```

Once installed, `nova-cells` will be added to the Nova service list as follows:

```
# nova service-list
+----+------------------+-------+----------+---------+-------+------------+
| Id | Binary           | Host  | Zone     | Status  | State | Updated_at |
+----+------------------+-------+----------+---------+-------+------------+
| 1  | nova-consoleauth | cc01  | internal | enabled | up    | 2016-09-26 |
| 2  | nova-scheduler   | cc01  | internal | enabled | up    | 2016-09-26 |
| 3  | nova-conductor   | cc01  | internal | enabled | up    | 2016-09-26 |
| 6  | nova-compute     | cn01  | AZ-1     | enabled | up    | 2016-09-26 |
| 7  | nova-cert        | cc01  | internal | enabled | up    | 2016-09-26 |
| 8  | nova-cells       | cc01  | internal | enabled | up    | 2016-09-26 |
+----+------------------+-------+----------+---------+-------+------------+
```

Let's take a closer look at how cells could be practically used and managed. The following schema considers the existence of many cells, including one parent cell that runs only compute APIs, excepting a `nova-compute` service that runs specifically in compute or child cells:

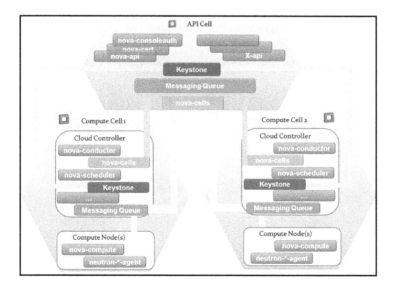

After deciding which cell will be assigned which role, configuring such a setup is fairly straightforward. We can start by looking at the first root cell that will be designated as the API cell:

1. The `nova.conf` file can be configured to dictate how requests should be forwarded across other cells through `nova-cells`, as follows:

```
[DEFAULT]
...
compute_api_class=nova.compute.cells_api.ComputeCellsAPI
```

2. Of course, each API and compute cell should have a `cells` directive enabled within a given name and type:

```
...
[cells]
enable=True
name=cell_api
type=api
```

3. You can restart a `nova-cells` service as follows:

```
# service nova-cells restart
```

4. Child cells can be adjusted as follows:

```
[DEFAULT]
quota_driver=nova.quota.NoopQuotaDriver
...
```

5. You can enable cell directive per compute cell for `Cell-OS1` and specify its type as follows:

```
...
[cells]
enable=True
name=Cell-OS1
cell_type=compute
```

6. You can restart the `nova-cells` service on `Cell-OS1` as follows:

```
# service nova-cells restart
```

7. The same can be performed for a second compute cell, `Cell-OS2` as follows:

```
...
[cells]
enable=True
name=Cell-OS2
cell_type=compute
```

8. You can restart the `nova-cells` service on `Cell-OS1` as follows:

```
# service nova-cells restart
```

 Although cell functionally reaches a high level of maturity within the latest releases of OpenStack, it still is considered experimental. At the time of writing, cells version 2 has became the default supported version for Nova cells in OpenStack.

Reasoning for workload segregation

A complementary approach to empower the scalability of large OpenStack deployment is to define policies as to how your compute nodes should be physically grouped and how they should dispatch instances. As we discussed in the previous section, segregating your large infrastructure based on AZs and host aggregates will help you to handle where a given instance will be hosted from a high-level perspective. Diving deeper, more use cases would raise the need to place a given virtual machine in a very particular fashion. Nova has an overwhelming list of features implemented to segregate workloads in a large OpenStack environment. The `nova-scheduler` service determines in which hypervisor host a virtual machine will be running. Based on preconfigured schedulers, compute scheduling services would apply certain filters based on them, and will consider hosts that meet certain predefined criteria.

Filtering the compute workload

Nova service depends on its scheduler to determine where to run a requested virtual machine. The decision as to which hypervisor machine an instance should be placed is made based on filters. The `nova-scheduler` service can use a variety of filters that can be pinpointed in the `/etc/nova/nova.conf` file. Scheduling in OpenStack is a very critical service that must be configured based on a well-documented, available hardware list and inventories in the overall infrastructure. By default, OpenStack supports the following filters:

- **ComputeFilter**: This returns a set of hosts with matched capabilities, and it is fully operational. It can be configured as follows:
    1. Edit the `/etc/nova/nova.conf` file by adjusting the following directive:

        ```
        scheduler_default_filters = ComputeFilter
        ```

    2. Restart the `nova-scheduler` service:

        ```
        # service openstack-nova-scheduler restart
        ```

- **CoreFilter**: This returns a set of hosts that have a sufficient number of available CPU cores on the physical machine. The `nova-scheduler` also allows configuring the value of the CPU overcommitment ratio.

     CPU overcommitment is a modern technique that allows launching instances that exceed the number of CPU cores available in a given hypervisor physical machine. OpenStack supports CPU, RAM, and disk overcommitment.

    CoreFilter can be configured as follows:

    1. Edit the `/etc/nova/nova.conf` file by adjusting the following directive:

        ```
        scheduler_default_filters = CoreFilter
        ```

    2. Adjusting the CPU overcommitment ratio so that it reads 24:1. This means the scheduler service is considering the existence of a pool of 24 virtual cores per physical core:

        ```
        cpu_allocation_ratio 24
        ```

3. Restart the `nova-scheduler` service:

```
# service openstack-nova-scheduler restart
```

- **RamFilter**: This returns a set of hosts that have a sufficient amount of memory available to fulfill requests of instance creation. Using `RamFilter`, Nova scheduler allows you to also configure the amount of the memory overcommitment ratio.

 Memory overcommitment is a modern technique that allows you to launch instances exceeding the memory resource available in a given hypervisor physical machine. In general, a resource is considered overcommitted when a virtual machine is using more resources than the hypervisor machine has available. OpenStack supports CPU, RAM, and disk overcommitment.

RamFilter can be configured as follows:

1. Edit the `/etc/nova/nova.conf` file by adjusting the following directive:

```
scheduler_default_filters = RamFilter
```

2. To adjust a RAM overcommitment to a ratio of 200%, set the `ram_allocation_ratio` to `2`. This means that if a physical node has X GB of RAM, then the scheduler allocates instances to that node until the sum of the RAM associated with the instances reaches double the amount of X memory size ($2*X$ GB):

```
ram_allocation_ratio 2
```

3. Restart the `nova-scheduler` service:

```
# service openstack-nova-scheduler restart
```

- **DiskFilter**: This returns a set of hosts with the available and sufficient disk space dedicated for instance root and ephemeral storage. Nova scheduler also allows you to configure the value of the disk overcommitment ratio:
    1. Edit the `/etc/nova/nova.conf` file by adjusting the following directive:

```
scheduler_default_filters = DiskFilter
```

2. Then adjust the disk overcommitment ratio to `1.5`. The scheduler allocates instances to that node until the sum of the disk space allocated to the instances root and ephemeral storage devices reaches 150% of the available disk:

```
ram_allocation_ratio 1.5
```

3. Restart `nova-scheduler` service:

```
# service openstack-nova-scheduler restart
```

- **RetryFilter**: This excludes any host that has been contacted by a service request and kept failing. It can be configured as follows:
    1. Edit the `/etc/nova/nova.conf` file by adjusting the following directive:

    ```
    scheduler_default_filters = RetryFilter
    ```

    2. The number of retries can also be adjusted when using the `RetryFilter` by adjusting the directive `scheduler_max_attempts`:

    ```
    scheduler_max_attempts = 5
    ```

    3. Restart the `nova-scheduler` service:

    ```
    # service openstack-nova-scheduler restart
    ```

- **AvailabilityZoneFilter**: This returns a set of hosts that belong to the requested AZ. It can be configured as follows:
    1. Edit the `/etc/nova/nova.conf` file by adjusting the following directive:

    ```
    scheduler_default_filters = AvailabilityZoneFilter
    ```

    2. The AZ name can be added by adjusting the following directive:

    ```
    node_availability_zone = pp_az_01
    ```

    3. Restart the `nova-scheduler` service:

    ```
    # service openstack-nova-scheduler restart
    ```

- **ComputeCapabilitiesFilter**: This returns a set of hosts that are capable of creating the requested instance type. If no extra specs are mentioned, all hosts pass the filter. It can be configured as follows:
    1. Edit the `/etc/nova/nova.conf` file by adjusting the following directive:

        ```
        scheduler_default_filters = ComputeCapabilitiesFilter
        ```

    2. The `ComputeCapabilitiesFilter` filters hosts based on an extra set of specs noted in a key-value pair format. For example, the following extra specs have the scope of checking the capabilities of a host supporting KVM as a hypervisor:

        ```
        capabilities:hypervisor_type = KVM
        ```

    3. Restart the `nova-scheduler` service:

        ```
        # service openstack-nova-scheduler restart
        ```

- **ImagePropertiesFilter**: This returns a set of hosts based on the supported images description in Glance. It can be configured as follows:
    1. Edit the `/etc/nova/nova.conf` file by adjusting the following directive:

        ```
        scheduler_default_filters = ImagePropertiesFilter
        ```

    2. Restart the `nova-scheduler` service:

        ```
        # service openstack-nova-scheduler restart
        ```

    3. Image properties can be adjusted based on the architecture or the hypervisor type. The following example instructs Glance to update an existing image by setting its architecture property to `arm` and Xen hypervisor:

        ```
        # glance image-update img-uuid --property
        architecture=arm --property hypervisor_type=xen
        ```

Let's say a cluster of web servers will be hosted in one or several compute nodes and should be highly available. A best practice is to run each web server in different compute node. If one physical machine goes down, the instances running on top will no longer be available. The bright side is that the rest of the instances are responsive and running on healthy compute nodes—do not put all your eggs in one basket. Nova joins two more filters to the default list designed for the collocation and distribution of a group of instances in OpenStack by the means of the `Affinity` and `Anti-Affinity` groups:

- **ServerGroupAffinity**: This dictates the scheduling on which to run virtual machines of the same group on the same physical machine (hypervisor host). It can be configured as follows:

    1. Edit the `/etc/nova/nova.conf` file by adjusting the following directive:

       ```
       scheduler_default_filters = ServerGroupAffinity
       ```

    2. Restart the `nova-scheduler` service:

       ```
       # service openstack-nova-scheduler restart
       ```

    3. Instructing Nova to spawn a new instance in a specific affinity group requires the usage of the `--hint` extra option in the `nova` command line tool. But first, make sure that you have created a new server group with the following affinity policy:

       ```
       # nova server-group-create --policy affinity pp_ag01
       # nova boot --image "CentOS 7.2" --hint
       group=471eab33-4a24-3372-bba2-537e529abe13 --flavor 5
       "instance 01"
       # nova boot --image "CentOS 7.2" --hint
       group=3452caa2-4552-4e34-cba2-63efad278301 --flavor 5
       "instance 02"
       ```

    This ensures that `instance 01` and `instance 02` will be running on the same hypervisor machine. `ServerGroupAffinity` is a recommended filter on which to run a set of cluster virtual machines that require a high performance rate, including intercommunication and throughput between them.

- **ServerGroupAntiAffinity**: This dictates the scheduling on which to run each virtual machine in a group on different physical machines (hypervisor host). It can be configured as follows:

  1. Edit the `/etc/nova/nova.conf` file by adjusting the following directive:

     ```
     scheduler_default_filters = ServerGroupAntiAffinity
     ```

  2. Restart the `nova-scheduler` service:

     ```
     # service openstack-nova-scheduler restart
     ```

  3. Instruct Nova to spawn a new instance in a different physical machine using the flag `--hint` in the `nova` command-line tool. Create a new server group with an anti-affinity policy as follows:

     ```
     # nova server-group-create --policy anti-affinity
     pp_aag01
     # nova boot --image "CentOS 7.2" --hint
     group=2255eabb-4733-9822-cab2-4221fe7eabee--flavor 5
     "instance 01"
     # nova boot --image "CentOS 7.2" --hint
     group=33e4c144-34e2-34ba-c3ea-763edba22230--flavor 5
     "instance 02"
     ```

  This ensures that `instance 01` and `instance 02` will be running on different hypervisor machines. `ServerGroupAntiAffinity` might be useful to design highly available application layers in OpenStack. Nova supports more customized filters for specific purposes. Depending on the use case of each, the list can be extended by editing the `nova.conf` file of each compute node.

 An exhaustive list of the available filters supported in OpenStack can be found at `http://docs.openstack.org/mitaka/config-reference/compute/scheduler.html`.

Weighting the compute power

The weighting mechanism in OpenStack Nova comes in the last stage in the scheduling process. Basically, `nova-scheduler` applies a rate per selected candidate host upon each request. The rate calculation is based on the monitored resource consumption measured across a specific period of time. By default, `nova-scheduler` elects the host with the highest weight on which to run the requested instance as demonstrated in the next sample figure:

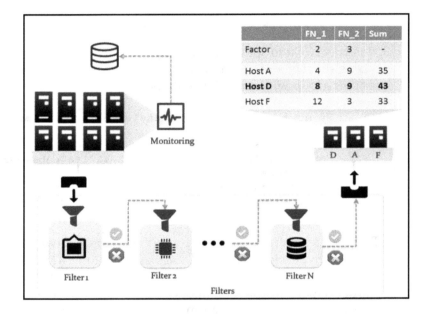

As illustrated in the previous diagram, every physical machine saves its monitored metrics in a database. That will help the scheduler to decide the best host fit based on the resources state saved in the database over all the compute nodes. The weight score is multiplied by a configured factor, and it will be calculated by the end of the weighting process.

The weighing code calculates the score of a given host using the formula *Score_Host-Filtered = $\sum$ (Factor_Cost_FN x Score_Value_FN)*. The features of this equation are detailed as follows:

- *Factor_Cost_FN*: This is the factor set for the cost function
- *Score_Value_FN*: This is the obtained score after applying the set of filters per host

The previous example promotes **Host D** as the elected physical compute node to fulfill the instance request. The score was calculated as *[(8*2) + (9*3)] = 43*.

Stacking or spreading

Although Nova exposes several filters for better computing workload distribution and management, you may encounter a problem where you are not able to spawn more instances even though Horizon is showing free resources. By default, instances will be spread across the selected compute nodes one by one. This ensures that the compute workload is fairly distributed across all hosts. Eventually, the behavior of the scheduler as to how to dispatch the instances across compute nodes can be tricky in this case. By default, filters provide a finely selected list of hosts. Requesting different instances with different flavors would create a sort of concurrency, and even prevent them from creating additional instances with larger flavor. In this case, spreading the compute workload can be adjusted by defining a scheduler-weighing policy. On the other hand, by referring to the last section, you can adjust the compute workload distribution by exploiting the available resources of the first host in the selected list as much as possible before moving to the next compute node. This stacking method can be performed by referring to the anti-affinity rules covered in the last section.

Weighing in action

The next wizard will go through some simple steps to enable weight-scheduling in Nova:

1. Edit the `nova.conf` file by editing the directive `compute_available_monitors`:

   ```
   ...
   compute_available_monitors = nova.compute.monitors.all_monitors
   ...
   ```

   This will activate the Nova `monitors` class to start collecting monitoring metrics for consumed resources per compute host.

2. In the same file, we can enable CPU monitoring:

   ```
   ...
   compute_monitors   ComputeDriverCPUMonitor
   ...
   ```

3. Enable the weighting for RAM and metrics:

```
. . .
scheduler_weight_classes    nova.scheduler.weights.all_weighers
nova.scheduler.weights.ram
. . .
```

4. As was discussed in the previous paragraph, stacking virtual machines can be preferred in our setup. We can instruct Nova to create new instances in new compute nodes only when all memory in the first is consumed:

```
. . .
ram_weight_multiplier=-1.0
. . .
```

 If you prefer to spread instances across hosts so memory will be consumed in all compute nodes per instance request order, set `ram_weight_multiplier` to a positive value `1.0`.

5. Add a new multiplier to calculate the weighing host I/O operations. We will instruct Nova to use the active host with the least I/O workload by setting a negative value as follows:

```
. . .
io_ops_weight_multiplier=-1.0
. . .
```

6. Additionally, weighing in Nova can be calculated on a named metric set by adding a new metric section in the `nova.conf` file as follows:

```
[metrics]
weight_multiplier = -0.1
weight_setting = cpu.iowait.percent=-1.0
```

The last example will stack a possibly new requested instance in the host with the metrics that has the lowest CPU I/O wait percentage value.

At the time of writing, only CPU monitoring is enabled for hosts. RAM monitoring will be included in the future versions, but no driver is available yet that can be integrated in the scheduler weighing options. The current available CPU metrics supported through the `ComputeDriverCPUMonitor` are as follows:

- `cpu.user.percent`
- `cpu.user.time`
- `cpu.iowait.percent`
- `cpu.iowait.time`
- `cpu.frequency`
- `cpu.idle.percent`
- `cpu.idle.time`
- `cpu.percent`
- `cpu.kernel.time`
- `cpu.kernel.percent`

Summary

The OpenStack compute service leverages many concepts and terminologies described in this chapter in order to enable additional OpenStack capabilities. We have learned how adding a new compute node can be performed from code using Ansible. More advanced layouts have been exposed to take advantage of several supported hypervisors by OpenStack. We have covered a few of them, such as Docker and Xen. VMware and HyperV are also powerful candidates to support Nova hypervisors in OpenStack, but they were not covered. This chapter demonstrates not only that adopting a hybrid hypervisor setup might expand your OpenStack environment, but also that you might expand it adopting compute segregation. It is a big plus to design a compute cluster setup by taking into consideration how they should be grouped locally and spread widely. We have covered a logical grouping layout using host aggregates supported by Nova. Of course, an expanded OpenStack operational infrastructure should think big by leveraging concepts as cells, regions, and AZs.

By the end of the chapter, a more granular study has been reinforced by putting compute service scheduling under the scope. We have seen how `nova-scheduler` works and demonstrated how instance requests will end up after applying a number of filters and weighing operations. As a compute service in OpenStack is overwhelmed by a variety of options, another spot in OpenStack has been kept by extending its functions—storage in OpenStack. In the next chapter, we will step up to explore more opportunities on using novelties of storage in OpenStack.

3
Enlarging the OpenStack Storage Capabilities

"He who performs not practical work nor makes experiments will never attain to the least degree of mastery."

–Jabir Ibn Hayyan

The first two chapters of this book were designed to cover the latest capabilities of the OpenStack ecosystem and its deployment in a large-scale environment. In the first part of the book, automation was presented as a must have craft tool chain to deploy an OpenStack environment. The second chapter took the compute service to the next level by bringing new opportunities to extend its first core service capabilities in the deployed OpenStack environment. The next part of the extension journey will cover the storage service in OpenStack. In this chapter, more storage options will be presented to tackle different use cases taking part in the OpenStack setup extension. This chapter will walk-through the following topics:

- Exploring the variety of backends existing in OpenStack block storage
- Diving into advanced block storage configurations including scheduling and weighing mechanisms
- Highlighting existing approaches for storage backups in OpenStack
- Extending the storage layout using Ceph
- Introducing the file share service in the OpenStack ecosystem

Varying the block storage backends

The block storage service in OpenStack , code named **Cinder**, has been extensively developed at every OpenStack release to come with new additions to support multiple storage vendors. As Cinder has become the default service for persistent storage in OpenStack, managing volumes for virtual machines has been simplified. This covers more operational commands for different use cases, including:

- Recovering instances due to hypervisor failure or instance termination events by attaching volumes to new ones.
- Resizing volumes size based on storage array capacity and flavor needs.
- Storage backup enhanced by the volume snapshot option.
- Creating volumes from snapshots.
- Enhanced block storage capabilities including quality of service, live migration, and performance requirements such as latency and input/output storage throughput. This can be adjusted depending on the vendor storage backend configured for Cinder.

When designing a storage solution in a private cloud environment based on OpenStack, one should revisit the direct and available options for Cinder. Let's get to grips and check out the most commonly used ones.

Managing block storage – Logical Volume Manager (LVM)

The LVM is a Linux kernel volume manager that adds an abstraction layer between the storage and logical devices in a Linux-based system. LVM is an independent Linux software that provides useful options including resizing, snapshotting volumes, and thin provisioning. Bear in mind that LVM is not a Cinder dependency. On the other hand, it is configured as the default block storage backend for OpenStack.

Under the hood, the `cinder-volume` service will check the volume group created in the storage host. To provide access, Cinder will use a path target by the means of multi transfer protocols supported by LVM, including iSCSI (SCSI over IP), iSER (SCSI over RDMA), and **Fiber Channel over Ethernet (FCoE)**.

Configuring the OpenStack block storage service to use LVM is straightforward. We will first need to install the LVM package if it is not installed yet. Follow these steps:

1. In a CentOS Linux distribution, LVM can be installed in the storage node using the following command line:

   ```
   # yum install lvm2
   ```

2. Any available and attached disk devices can be listed in the storage node as follows:

   ```
   # fdisk -la /dev/disk/by-path
   ...
   pci-0000:00:0d.0-ata-3.0 -> ../../sdc
   ```

3. We will start by creating the physical available LVM disk using the pvcreate option:

   ```
   # pvcreate /dev/sdc
   Physical volume "/dev/sdc" successfully created
   ```

4. Check out if the new disk is being successfully created and is ready to go with LVM using the pvscan or pvdisplay commands:

   ```
   # pvdisplay
   ...
   "/dev/sdc" is a new physical volume of "9.77 GiB"
   --- NEW Physical volume ---
   PV Name                 /dev/sdc
   VG Name
   PV Size                 9.77 GiB
   Allocatable             NO
   PE Size                 0
   Total PE                0
   Free PE                 0
   Allocated PE            0
   PV UUID                 BJ5r75-qAeU-AFVf-cbzT-d3HZ-1vYX-JyHBZ4
   ```

5. For the new added physical volume, it is possible to create the volume group using LVM assigned as the pool of storage ready to allocate for the block storage service named cinder-ext-volumes:

   ```
   # vgcreate  cinder-ext-volumes /dev/sdc
   Volume group "cinder-ext-volumes" successfully created
   ```

6. The new volume group can be verified from the `vgdisplay` LVM command line:

```
...
--- Volume group ---
  VG Name               cinder-ext-volumes
  System ID
  Format                lvm2
  Metadata Areas        1
  Metadata Sequence No  1
  VG Access             read/write
  VG Status             resizable
  MAX LV                0
  Cur LV                0
  Open LV               0
  Max PV                0
  Cur PV                1
  Act PV                1
  VG Size               9.76 GiB
  PE Size               4.00 MiB
  Total PE              2499
  Alloc PE / Size       0 / 0
  Free  PE / Size       2499 / 9.76 GiB
  VG UUID               RGPiI9-VQ81-1ONA-j4dY-2cTt-riDG-XQeOOE
```

7. The next step requires addressing in the main configuration file the type of the
   storage driver, the target transport protocol, and the name of the volume group
   created in the previous step. This can be adjusted in the `lvm` section of the
   `/etc/cinder/cinder.conf` file:

```
# vi /etc/cinder/cinder.conf
...
[lvm]
volume_group=cinder-ext-volumes
volume_driver=cinder.volume.drivers.lvm.LVMVolumeDriver
iscsi_protocol=iscsi
```

Optionally, the `iscsi_helper` directive can be adjusted to `tgtadm`,
`scstadmin`, or `lioadm` for LIO iSCSI. By default, it is configured to use
`tgtadm` allowing various SCSI target drivers that include iSCSI, SRP, and
FCoE to assign block volumes.

8. Restart the `cinder-volume` service to reflect the latest configuration update:

   ```
   # systemctl restart cinder-volume
   ```

9. Create the first volume with 4 GB size using the `cinder` command line interface as follows:

   ```
   # cinder create --display-name "extended volume 01" --display-
   description "Extending Cinder PacktPub" 4
   ```

```
+---------------------------------------+-------------------------------------+
|              Property                 |              Value                  |
+---------------------------------------+-------------------------------------+
|             attachments               |               []                    |
|          availability_zone            |              nova                   |
|              bootable                 |              false                  |
|          consistencygroup_id          |              None                   |
|             created_at                |   2017-07-16T19:41:40.000000        |
|            description                |   Extending Cinder PacktPub         |
|             encrypted                 |              False                  |
|                id                     | 40683bde-36f5-4bea-83c2-dca093441ac1 |
|             metadata                  |               {}                    |
|          migration_status             |              None                   |
|            multiattach                |              False                  |
|               name                    |       extended volume 01            |
|        os-vol-host-attr:host          |              None                   |
|     os-vol-mig-status-attr:migstat    |              None                   |
|     os-vol-mig-status-attr:name_id    |              None                   |
|       os-vol-tenant-attr:tenant_id    |   6fa47a2b492e48548c2c9596d1c2a5a2  |
|   os-volume-replication:driver_data   |              None                   |
| os-volume-replication:extended_status |              None                   |
|          replication_status           |             disabled                |
|               size                    |               4                     |
|             snapshot_id               |              None                   |
|            source_volid               |              None                   |
|               status                  |             creating                |
|              user_id                  |  375ae5b3359a4a1ba835825fcc3fc8c3   |
|             volume_type               |              None                   |
+---------------------------------------+-------------------------------------+
```

10. The volume created has ID `40683bde-36f5-4bea-83c2-dca093441ac1`. The creation of a new Cinder volume is accompanied with the creation of a new logical volume that can be managed and traced through LVM. That can be verified using the `lvdisplay` LVM command-line tool:

   # **lvdisplay**

```
--- Logical volume ---
LV Path                /dev/cinder-ext-volumes/volume-40683bde-36f5-4bea-83c2-dca093441ac1
LV Name                volume-40683bde-36f5-4bea-83c2-dca093441ac1
VG Name                cinder-ext-volumes
LV UUID                9Qz44p-pwIR-f80t-w41h-Cpsa-M2qp-16g5Yw
LV Write Access        read/write
LV Creation host, time cloud, 2017-07-16 21:41:41 +0200
LV Status              available
# open                 0
LV Size                4.00 GiB
Current LE             1024
Segments               1
Allocation             inherit
Read ahead sectors     auto
- currently set to     8192
Block device           253:2
```

11. This also can be checked from the `cinder` command-line tool interface by applying the following command line:

   # **cinder list**

```
+--------------------------------------+-----------+------------------+------------------+------+-------------+----------+-------------+-------------+
|                  ID                  |  Status   | Migration Status |       Name       | Size | Volume Type | Bootable | Multiattach | Attached to |
+--------------------------------------+-----------+------------------+------------------+------+-------------+----------+-------------+-------------+
| 40683bde-36f5-4bea-83c2-dca093441ac1 | available |        -         | extended volume 01 |  4  |      -      |  false   |    False    |             |
+--------------------------------------+-----------+------------------+------------------+------+-------------+----------+-------------+-------------+
```

Managing block storage – Network File System (NFS)

Cinder also supports the NFS driver, which can use NFS as a storage backend. During the last few decades, most IT organizations have started using heavily shared storage that can be easily managed from one central point. Cinder provides a driver that maps its API to the NFS backend storage. It mounts the mapped NFS and creates and stores disk images on it so compute nodes require NFS mounts to access the image files:

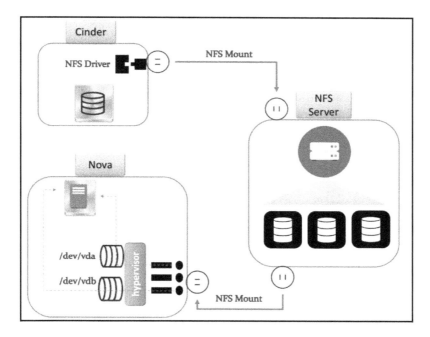

The usage of the driver requires the existence of an NFS server already in place. Depending on your server vendor, NFS protocol should be supported. On the OpenStack block storage and compute servers, make sure that an NFS client is installed.

If using Ansible to deploy and manage OpenStack servers, make sure to have nfs-utils and nfs-utils-lib installed in the block storage and compute playbooks. For more details refer to https://docs.openstack.org/openstack-ansible-os_cinder/latest/configure-cinder.html#nfs-backend

1. Install the NFS client in both the block storage and compute servers as follows:

   ```
   # yum install nfs-utils nfs-utils-lib
   ```

2. Add a new NFS share file /etc/cinder/nfs_shares in the block storage server. The file should contain a list of the accessible shares in the NFS by providing the hostname and share name in the NFS server as follows:

   ```
   nfs-server-pp:/sync/share1
   ```

   Where nfs-server-pp is the hostname of the NFS server and /sync/share1 is the path of the NFS share in the server.

3. Adjust the permission rights for the Cinder service to access the NFS share file:

```
# chown  root:cinder /etc/cinder/nfs_shares
# chmod 0640 /etc/cinder/nfs_shares
```

4. Add `nfs` as an additional default storage backend and specify the NFS driver name in the Cinder configuration file by adjusting the `volume_driver` directive as follows:

```
...
enabled_backends=nfs
volume_driver=cinder.volume.drivers.nfs.NfsDriver
```

5. Make sure to include the NFS share path specified in step 1 and the mount point:

```
...
nfs_shares_config=/etc/cinder/nfs_shares
nsf_mount_point_base=/var/lib/cinder/mnt
```

6. Restart the `cinder-volume` service to reflect the new driver change:

```
# systemctl restart cinder-volume
```

7. Once the new configuration has reloaded, the new NFS share directory should be mapped and visible in the block storage server:

```
# mount | grep nfs
nfs-server-pp:/sync/share1 on
/var/lib/cinder/mnt/26adf398409d4f6e9c44918779d8f57f
 type nfs4
(rw,relatime,vers=4.1,rsize=81921,wsize=81921,namlen=255,hard,proto
=tcp,port=0,clientaddr=10.10.255.1,local_lock=none,addr=10.10.255.1
)
```

8. A new hashed directory, `26adf398409d4f6e9c44918779d8f57f`, has been created under the Cinder mount path for the share declared in the NFS share file `/etc/cinder/nfs_shares`. Any new created volume will reside under the new directory mapped as follows:

```
# cinder volume create --display-name Vol_In_NFS 5
...
id             |      a1bd4ce0-6f41-44db-84e7-b71b50ba90de
...
# ls /var/lib/cinder/mnt/26adf398409d4f6e9c44918779d8f57f
volume-a1bd4ce0-6f41-44db-84e7-b71b50ba90de
```

Managing block storage – Ceph RADOS Block Device (RBD)

Ceph has been an attractive open source **Software Defined Storage** (**SDS**) solution since its earliest release. This can be justified by its massive scalability and high performance capabilities that puts all defined patterns for block, object, and file storage in one unified software. Ceph was designed to scale up to Exabyte storage pools and even more, and run on commodity hardware.

If you are already running a Ceph storage cluster, there are still areas to extend its layout when operating a private cloud running OpenStack. As mentioned earlier, Ceph takes care of block storage that can be used as backend storage for OpenStack. This can be achieved by including the RBD backend driver implemented by Cinder. In this way, operators can enjoy the power of Ceph where instances and disks live and be managed by Cinder.

In this section, we will walk-through how to use Ceph as storage backend for OpenStack block storage:

 If using Ansible, check out the latest stable Ceph playbooks hosted at `https://github.com/ceph/ceph-ansible`. A detailed setup description can be found at `http://docs.ceph.com/ceph-ansible/master/`.

1. Make sure to have Ceph client packages installed in the OpenStack controller and compute nodes:

   ```
   # yum install ceph
   ```

2. We will also need to install the Python `rbd` binding library in the same hosts to connect to the Ceph cluster:

   ```
   # yum install python-rbd
   ```

3. Before proceeding to manipulate the Cinder configuration file, we will need to first configure our OpenStack nodes as Ceph clients. If you have the `ceph-deploy` command-line tool installed, push the `/etc/ceph/ceph.conf` file from any Ceph node to the OpenStack nodes as follows:

   ```
   # ceph-deploy config push cc-01 cn-01
   ```

The `ceph-deploy push` command requires an `ssh password-less` login to any cloud controller or compute nodes. Make sure that the ceph cluster node can have SSH access to OpenStack nodes where the configuration file will be pushed.

4. On the Ceph cluster node, create a new Cinder pool named `ext-volumes`:

```
# ceph osd pool create ext-volumes 256
```

5. As a client, OpenStack Cinder users will need to authenticate against the Ceph authentication system. On the Ceph node, create a new Cinder user named `cinder` that is allowed to have access to the `ext-volumes` pool previously created:

```
# ceph auth get-or-create client.cinder mon 'allow r' osd ' allow
rwx pool=ext-volumes'
[client.cinder]
        key = QA7sduw73dx83ks02210dj9Lmfj00sdju3ndoy==
```

6. Copy the keyring created to the OpenStack nodes and change its ownership to `cinder` user:

```
# ceph auth get-or-create client.cinder | ssh cc-01 sudo tee
/etc/ceph/ceph.cinder.keyring
# ceph auth get-or-create client.cinder | ssh cn-01 sudo tee
/etc/ceph/ceph.cinder.keyring
# ssh cc01 sudo chown cinder:cinder /etc/ceph/ceph.cinder.keyring
# ssh cn01 sudo chown cinder:cinder /etc/ceph/ceph.cinder.keyring
```

7. Make sure that the Cinder client can access the Ceph cluster by running the following command line from the cloud controller node:

```
# ceph -s --name client.cinder --keyring
/etc/ceph/ceph.cinder.keyring
```

```
cluster 93efca28-4b1b-4eae-bfaa-ef159d654e73
 health HEALTH_WARN
        64 pgs degraded
        64 pgs undersized
 monmap e1: 1 mons at {mon0=172.28.128.133:6789/0}
        election epoch 3, quorum 0 mon0
 osdmap e5: 1 osds: 1 up, 1 in
        flags sortbitwise,require_jewel_osds
  pgmap v8: 64 pgs, 1 pools, 0 bytes data, 0 objects
        34004 kB used, 986 MB / 1019 MB avail
              64 undersized+degraded+peered
```

8. Now that we have completed the Ceph configuration part, we adjust our block storage service to use Ceph as a storage backend. Add `rbd` to the `enabled_backends` option in the `/etc/ceph/ceph.conf` file:

```
...
enabled_backends= rbd
volume_driver=cinder.volume.drivers.nfs.NfsDriver
```

9. In a new section, add a new `rbd` block with the following set of configuration options:

```
...
[rbd]
volume_driver = cinder.volume.drivers.rbd.RBDDriver
rbd_pool = ext-volumes
rbd_user = cinder
rbd_ceph_conf = /etc/ceph/ceph.conf
rbd_store_chunk_size = 4
```

That specifies in the order of the RBD driver, the name of the target Ceph pool, the Cinder user, the path of the Ceph configuration file, and optionally the size of chunked stored objects in megabytes.

 The latest list of Cinder and Ceph options for the Ocata release can be found at the official OpenStack reference page: `https://docs.openstack.org/ocata/config-reference/block-storage/samples/cinder.conf.html`.

10. Restart the `cinder-volume` service:

    ```
    # systemctl restart cinder-volume
    ```

11. Test the new updated configuration by creating a new Cinder volume that should be created and stored on the Ceph cluster as follows:

    ```
    # cinder create –display-name rbd 5
    ```

ID	Status	Migration Status	Name	Size	Volume Type	Bootable	Multiattach
1848e828-b3d7-4829-8411-1756233fa60f	available	-	rbd	5	-	false	False

12. From the controller node, check the creation of the new `rbd` volume in the Ceph `ext-volumes` pool:

    ```
    # rados -p volumes -name client.cinder –keyring
    /etc/ceph/client.cinder.keyring ls | grep -i id
    rbd_id.volume-1848e828-b3d7-4829-8411-1756233fa60f
    ```

Scheduling and filtering

Cinder provides a mechanism to assign volume management to a specific backend. As we have iterated previously through some of the most commonly used Cinder backends, an OpenStack operator could control the creation of different volumes that correspond to specific backends available in the storage pool. This becomes a very essential part of block storage operation when using a variety of multiple backends. The key component that takes care of automating the placement of new volumes is the **cinder-scheduler** service.

As shown in the following figure, the cinder-scheduler decides the best backend fit of a newly created volume based in the first place on filter policies. Filters can be applied according to a few storage information capabilities such as drive state, health, space, and types. The second scheduler stage will apply weighing policy if more than one backend candidate has fulfilled the first stage requirements. The weighing mechanism will assign each filtered storage backend a weight (integer) and sort them out based on specific criteria such as the available free space. Keep in mind that the candidancy list will be continuously updated based on the state of each storage backend reported by the scheduler. The latest OpenStack releases provide more enhanced filtering and weighing algorithms allowing operators to refine the scheduling process in Cinder:

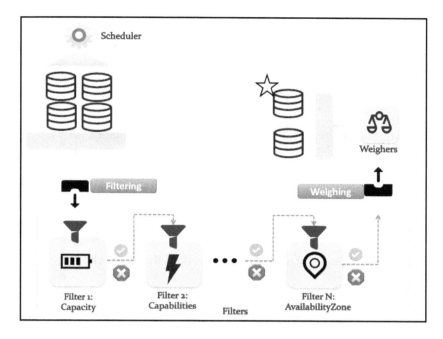

By default, both filter `CapacityFilter` and weigher `CapacityWeigher` are enabled. This promotes the backend with more storage space capacity.

> The latest available Cinder scheduler filters and weights can be found respectively at: `https://docs.openstack.org/cinder/pike/scheduler-filters.html` and `https://docs.openstack.org/cinder/pike/scheduler-weights.html`. Make sure to check the latest update of the Cinder scheduler filters and weights by referring to the latest OpenStack release web page.

Hybrid storage scheduling

In this section, we will be extending our block storage layout by introducing a filtering and weighing mechanism for two of the storage backends elaborated in the first part of this chapter—LVM and Ceph RBD:

1. Review the Cinder configuration settings to enable `lvm` and `rbd` drivers within their respective sections:

```
[default]
enabled_backends = lvm,rbd
```

```
[lvm]
volume_group=cinder-ext-volumes
volume_driver=cinder.volume.drivers.lvm.LVMVolumeDriver
iscsi_protocol=iscsi
volume_backend_name=lvm
iscsi_ip_address=192.168.47.50
volumes_dir=/var/lib/cinder/volumes
[rbd]
volume_driver = cinder.volume.drivers.rbd.RBDDriver
rbd_pool = volumes
rbd_user = cinder
rbd_ceph_conf = /etc/ceph/ceph.conf
rbd_store_chunk_size = 4
rados_connect_timeout = -1
volume_backend_name=rbd
    ...
```

2. Restart the `cinder-volume` service to reflect the latest changes:

```
# systemctl restart cinder-volume
# systemctl restart cinder-api
```

3. Declare a new storage type for each storage backend. This allows us to label each configured Cinder storage backend. One can, for example, assign a label `medium_store` to the `lvm` backend as a limited storage capacity of 200 GB that can be used for caching. Make sure to assign the new Cinder volume type to the LVM backend created previously:

```
# cinder type-create  medium_store
# cinder type-key medium_store set volume_backend_name=lvm
```

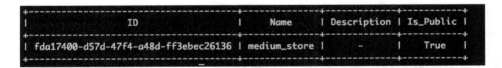

4. Create a new storage type for the Ceph backend pool with a label `large_store` as default for large storage capacity over 1 TB:

```
# cinder type-create large_store
```

5. So far, we have two different storage backends enabled for Ceph and LVM. We will need to adjust the Cinder scheduler to place any newly created Cinder volume in the right storage pool. For this purpose, we will use two sophisticated filters and weighers named respectively: DriverFilter and GoodnessWeigher. Make sure to enable the DriverFilter filter and the GoodnessWeigher weigher to be used as default ones for scheduling in the Cinder configuration file:

```
[default]
scheduler_default_filters = DriverFilter
scheduler_default_weighers = GoodnessWeigher
```

6. The former filter is configured by the directive filter_function. The next configuration will update the Cinder scheduler to place new volumes smaller than 20 GB on lvm and volumes larger than 50 GB on the rbd backend:

```
[lvm]
...
filter_function = "volume.size < 20"
...
[rbd]
...
filter_function = "volume.size >= 50 "
```

7. Staying with the same configuration section, use the goodness_function directive to define weighing rules for the filtered volumes. The following configuration will check if the filtered volume size is larger than 20 GB and then lvm will be ranked as 50 and rbd is rated as 100. The volume requested will then be placed in the rbd storage backend. If the filtered volume size is 15 GB then lvm is ranked as 100 and it will be the ideal candidate for the new volume placement while rbd will be rated 10:

```
[lvm]
...
goodness_function = "(volume.size < 20) ? 100 : 50"
...
[rbd]
...
goodness _function = "(volume.size >= 50) ? 100 : 10"
```

8. Restart the `cinder-volume` and `api` services to reflect the new configuration update:

```
# systemctl restart cinder-volume
# systemctl restart cinder-api
```

9. As we have our Cinder types, we can provision a Cinder volume to check out the correctness of the filter and weight set in the previous steps:

```
# cinder create -display-name vol_10g 10
```

10. Verify the new created volume type and which storage backend it has been assigned to:

```
# cinder list
```

Navigating the storage backup alternatives

Finding the right backup solution can be a complicated task if it is not handled from the very beginning of the private cloud design phase. Typically, backup and recovery options can be seen from different levels that vary from storage, filesystem, to application level. Most of the open source solutions in the community might help to achieve this goal, but that would require a junction of tool sets and a proper automation stack. For this reason, it is necessary to pinpoint to a simple and efficient backup and recovery solution that ensures the safety of critical production data. Prior to the Havana release, the OpenStack ecosystem had one key operational gap to provide a simple backup solution to the world that needed tweaking, home-made tools. One common option with some extensions was using heavy snapshots to compute instances and block storage. Although this feature can help partially to have point in time copies of images and data, it is still not considered a very proper way to back up a production workload.

Today, due to the amazing development of the OpenStack ecosystem, it might be tempting to extend its built-in backup and restore advancements. One of the major trends of backup in OpenStack is to rely on the new block storage service capabilities. Starting from the Juno release, the Cinder backup service has become more mature by providing an API to import and export service metadata as well as supporting volume replication at the block level.

The new way of operating backups in OpenStack has amazingly improved the flexibility of handling critical data by defining storage and replication policies. Besides its simplicity, there are more backup drivers developed around Cinder. Ceph and Swift were the first candidates to perform volume backups. The list of backup drivers is being enlarged to cover more open source options such as NFS, GlusterFS, public cloud as Google Cloud Storage, and vendor storage solutions such as IBM Tivoli Storage Manager.

Ideally, exploring more than one single option to back up data is a trivial way to keep business continuity. OpenStack offers you that. Let's explore dual backup options using Ceph and Swift.

Ceph as backup

So far, we have extended our Cinder storage layout to use Ceph as a storage backend. As shown previously, the latest releases of Cinder have integrated a new Cinder mechanism to back up volumes on external storage targets by means of the `cinder-backup` service. In this section, we will use an additional Cinder driver for Ceph RBD backup:

1. Starting by the Ceph storage nodes, make sure to provide a storage pool for the Cinder backup volumes as follows:

   ```
   # ceph osd pool create cinder-ext-backups 256
   ```

2. To authenticate against the Ceph API, create a new `cinder-backup` user to enable read and write permissions in the new pool created in the previous step:

   ```
   # ceph auth get-or-create client.cinder-backup mon 'allow r' osd
   'allow class-read object_prefix rbd_children, allow rwx pool=
   cinder-ext-backups '
   [client.cinder-backup]
     key = AQCQJuFZ7q75AhAAcP78U4VcDt6bNHkUxzg0ow==
   ```

 Ceph Authentication (Cephx) is used by default as the authentication protocol for the cryptographic authentication between client and server hosts in a Ceph cluster. Cephx requires having keys for Ceph monitors and OSDs.

3. Generate and add the `keyring` for the `client.cinder-backup` user to the controller node `cc01.pp` running the Cinder backup service:

```
# ceph auth get-or-create client.cinder-backup | ssh cc01.pp sudo
tee /etc/ceph/ceph.client.cinder-backup.keyring
```

4. On the controller node, make sure to change ownership of the newly copied `keyring` to the Cinder user:

```
# chown cinder:cinder /etc/ceph/ceph.client.cinder-backup.keyring
```

5. In the Cinder main configuration file, set the default backup driver to use Ceph as follows:

```
[DEFAULT]
...
backup_driver=cinder.backup.drivers.ceph
```

6. In the same section, set the Ceph configuration path, the backup pool name target, and the Ceph backup user respectively as the following:

```
...
backup_ceph_conf=/etc/ceph/ceph.conf
backup_ceph_pool=cinder-ext-backups
backup_ceph_user=cinder-backup
```

7. Additionally, adjust a few Ceph storage options such as the number of bytes per transfer, and the RBD stripe unit and count when creating a backup image, respectively as follows:

```
...
backup_ceph_chunk_size=100500000
backup_ceph_stripe_unit=0
backup_ceph_stripe_count=0
```

8. Restart the `cinder-backup` service:

```
# systemctl restart cinder-backup
```

9. Create a backup for a volume using the Cinder `backup-create` option:

```
# cinder backup-create --name backup_ceph_01
40683bde-36f5-4bea-83c2-dca093441ac1
```

10. From a Ceph cluster node, verify that the backed-up volume exists in the Ceph storage cluster using client tools as follows:

```
# rbd -p cinder-ext-backups ls
volume-40683bde-36f5-4bea-83c2-dca093441ac1
```

Swift as backup

Swift is a revolutionary object storage solution that started with the earliest release of OpenStack. Besides other storage systems integrated in the OpenStack ecosystem, Swift has mainly been designed to store data in the form of objects and it is exposed in a flat hierarchy. This new design compared to block storage, file-based systems, and object storage systems handles data placement and their availability very well. Since its earliest release, Swift has been used for archiving, repository stores, and backups. In this section, we will explore how Swift can be useful to back up volumes. Unlike other systems, Swift provides an optimized way to perform full back up in a short time window. Cinder supports the Swift backup driver by default:

1. On the Swift nodes, install the `cinder-backup` service as follows:

```
# yum install cinder-backup
```

2. Create a Swift container to be used as our volume backup store:

```
# swift post vol-ext-backups
```

3. Edit the default Cinder configuration file to use the Swift backup driver:

```
[DEFAULT]
...
backup_driver= cinder.backup.drivers.swift
```

4. In the same section, adjust the Swift options including the Swift user, the name of the Swift container to store the backups, the size in bytes of each Swift backup transferred object, and the address of the Swift cluster endpoint respectively:

```
...
backup_swift_user=cinder
backup_swift_container=vol-ext-backups
backup_swift_object_size=52428800
backup_swift_url=http://swift-cc:8080/v1/AUTH
```

5. Restart the `cinder-volume` and `cinder-backup` services:

```
# systemctl restart cinder-volume
# systemctl restart cinder-backup
```

6. We can start creating our second backup volume to the Swift storage cluster as follows:

```
# cinder backup-create 40683bde-36f5-4bea-83c2-dca093441ac1
```

| 40683bde-36f5-4bea-83c2-dca093441ac1 | backing-up | - | extended volume 01 | 4 | - | false | False |

7. Verify the end of the backup process by checking the Cinder backup list. A successful Swift backup must show the creation of a new volume ID in available state as follows:

ID	Volume ID	Status	Name	Size	Object Count	Container
da01bffd-ed20-443a-8174-96493a9ee860	40683bde-36f5-4bea-83c2-dca093441ac1	available	None	1	22	vol-ext-backups

The Cinder backup service creates `22` objects for the volume that will be spread across the Swift cluster nodes. Swift will do the rest, preparing the ring, and object mappings for a faster backup and recovery process.

8. To validate what has been done from the Swift side, check the object list of the `vol-ext-backups` container in one of the Swift nodes:

```
# swift list vol-ext-backups
volume_40683bde-36f5-4bea-83c2-
dca093441ac1/20171020142814/az_nova_backup_da01bffd-
ed20-443a-8174-96493a9ee860-00001
volume_40683bde-36f5-4bea-83c2-
dca093441ac1/20171020142814/az_nova_backup_da01bffd-
ed20-443a-8174-96493a9ee860-00002
volume_40683bde-36f5-4bea-83c2-
dca093441ac1/20171020142814/az_nova_backup_da01bffd-
ed20-443a-8174-96493a9ee860-00003
...
volume_40683bde-36f5-4bea-83c2-
dca093441ac1/20171020142814/az_nova_backup_da01bffd-
ed20-443a-8174-96493a9ee860-00022
```

Automating the creation of backups in Cinder was quite limited prior to the OpenStack Liberty release. This means it was only possible to create backups of volumes in an `available` state. The latest Ocata release has improved the backup feature and it becomes a non-disruptive operation. It becomes possible to take advantage of incremental backups from the generic Cinder backup service, whereas most of the drivers did not have this feature implemented prior to the Kilo release. By default, the `cinder-backup` services creates a full backup of the volume. Any attached volume to an instance would not be backed up. This limitation has been resolved and leaves the cloud administrator to choose how to perform backups either from CLI or API in an automated fashion.

For example, creating an incremental backup for an attached volume can be achieved by using two newly introduced flags, `incremental` and `force`, as follows:

```
# cinder backup-create -name vol001-backup-1 --description vol001-
incremental-backup --incremental --force vol001
```

The previous command line will create an incremental backup of the volume `vol001` either if it is attached to an instance or in an available state.

On the other hand, these types of storage cloud operations must be performed with care and require deep insight on how to set up a strategy for backups. The latest releases support more options to facilitate a successful backup experience.

 As best practice, it is recommended to initially take a snapshot of the Cinder volume before starting the backup process. You may face an error or non-ending snapshot creation process when the volume is attached and being used by a virtual machine. For this reason, make sure to unmount the volume to avoid data corruption. Additionally, Cinder snapshot targets can be backed by LVM and use less volume size in an incremental way. Bear in mind that you have enough space to store snapshots.

Exploring Manila – shared file service

Since the Liberty release, the OpenStack community recognises the integration of a new storage project in its ecosystem–shared file service code named `Manila`.

It adds a complementary storage offer to the existing facilities by allowing simultaneous access to a shared-file based storage for different clients, including compute instances. Unlike Swift, Cinder, or Ceph, Manila sits on top of the basic core services of OpenStack. It is considered as a storage backend agnostic, so it can use different storage backends, as we have explored in Cinder. Manila supports several sharing protocols including NFS, CIFS, CephFS, GlusterFS, and HDFS. Bear in mind that the storage backends use drivers to serve shares and should use one of the mentioned protocols.

 Manila can also be integrated with other third-party storage vendors such as IBM, Hitashi, EMC, NetApp, and many more. The complete list of supported Manila share storage drivers can be found here at `https://docs.openstack.org/ocata/config-reference/shared-file-sy stems/drivers.html`.

Before introducing share storage services in our running OpenStack environment, let's explore how Manila orchestrates the file shares and manages their life cycle from an architectural perspective.

Manila presents four main components:

- **Share server**: The storage appliance hosting the shares
- **API server**: A REST API interface to handle client requests
- **Scheduler**: A Manila service handling the selection of the best share server fit for any new file share request
- **Data service**: A Manila service handling data backups, recovery, and migration

As shown in the following diagram, Manila communicates with three OpenStack core services:

- **Nova** to host the Manila share server.
- **Cinder** to create the file shares in block storage.
- **Neutron** to provide access of the file shares to the compute nodes through the tenant network.

Manila service could use different storage backends if configured with the supported ones. The share server will handle the storage access through the Manila service once the storage driver is enabled:

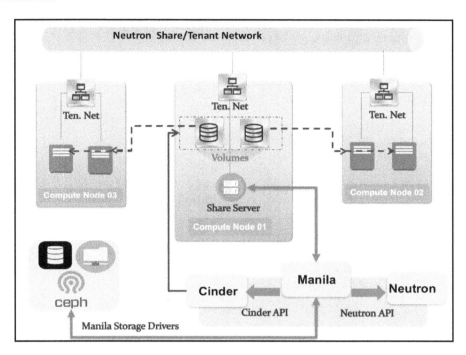

Configuring the shared file service

Similarly, Manila can be configured to use multiple storage backends and it is able to handle them at the same time. This can be achieved by enabling drivers supported by Manila in the main configuration file `/etc/manila/manila.conf`.

Configuring block storage for the Manila backend

The driver backend can be specified using the flag `driver_handles_share_servers`.

In the following configuration, we will enable the generic driver for Manila that uses a combination of volume and compute services:

1. Edit the `/etc/manila/manila.conf` configuration file to specify the desired generic driver to be used. Additionally, specify the types of protocols for share communication as follows:

   ```
   [Default]
   enabled_share_backends = generic
   enabled_share_protocols = NFS
   ```

2. For each backend driver, add a new section named as specified in the `enabled_share_backends` directive initially for a generic driver:

   ```
   ...
   [generic]
   share_backend_name = generic_backend01
   share_driver = manila.share.drivers.generic.GenericShareDriver
   driver_handles_share_servers = True
   service_instance_flavor_id = 2
   service_image_name = manila-service-image
   service_instance_user = manila
   service_instance_password = manila
   ```

    The previous settings assume the existence of a Manila image in Glance named `manila-service-image`. Use Glance or OpenStack command-line tools to create a Manila service image. The disk image of the default Manila service can be found here at `http://tarballs.openstack.org/manila-image-elements/images/manila-service-image-master.qcow2`.

3. Restart the Manila services so the latest configuration update will take effect:

```
# systemctl restart manila-api
# systemctl restart manila-scheduler
# systemctl restart manila-share
```

4. We can start by creating our share types. The first command will create the generic type that provisions Manila share onto any generic pool drives:

```
# manila type-create generic True
```

5. The new created type can be associated with each backend listed in the Manila configuration file generic_backend001:

```
# manila type-key generic set
share_backend_name=generic_backend001
driver_handles_share_servers=True
```

6. In the previous step, the generic type is configured with the additional argument driver_handles_share_servers set to True. This requires additional information to be provided that includes network and subnet to start creating shares and access them. By default, Neutron is used for the networking service. The network and subnet IDs can be saved in environment variables to be used later:

```
# NET_ID=$(openstack network list | grep 'int_net' | awk '{print
$2}')
# SUBNET_ID=$(openstack subnet list | grep 'subnet1' | awk '{print
$2}')
```

7. Create our first network share generic_manila_share by specifying the network and subnet IDs as follows:

```
# manila share-network-create --neutron-net-id $NET_ID --neutron-
subnet-id $SUBNET_ID --name manila_share_net
```

8. Using the new Neutron share network created in the previous step, create a new NFS share as follows:

```
# manila create --name gen_share --share-network manila_share_net
NFS 5
```

9. To allow a new Nova instance to gain access to the newly created share, create an access rule for the share. The following command line allows any Nova instance with an IP address in the `10.0.2.0/24` range access to the `gen_share` share:

```
# manila access-allow gen_share ip 10.0.2.0/24 --access-level rw
```

10. Collect the access path of a newly created share:

```
# manila show gen_share | grep path | cut -d    '|' -f3
path = 10.0.2.50:/shares/gen_share-0d42f645-5adb-4708-85f3-
d1aa56eb16ac
```

11. On any virtual machine that has gained access to the new created share, mount the new Manila shared storage using NFS from the collected access path in the previous step as follows:

```
# ssh user@10.0.2.47
# mount -t nfs 10.0.2.50:/shares/share-0d42f645-5adb-4708-85f3-
d1aa56eb16ac /mnt
# df -hT
Filesystem Type Size Used Avail Use% Mounted on
...
10.254.0.7:/shares/share-35353aa3-389c-4274-a28a-14563b28fc2a nfs4
5076M 1.7M 5022M 1% /mnt
```

The `GenericShareDriver` uses Cinder to create new volumes. Once the Manila instance is launched, the Cinder volume will be attached, formatted, and mounted to the Manila instance. In the last step, the Manila share will export the Cinder volume as NFS export.

Configuring CephFS for the Manila backend

In the next configuration exercise, we will use the CephFS driver for Manila to map shared file systems to instances using the Ceph native protocol:

1. Edit the `/etc/manila/manila.conf` configuration file to specify the desired CephFS driver to be used. Additionally, specify the types of protocols for share communication as follows:

```
[Default]
enabled_share_backends = generic,cephfs
enabled_share_protocols = NFS,CEPHFS
```

2. Add a new backend driver section named as specified in the `enabled_share_backends` directive for `cephfs`:

```
...
[cephfs]
share_backend_name = cephfs_backend002
share_driver=
manila.share.drivers.cephfs.cephfs_native.CephFSNativeDriver
driver_handles_share_servers = False
cephfs_conf_path = /etc/ceph/ceph.conf
cephfs_auth_id = manila
cephfs_cluster_name = ceph
```

3. Restart the Manila services so the latest configuration update will take effect:

```
# systemctl restart manila-api
# systemctl restart manila-scheduler
# systemctl restart manila-share
```

 The `manila-scheduler` is restarted to update the service of the existence of more than one backend that needs to be handled upon each share request.

4. Create the `cache` type that provisions the Manila share onto any pool exposing SSD disks:

```
# manila type-create cache False
```

5. The newly created type can be associated with the `cephfs` backend listed in the Manila configuration file `cephfs_backend002`:

```
# manila type-key generic set \
share_backend_name=cephfs_backend002 \
driver_handles_share_servers=False
```

6. In the Ceph Monitor node, create a new `keyring` and authentication key for the Manila service and then copy the `keyring` file to the OpenStack node running the share service:

```
# ceph auth get-or-create client.manila  -o manila.keyring mon
'allow rwx' osd 'allow rw' | ssh cc01.pp sudo tee
/etc/ceph/ceph.client.manila.keyring
```

7. Update the file ownership of the `keyring` file for a Manila user:

```
# chown manila:manila /etc/ceph/manila.keyring
```

8. Edit the existing Ceph configuration file in a controller node to support the new Manila user where the keyring will be set:

```
#  vim /etc/ceph/ceph.conf
...
[ceph.manila]
client mount uid = 0
client mount gid = 0
keyring = /etc/ceph/manila.keyring
```

 Make sure that the Manila client can successfully authenticate against the Ceph authentication system. At the time of writing, only `cephx` is supported to control access of clients to shares.

9. Create a new Manila share using the `cache` share type:

```
# manila create --share-type cache --name ceph_share cephfs 5
```

10. Locate the new Manila share export using the `share-export-location-list` Manila command line as follows:

```
# manila share-export-location-list ceph_share
```

11. Create a new user `pp_user` to gain access to the created share `ceph_share`:

```
# manila access-allow ceph_share cephx pp_user
```

12. The new user will need a `keyring` to authenticate against `cephx`. The client `keyring` can be initiated from the OpenStack Manila share server:

```
# ceph --name=client.manila --keyring=/etc/ceph/manila.keyring
auth get-or-create client.pp_user -o pp_user.keyring
    [client.pp_user]
            key = B6sdsdi/zdjhTARGgBfDBCDsfJaaOKaqgKsdDu==
```

13. Make sure to copy both the `pp_user.keyring` and main Ceph configuration files to a running instance in the OpenStack environment. To start using the new share, install a Ceph client such as a FUSE client in the virtual instance:

```
# ssh user@10.0.2.47
$ sudo yum install ceph-fuse
```

14. Mount the new share to the instance using the `ceph-fuse` command line:

```
$ sudo ceph-fuse /mnt/cephfs --idk=pp_user \
--conf=/home/ user/ceph.conf --keyring=/home/ user/pp_user.keyring \
--client-mountpoint=/volumes/_nogroup/ a1334114-
fe11-38fe-11a1-1a1a1a3dee22
$ df -k
Filesystem 1K-blocks Used Available Use% Mounted on
...
ceph-fuse 5368720 0 5368720 0% mnt/cephfs
```

Summary

In this chapter, we have highlighted a few possibilities of extending the storage layout around OpenStack by taking advantage of the usage of a variety of storage drivers. As has been demonstrated, a cloud operator can define multiple storage backends that can be used at the same time. Keep in mind that there is not only Ceph, NFS, or LVM that can be used as a storage backend for the block storage in OpenStack; Ocata release brings dozens of storage drivers supported by Cinder. With this tremendous growth of the storage support options around OpenStack, we have walked-through a combination of storage backends usage and covered filters and weighing mechanisms and how they work. At this stage, you should be comfortable to start integrating such useful functions in the storage scheduler service. It is important to add more intelligent storage backend in a private cloud by tweaking scheduling, filtering, and weighing mechanisms in OpenStack.

This chapter also covered the new novelty of storage backups in OpenStack. Bear in mind that the old limitations of backup features in OpenStack won't discourage you anymore to define a simple, efficient, and straightforward backup strategy for your cloud data. As demonstrated in the chapter, Cinder backup can use different storage backends. Hence, a cloud operator could manipulate different backup storage backends from one central OpenStack service. Finally, we have covered a new file share as a service project code named Manila. That brings another storage facility to the OpenStack ecosystem. With the overwhelming storage glossary in the latest release of OpenStack, you should be capable of distinguishing different use cases of each storage option in the OpenStack setup. As this chapter highlighted several options around storage solutions supported by OpenStack, we will tackle the same topic, but for networking services in the next chapter.

4
Harnessing the Power of the OpenStack Network Service

"Education is the passport to the future, for tomorrow belongs to those who prepare for it today."

–Malcolm X

The networking service in OpenStack has reached a level of extensibility allowing users and cloud administrators to build a variety of networking topologies, as well as to exploit more advanced network setups in a cloud environment. There are two different networking services in OpenStack:

- **Nova-network**: The legacy network solution taking part of the Nova compute component
- **Neutron**: A standalone network service that exposes overwhelming features and functionalities

In this chapter, we will focus on a Neutron project in an existing OpenStack environment and will go through its reference implementation to explore more features, including:

- The novelty of Neutron architecture and plugins
- Iteration through its core and service plugins
- Configuring plugins and drivers including their respective agents
- Writing and integrating our first custom plugin ML2 extension

- Exploring how to provide a highly-available routing solution using VRRP and DVR
- Introducing **Network Function Virtualization** (**NFV**) concepts
- A guide through the installation of NFV platform in an OpenStack named Tacker

Neutron plugins reference

Implementing a custom network layout in an OpenStack environment can be achieved by acquiring the usage of plugins within the Neutron architecture. It is important to differentiate between two types of plugins in Neutron as follows:

- **Core plugins**: These enable layer 2 connectivity, IP addressing management, and orchestration of the logical elements of a virtual network, including networks, ports, and subnets.
- **Service plugins**: These enable a higher implementation of network services at layer 3 including routings, load balancing, firewalling, and VPN services.

By exploiting the plugin-based architecture design of Neutron, a cloud administrator can go beyond basic network implementations and extend its layout to support additional network functionalities.

Before diving into this exercise, let's have a look at the current state of art of the new Neutron modular plugin-based architecture.

Driving the sole plugin – ML2 under the hood

Prior to the Havana release, Neutron did not allow the integration of multiple core plugins at the same time. Thus, to extend the network layout and use third party software and hardware network features, cloud operators had to harden additional design customization in the existing OpenStack environment. That adds more complexity to distinguish which part of the core OpenStack network service would use which plugin.

 From the code perspective, plugins are extensible Python classes that can be customized and written to integrate a specific network type and vendor device. A new plugin can be invoked through the Neutron APIs.

Most common used monolithic core plugins in Neutron are LinuxBridge, Open vSwitch, and other third-party network vendors. Starting from Havana release, the Neutron plugin hub has changed drastically to come up with one core plugin **Modular Layer 2 (ML2)** allowing the integration of multiple L2 technologies at the same time by just referencing them in the Neutron configuration.

Bundling the ML2 plugin into the network service offers a variety of network types to create more segmented and segregated networks. This includes layer 2 functionalities such as VLAN, VXLAN, GRE, Flat, and local network types. They are referred in the Neutron plugin glossary as ML2 type driver.

 To review different and existing network types in the latest release of OpenStack, refer to the URL `https://docs.openstack.org/newton/networking-guide/config-ml2.html`.

Besides this major switch of Neutron core plugin, ML2 comes with a second support driver referred to as **mechanism driver**. That encapsulates the standalone core plugins existing prior to Havana release including LinuxBridge, and Open vSwitch, plus multiple co-existing vendor technologies such as OpenContrail, Cisco NXOS, and more.

 Replacing origin plugins with ML2 does not affect the usage of their respective agents from an architectural perspective.

Bear in mind that each of the mechanism driver's supports a specific set of networks driver's types. An example of the latest OpenStack Pike release for the ML2 support mechanism drivers matrix can be found here
at `https://docs.openstack.org/neutron/pike/admin/config-ml2.html#ml2-driver-support-matrix`.

Let's summarize where the ML2 core plugin sits in the OpenStack networking service and how it reflects a wide number of options for users and vendors to leverage different network layout possibilities, including both hardware and software resources:

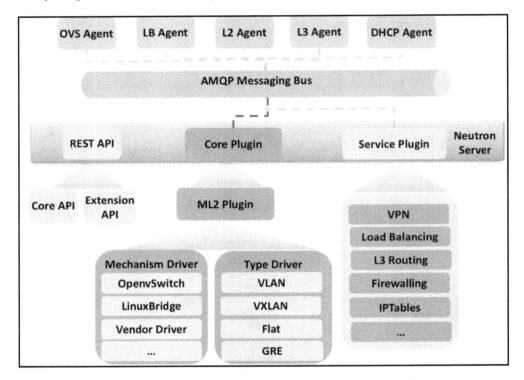

Extending ML2 – customizing your own plugin

The ML2 plugin is mainly designed to expose APIs for writing drivers of different devices and network types. That creates new opportunities for cloud administrators to implement their custom plugin that meets their network needs and features. As mentioned previously, Neutron plugins are a set of pluggable and extensible python classes invoked while intercepting API requests. As ML2 exposes multiple types of drivers and mechanism drivers; in the next section, we will demonstrate the implementation of a custom ML2 mechanism driver and integrate it in the existing Neutron setup.

The sole part of the ML2 plugin is the mechanism driver that ensures the correctness and functionality of the applied networking mechanism. The ML2 plugin will make sure to process any received requests and invokes necessary database updates before dispatching them to the desired mechanism driver. It mainly exposes two methods invoked in two different phases to handle network resources for the new mechanism driver as follows:

- ACTION_RESOURCE_precommit: This is a method called within the database transactional context state. The new driver will only validate any resource change privately in the database and will not reflect it outside of Neutron.
- ACTION_RESOURCE_postcommit: This is a method called to persist the resource state in the database and mark the transaction as complete. The driver will relay the updated information outside of Neutron to the external network controller. Possible ACTION and RESOURCE values can be as follows:
  - ACTION: create, delete, or update
  - RESOURCE: network, subnet, or port

Writing a specific mechanism driver depends on elaborating new python classes to handle API calls that will use the predefined methods in the ML2 plugin. The new demo driver will simply log each API request to trace the Neutron calls as follows:

1. Create a new Python file ext_pp.py under the /usr/lib/python2.7/site-packages/neutron/plugins/ml2/drivers/ source directory with the following content:

```
from neutron.plugins.ml2 import driver_api as api
from neutron.db import api as db_api
from oslo_log import log as pp_logger
LOG = pp_logger.getLogger(__name__)

class MyExtDriver(api.MechanismDriver):
    def initialize(self):
  LOG.info("Initializing MyExtDriver driver ")
```

Note that the new class driver MyExtDriver uses the Neutron API class MechanismDriver. As discussed previously, the MechanismDriver class exposes all necessary methods to manage network resources that can be found in the /usr/lib/python2.7/site-packages/neutron/plugins/ml2/driver_api.py file.

2. Let's make sure that our new mechanism driver can be recognized by the ML2 plugin. This can be checked by adding the new driver name in the `/etc/neutron/plugins/ml2/ml2_conf.ini` file. Edit the `[ml2]` stanza in the configuration file, as follows:

```
...
[ml2]
...
mechanism_drivers = openvswitch,linuxbridge,pp_ext_driver
```

3. The next step requires the update of the `/usr/lib/python2.7/site-packages/neutron-7.0.1-py2.7.egg-info/entry_points.txt` file to load the new `pp_ext_driver` mechanism driver, added recently in the `ml2_conf.ini` file:

```
[neutron.ml2.mechanism_drivers]
...
pp_ext_driver = neutron.plugins.ml2.drivers.ext_pp:MyExtDriver
```

Each added new mechanism driver in the `entry_points.txt` file is specified as follows:

`NAME_DRIVER = PATH_DRIVER:MECHANISM_DRIVER` where

- `NAME_DRIVER`: This is the name of the driver as referred in the `ml2_conf.ini` file
- `PATH_DRIVER`: This is the path of the Python driver file starting with the `neutron.plugins.ml2.drivers` string
- `MECHANISM_DRIVER`: This is the name of the class mechanism driver as mentioned in the Python file

4. Restart the `neutron-server` service to register the new mechanism driver:

```
# systemctl restart neutron-server
```

5. Tail the Neutron server log file to verify whether our new mechanism is being detected and recognized successfully or not:

```
# tail -f /var/log/neutron/server.log | grep pp_ext_driver
...
INFO neutron.plugins.ml2.managers [-] Loaded mechanism driver
names: ['openvswitch', 'linuxbridge', 'pp_ext_driver']
INFO neutron.plugins.ml2.managers [-] Registered mechanism driver
```

```
names: ['openvswitch', 'linuxbridge', 'pp_ext_driver']
INFO neutron.plugins.ml2.drivers.pp_ext [-] Initializing
MyExtDriver driver
...
```

6. Like all other OpenStack components, Neutron exposes a REST API that can be used to implement custom methods and handle the specific needs of network resources including networks, subnets, and ports. Based on this approach, we will enhance our first mechanism driver skeleton by including additional methods to process API requests for a port resource. This example assumes the presence of a network and subnet in the OpenStack environment that inherits their post and pre CRUD methods by default from the ML2 plugin. In the following section, we will elaborate on the ext_pp.py file by adding the create, delete, and update methods for the port resource within an existing network:

```
...
def create_port_precommit(self, context):
        port = context.current
        network = context.network
        LOG.info("Create Network Port Precommits with associated
network: %s " %(network.current['name']))

def create_port_postcommit(self, context):
        port = context.current
        network = context.network
        LOG.info("Create Network Port Postcommits with associated
network: %s " %(network.current['name']))

def delete_port_precommit(self, context):
        port = context.current
        LOG.info("Delete Network Port Precommits with associated
network: %s " %(network.current['name']))

def delete_port_postcommit(self, context):
        port = context.current
        network = context.network
        LOG.info("Delete Network Port Postcommits with associated
network: %s " %(network.current['name']))

def update_port_precommit(self, context):
        port = context.current
        network = context.network
        LOG.info("Update Network Port Precommits with associated
network: %s " %(network.current['name']))

def update_port_postcommit(self, context):
```

```
port = context.current
network = context.network
LOG.info("Update Network Port Postcommits with associated
network: %s " %(network.current['name']))
```

7. Save the new addition and restart the Neutron server service:

```
# systemctl restart neutron-server
```

8. To verify the log output of the new driver mechanism, we will need to create a new port using Neutron CLI or Horizon dashboard:

```
# neutron router-create ExtendedRouter
```

```
Created a new router:
+----------------------------+------------------------------------------+
| Field                      | Value                                    |
+----------------------------+------------------------------------------+
| admin_state_up             | True                                     |
| distributed                | False                                    |
| external_gateway_info      |                                          |
| ha                         | False                                    |
| id                         | 63880d49-7bc0-4384-a5e7-35ba9d6c00a7     |
| name                       | ExtendedRouter                           |
| routes                     |                                          |
| status                     | ACTIVE                                   |
| tenant_id                  | 6fa47a2b492e48548c2c9596d1c2a5a2         |
+----------------------------+------------------------------------------+
```

9. Create a new port resource by creating a new router interface associated with a given subnet network resource. In this example, we use an existing subnet named extended_subnet corresponding to the extended_network network:

```
# neutron router-interface-add ExtendedRouter extended_subnet
Added interface a3484b3a-8ff3-442b-bc24-b414abfaed14 to router
ExtendedRouter.
```

10. In the Neutron server log file, check the execution of the new mechanism driver that triggers the creation of a new port within a network interface as per both methods create_port_precommit and create_port_postcommit:

```
...
INFO neutron.plugins.ml2.drivers.ext_pp
[req-35e9ff56-7742-4dc9-9f65-fe7c0096fedc admin admin] Create
Network Port Precommits with associated network: extended_network
```

```
INFO neutron.plugins.ml2.drivers.ext_pp
[req-35e9ff56-7742-4dc9-9f65-fe7c0096fedc admin admin] Create
Network Port Postcommits with associated network: extended_network
...
```

The Neutron ML2 API module,
at https://docs.openstack.org/neutron-lib/latest/reference/modules/neutron_lib.p
lugins.ml2.html, has a rich submodules reference to extend the network resources by
extending the ML2 plugin methods. As demonstrated previously, we used port and
network contexts to extract network information from the port entity. Modern mechanism
drivers extend the ML2 methods, by extracting resources information in more customized
ways using the predefined Neutron API attributes. For example, the port methods in our
first mechanism driver can be more enhanced by extracting a variety of information of the
current port context using port attributes.

A full collection of predefined port attributes can be found here at
https://github.com/openstack/neutron/blob/master/neutron/api/v2/attributes.py#L
87.

Maximizing network availability

The ML2 plugin offers a wide range of possibilities to handle different virtual network
topologies in an OpenStack environment. The implementation of virtual networks can be
more complex, depending on how traffic will be segmented based on tunneling.

> Tunneling in OpenStack networking jargon can be classified into two
> network types:
>
> - **Underlay network**: IP fabric network connectivity between
>   network and compute nodes
> - **Overlay network**: A virtual layer-2 domain for connectivity
>   between VMs

Depending on which mechanism driver is being used, any virtual network in Neutron acts as a layer-2 broadcast domain. To manage and operate any type of virtual network resources, refer to the basic pieces in Neutron forming a virtual network infrastructure as follows:

- **Virtual network switches**: These connect virtual and physical networks by the means of virtual ports. By default, they are implemented in built-in virtual switching mechanisms, in OpenStack they are Open vSwitch and LinuxBridge.
- **Virtual network interfaces**: These connect an instance to a network interface on boot.

The last piece of the network jargon in Neutron operates in layer 3 by means of **virtual routing**. More expanded network layouts make extensive use of virtual routers to establish connectivity between VMs residing in different networks or across cloud environments. Prior to the OpenStack Juno release, routers in Neutron pictured a single point of failure. A few options existed to tackle the routing and L3 agent HA challenge by tweaking a custom setup using a Linux clustering software solution such as Pacemaker, HAProxy, and Corosync. Since Juno's release, Neutron includes a few native options to address the single point of failure issue with legacy routers:

- **Distributed Virtual Routing (DVR)**
- **Virtual Router Redundancy Protocol (VRRP)**

In the next sections, we will expand an existing network setup in OpenStack using DVR and VRRP, and highlight the major differences between both of HA solutions.

Neutron HA – DVR

Legacy routers in Neutron provide the following connectivity scenarios:

- Traffic flow between VMs (east-west)
- Traffic flowing between VMs and an external network (north-south) using floating IP addresses
- Traffic flowing from a VM to an external network (north-south) using **Source Network Address Translation (SNAT)**

SNAT is a network method consisting of replacing the source IP address of a TCP packet when reaching an external network, the source IP of the VM will be translated and used as the router's address.

As the traffic flowing through the whole OpenStack environment must hairpin through the same network nodes, this routing design exposes major performance issues with the increase in the amount of traffic. Besides to the latter performance bottleneck problem, centralizing routing decisions in a single node (one route instance) limits scaling traffic and retains a single point of failure in an OpenStack private cloud environment.

The DVR approach brings an extensible design of the former legacy routing in Neutron, by reducing the traffic load on the network node. The idea behind it is to distribute simply the Neutron L3 agents service across the compute nodes. The traffic flow will be traversing the compute nodes instead of the network node for east-west and north-south. Hence, scaling the network will be limited only by the size of the compute pool in an OpenStack environment, while the network L3 failure is narrowed to the compute farm as every compute node will be running an L3 agent service. Under the hood, the compute nodes will have the same floating IP namespaces. Thus, VMs will reach external networks or vice-versa (north-south) through the compute nodes connected directly to the external network.

Configuring DVR

Expanding the existing network layout for Neutron using DVR requires a few configuration updates in both network and compute nodes as follows:

1. On the network node, set the `router_distributed` directive to `True` in the `/etc/neutron/neutron.conf` file to enable DVR by default for newly created routers:

   ```
   ...
   [DEFAULT]
   ...
   router_distributed = True
   ```

2. On the network node, set the `enable_distributed_routing` directive to `True` in the `/etc/neutron/plugins/ml2/openvswitch_agent.ini` file to support DVR for the ML2 plugin using the OVS driver mechanism:

   ```
   ...
   [agent]
   ...
   enable_distributed_routing = True
   ```

3. Adopting the DVR mode requires updating the L3 agent running mode on the network node from `legacy` to either `dvr` or `dvr_snat`. In the next configuration update, we will keep our L3 agent handling SNAT service in addition to DVR support by changing legacy to `dvr_snat` for `agent_mode` directive in the `/etc/neutron/l3_agent.ini` configuration file as follows:

```
[DEFAULT]
...
agent_mode = dvr_snat
```

4. On the compute node, make sure to have the L3 agent service installed. To install the Neutron L3 agent on the compute nodes, run the following command line:

```
# yum install openstack-neutron openstack-neutron-ml2 openstack-openvswitch
```

5. On the compute node, enable DVR mode by setting the `agent_mode` directive to `dvr` in the `/etc/neutron/l3_agent.ini` file to support DVR for the ML2 plugin using the OVS driver mechanism:

```
[DEFAULT]
...
agent_mode = dvr
```

6. Make sure to enable the distributed routing mode in the compute node in the `/etc/neutron/plugins/ml2/ml2_conf.ini` file:

```
[agent]
...
enable_distributed_routing = True
```

7. On the compute nodes, set the `interface_driver` directive to use the Open vSwitch driver mechanism in the `/etc/neutron/l3_agent.ini` configuration file:

```
[DEFAULT]
...
interface_driver = openvswitch
```

8. Unset the `external_network_bridge` directive in the compute node, so it will not contain any value:

```
[DEFAULT]
...
external_network_bridge =
```

9. On the network node, restart the Neutron server, L3 agent, and Open vSwitch agent services as follows:

```
# systemctl restart neutron-l3-agent
# systemctl restart neutron-server
# systemctl restart neutron-openvswitch-agent
```

10. On the compute node, restart the Open vSwitch and L3 agents services, as follows:

```
# systemctl restart neutron-openvswitch-agent
# systemctl restart neutron-l3-agent
```

11. Using the Neutron CLI, check the running state of the added agents in the OpenStack compute nodes. L3 and Open vSwitch agents should be available and can be checked from the controller or compute node as follows:

```
# neutron agent-list
```

12. To demonstrate the new DVR setup, create a new distributed virtual router using the following command:

```
# neutron router-create --distributed True dvr_router
```

13. The `neutron-l3-agent` service is running on each compute node; in the following example, we will verify that every compute node uses the same router namespace created in the previous step:

```
cc01:~# neutron router-list | grep dvr_router
|a029775e-204b-45b6-ad86-0ed2e507d5bf |dvr_router| null | True
```

Based on the router ID, we can use the `ip netns` command line to verify the namespaces on each compute and controller host:

```
cc01:~# ip netns exec qrouter-a029775e-204b-45b6-ad86-0ed2e507d5bf ip a
...
13: qr-c2902c14-3b: <BROADCAST,MULTICAST,UP,LOWER_UP> mtu 1500 qdisc
noqueue state UNKNOWN
link/ether fa:16:3e:df:7a:9d brd ff:ff:ff:ff:ff:ff
inet 10.15.15.1/24 brd 10.15.15.255 scope global qr-c2902c14-3b
        ...
16: qr-d8e8a74b-6c: <BROADCAST,MULTICAST,UP,LOWER_UP> mtu 1500 qdisc
noqueue state UNKNOWN
link/ether fa:16:3e:6f:cd:0d brd ff:ff:ff:ff:ff:ff
   inet 10.0.2.20/24 brd 10.0.2.255 scope global qr-d8e8a74b-6c
   ...
```

The `qrouter` namespace on the controller node exposes mainly two interfaces `qr-c2902c14-3b` and `qr-d8e8a74b-6c` to connect instances sitting in different networks.

 The router namespace noted as `qr` enables traffic forwarding between subnets connected to the same virtual router, using route table entries.

The same router namespace with exact same interfaces IDs, IP, and MAC addresses can be verified on each compute node:

```
cn01:~# ip netns exec qrouter-a029775e-204b-45b6-ad86-0ed2e507d5bf ip a
17: qr-c2902c14-3b: <BROADCAST,MULTICAST,UP,LOWER_UP> mtu 1500 qdisc
noqueue state UNKNOWN
link/ether fa:16:3e:df:7a:9d brd ff:ff:ff:ff:ff:ff
inet 10.15.15.1/24 brd 10.15.15.255 scope global qr-c2902c14-3b
...
18: qr-d8e8a74b-6c: <BROADCAST,MULTICAST,UP,LOWER_UP> mtu 1500 qdisc
noqueue state UNKNOWN
link/ether fa:16:3e:6f:cd:0d brd ff:ff:ff:ff:ff:ff
    inet 10.0.2.20/24 brd 10.0.2.255 scope global qr-d8e8a74b-6c

cn02:~# ip netns exec qrouter-a029775e-204b-45b6-ad86-0ed2e507d5bf ip a
20: qr-c2902c14-3b: <BROADCAST,MULTICAST,UP,LOWER_UP> mtu 1500 qdisc
noqueue state UNKNOWN
link/ether fa:16:3e:df:7a:9d brd ff:ff:ff:ff:ff:ff
inet 10.15.15.1/24 brd 10.15.15.255 scope global qr-c2902c14-3b
    ...
21: qr-d8e8a74b-6c: <BROADCAST,MULTICAST,UP,LOWER_UP> mtu 1500 qdisc
noqueue state UNKNOWN
link/ether fa:16:3e:6f:cd:0d brd ff:ff:ff:ff:ff:ff
    inet 10.0.2.20/24 brd 10.0.2.255 scope global qr-d8e8a74b-6c
    ...
```

The DVR solution is widely used to isolate failure domain that exists in the legacy router design. Moving traffic routing to be handled on the compute hosts, rather than network nodes, improves traffic distribution in a highly optimized way. It is important to note that using DVR requires more understanding of how traffic flows on each of the following network scenarios, presenting different levels of complexity:

- East-west traffic
- North-south traffic without floating IPs
- North-south traffic with floating IPs

A detailed explanation of each of the previous network flow for DVR setup is available at the official OpenStack network guide
at `https://docs.openstack.org/ocata/networking-guide/deploy-ovs-ha-dvr.html`.

Neutron HA – VRRP

The other way of handling high availability of the network service in OpenStack is based on the concept of VRRP. Unlike legacy and DVR-based routers, using VRRP has different requirements, as follows:

- VRRP groups set up for virtual routers
- Multiple network nodes
- An additional dedicated network for high availability traffic
- Designation of master and slave routers using virtual IPs

In a VRRP setup, a master router is configured with a **virtual IP** (**VIP**) that represents the next route hop acting as the default IP address for the routers pool. The network traffic load can also be spread amongst the available routers within the VRRP router group that can be configured based on the scheduler mechanism in the master router. In case of a failover event, a new master router will be elected and set as *active*. The VIP will be associated to the new master and immediately starts handling routing decisions.

It is important to note that the *active/standby* routers use the following essential terminologies to achieve a successful failover event:

- **Priority**: An assigned router with the highest priority is marked as master. The priority range in a VRRP router group starts from 0 up to 255. The highest priority is 255.
- **Preemptive election mode**: In case of a failed master router, the latter can be reassigned to resume its activity again if it is associated with the highest priority in the VRRP router group.
- **Non-preemptive election mode**: An active router keeps operating as master although the presence of a backup router with highest priority was assigned during a normal operational network exercise. Switching to a new master occurs only if the currently active master fails.
- **Preemptive delay timer**: The waiting time before starting an election for a new master.

- **Advertisement interval timer**: The active router keeps informing the standby routers within the same VRRP router group about its health state. If backup routers do not receive an indication of state from the master once in a window of X times, a new election process will be started by sending VRRP advertisements and priority selection.

In the following section, we will configure an HA routing setup in an existing OpenStack environment:

1. Add a new network instance, nn02, by installing Neutron packages:

   ```
   # yum install openstack-neutron openstack-neutron-openvswitch
   openstack-neutron-ml2
   ```

2. Update the new node to use the Open vSwitch driver mechanism in the /etc/neutron/l3_agent.ini file:

   ```
   . . .
   [DEFAULT]
   interface_driver = neutron.agent.linux.interface.OVSInterfaceDriver
   . . .
   ```

   Make sure that the new Neutron node can reach the same network segments as the running one, including management and tenant networks in OpenStack. The new Neutron agent needs also point to the same queuing messaging, database, and Keystone services in OpenStack. This can be configured from the main /etc/neutron/neutron.conf file.

3. Restart the L3 agent service in the new node and check it is registered and visible to the network service:

   ```
   # neutron agent-list --agent-type= "L3 Agent"
   ```

4. On the cloud controller node (running initially the network service), change the HA mode in the main Neutron configuration file /etc/neutron/neutron.conf file, from False to True, as follows:

   ```
   . . .
   l3_ha = True
   . . .
   ```

5. Set the minimum and maximum number for L3 Agents running in each VRRP router group:

```
. . .
min_l3_agents_per_router = 2
max_l3_agents_per_router = 3
. . .
```

6. Restart the `neutron-server` service running in the cloud controller node to reflect the latest configuration update:

```
# systemctl restart neutron-server
```

7. By default, the newly created router will be tagged as an HA router. The default command line to create the HA router adds the flag setting `--ha` to true:

```
# neutron router-create router-ext-ha --ha=true
```

8. A new router namespace will be added within the creation of the router that should be visible across the L3 agent nodes:

```
cc01 ~# ip netns
nn02 ~# ip netns
```

The Neutron server service might fail to restart due to requirements set for the minimum and maximum number of L3 agents available across the network service. A typical error message when creating a new router can be as follows:

Not enough L3 agents available to ensure HA. Minimum required 2, available 1

In such cases, make sure that the newly installed L3 agents are running and visible.

9. The new HA router will automatically create a new HA network. By default, the HA CIDR is `169.254.192.0/18` and it can be adjusted in the Neutron configuration file by updating the `l3_ha_net_net_cidr` directive. The router interface will be prefixed with `ha` that can be visualized from the namespace in each Neutron L3 agent host:

```
cc01 ~# ip netns exec qrouter- ip a
nn02 ~# ip netns exec qrouter- ip a
```

10. To demonstrate how HA using VRRP in Neutron functions, we can stop the network service running for example on the second network node. As noted in steps *8* and *9*, nn02 is elected as the master router that is holding the VIP. A failover event must be triggered to bounce the VIP to the standby router in cc01. The election process can be followed in the router namespace log files as follows:

```
# tail -f /var/lib/neutron/ha_confs/R/neutron-keepalived-state-
change.log
...
Debug neutron.agent.l3.keepalived_state_change [-] Wrote router
b122553e-232b-b653-83df-93e1da33d3a1 state master
write_state_change
...
```

The Neutron VRRP method uses keepalived to assign VIP to the active router. By default, Neutron creates and updates the HA routing keepalived setup under /var/lib/neutron/ha_confs/ROUTER_NAMESPACE/keepalived.conf file where ROUTER_NAMESPACE designates the namespace ID of a given virtual router.

The era of network programming

The Neutron project bundles different implementations of network services and solutions, such as routing, security, load balancing, and VPNs. We have explored its great extensibility by developing our own plugins and mechanism driver to fit to a certain network topology. This brings us to a new checkpoint in the network virtualization concept—programming the network flow. With the emergence of the **Software Defined Network (SDN)** technology, a physical network infrastructure can be programmatically operated. The SDN concept complies with the OpenStack networking service by abstracting the network resources. A major advantage of this approach is the flexibility added to the network management from user and operator perspectives. Traditional network implementations based on pure physical layouts exposes different barriers when it comes to deploying applications in a cloud environment. Especially, with the emergence of containerized applications, handling the network traffic granularly through network appliances might be cumbersome. Additionally, traditional networks present a lack of API compatibility when integrating with other infrastructure resources, such as storage and computation.

As we will not elaborate further on the SDN technology, it is worth highlighting the basic ingredients of its implementation. The network flow in an SDN based environment is programmed and controlled by the means of a standard protocol **OpenFlow**. It defines how packets will be forwarded across the networking devices based on flow rules and proactive programming.

In the previous section, we have already used the Open vSwitch driver mechanism. As a virtual multilayer switching implementation, Open vSwitch uses under the hood flow programming standards of the OpenFlow protocols.

In the next section, we will keep exploiting another great point of the OpenStack design grounds, to smoothly integrate SDN implementation and virtual network provisioning.

Orchestrating the network function virtualization (NFV)

Converging to a network infrastructure based on SDN leverages elasticity of handling network resources. Commissioning and decommissioning network hardware appliances in a data center does not respond to the scaling question when facing an increased appetite of network resources. In addition, scaling down is not a common practice in a static data center environment space, as connectivity demand is not predictable.

This is where the NFV concept comes into the picture. The NFV approach is based on the conversion of the data center networking functionalities to the virtual world. Essentially, it decouples the network function of hardware through virtualization technology known as **Virtual Network Function (VNF)**.

Any network device, such as a router, firewall, or a load balancer, can be turned into a VNF simply by running the software of its network service in a VM. VNFs offer the following advantages:

- They have the ability to scale up and scale down network resources when needed
- They are cost effective, as hardware resources will be reduced
- They embrace network orchestration in a cloud environment

Now, we reach the heart piece of the NFV concept, which is management and orchestration. Obviously, with a variety and number of types of VNF instances, there should be an orchestrator engine that takes care of spawning, terminating, and monitoring them. The **ETSI Industry Specification Group (ETSI ISG)** replied to this query by defining a management framework, **Management and Orchestration (MANO)**.

The MANO standard specifies essentially three blocks around NFV architecture:

- **VNF Manager (VNFM)**: This manages the lifecycle of VNFs instances-related events
- **Virtual Infrastructure Manager (VIM)**: This manages the underlying infrastructure resources availability including compute, network, and storage for NFV
- **NFV Orchestrator (NFVO)**: This manages virtual network functions and different NFV infrastructure resources in different VIMs

VNFs in MANO NFV-base can be described in the form of simple templates, known as **Topology and Orchestration Specification for Cloud Applications (TOSCA)** templates. Users and operators can choose any NFV resources and deploy the network service from a simple template, based on specific VNF artefacts. We are going to change gears now and have a look at a real state of the NFV art in OpenStack, the **Tacker** project.

Another incubated project that extends the OpenStack ecosystem to manage and orchestrate NFV, Tacker was introduced in 2015 and has been fully integrated into the OpenStack ecosystem since the *Mitaka* release.

Tacker implies the same MANO specifications and leverages the NFV building blocks for the OpenStack environment by collectively using Neutron, Nova, and Cinder as base VIM components. The sole engine of NFVO in the case of Tacker is Heat by providing an automated end-to-end deployment of VNFs based on templates. The VNFM enables VNF catalog and configuration in the form of VNF descriptors.

Let's unleash the power of NFV in OpenStack using Tacker, through the following steps:

1. We will be installing the Tacker server in the cloud controller manually. The installation is performed in the Ocata release. This will help you to understand how it will interact with the rest of the OpenStack ecosystem and figure out the workflow between Tacker and the rest of the OpenStack services. We will need, initially, to create a Tacker database and an identified Tacker user, as follows:

```
# mysql -u root
GRANT ALL PRIVILEGES ON tacker.* TO 'tacker'@'localhost' \
    IDENTIFIED BY 'tacker ';
GRANT ALL PRIVILEGES ON tacker.* TO 'tacker'@'%' \
    IDENTIFIED BY 'tacker';
```

2. As an admin, create a new user named `tacker` with admin privileges and assign it to the default `services` project and `admin` role using the OpenStack command line interface:

```
# openstack user create --domain default --password tacker tacker
# openstack role add --project services --user tacker admin
```

Note that the domain name used is `default` and the password is created as `tacker`. We will need this information for the next steps. Make sure to use the exact project name listed in the `openstack project list`. In our example, we use `services`. In different OpenStack releases prior to Ocata, this might be `service`.

3. Add a new Tacker service in OpenStack:

```
# openstack service create --name tacker --description \ "Tacker
Project" NVF-Orchestration
```

4. As a new service created in OpenStack, it must authenticate against Keystone. This can be achieved by creating necessary endpoints operating on default Tacker port `9890` as follows:

```
# openstack endpoint create --region RegionOne
NFV -Orchestration public http://172.28.128.5:9890/
# openstack endpoint create --region RegionOne
NFV -Orchestration internal http://172.28.128.5:9890/
# openstack endpoint create --region RegionOne
NFV-Orchestration admin http://172.28.128.5:9890/
```

5. Download the stable Tacker repository for Ocata release:

```
# git clone https://github.com/openstack/tacker -b \ stable/ocata
```

6. Run the `setup.py` script in the `tacker` directory, by initiating the installation of the necessary requirements and dependencies as follows:

```
# cd tacker
# pip install -r requirements.txt
# python setup.py install
```

 Make sure that `pip` is installed in the current OS. To install `pip`, run the `easy_install pip` command line.

7. In the same `tacker` directory, generate an initial tacker configuration file by executing the following command line:

   # tools/generate_config_file_simple.sh

   The sample configuration file will be located in the `etc/tacker/` directory.

8. Rename the generated sample `tacker.conf.sample` to `tacker.conf` with the following configuration directives:

```
[DEFAULT]
auth_strategy = keystone
policy_file = /usr/local/etc/tacker/policy.json
debug = True
use_syslog = False
bind_host = 172.28.128.5
bind_port = 9890
service_plugins = nfvo,vnfm
state_path = /var/lib/tacker

[nfvo]
vim_drivers = openstack

[keystone_authtoken]
memcached_servers = 11211
region_name = RegionOne
auth_type = password
project_domain_name = Default
user_domain_name = Default
username = tacker
project_name = services
password = tacker
auth_url = http://172.28.128.5:35357
auth_uri = http://172.28.128.5:5000

[agent]
root_helper = sudo /usr/local/bin/tacker-rootwrap
/usr/local/etc/tacker/rootwrap.conf

[database]
connection =
mysql://tacker:tacker@172.28.128.5:3306/tacker?charset=utf8

[tacker]
 monitor_driver = ping,http_ping
```

9. To keep the sanity of the Tacker service, create a new log directory for tacker under /var/log/tacker:

```
# mkdir /var/log/tacker
```

10. Locate the default path of the installed run binaries of tacker and use tacker-db-manage to populate the Tacker database, as follows:

```
# /usr/bin/tacker-db-manage --config-file \
/tacker/etc/tacker/tacker.conf upgrade head
```

11. To run the Tacker command line interface, proceed by installing the Tacker client from the Ocata stable branch:

```
# git clone https://github.com/openstack/python-tackerclient \
-b stable/ocata
# cd python-tackerclient
# python setup.py install
```

12. To configure Tacker from the Horizon dashboard, download and install the stable branch of the Tacker horizon asset for Ocata release:

```
# git clone https://github.com/openstack/tacker-horizon \
-b stable/ocata
# cd tacker-horizon
# cp tacker_horizon/enabled/* /usr/share/openstack-dashboard/\
openstack-dashboard/enabled/
```

13. Depending on which platform is running OpenStack, restart the web server in the controller node. For this example, we are using httpd:

```
# systemctl restart httpd
```

14. Now, you should be able to explore the new NFV tab in Horizon:

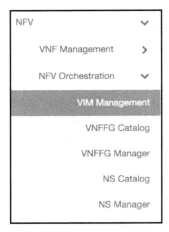

15. Before running the Tacker server, we will need to ensure that the tacker user has the right roles as project member for **admin, heat_stack_owner**. This can be configured from Horizon. Navigate to the **Identity tab** | **Projects** and select **services**. Then, assign the **admin** and **heat_stack_owner** to the tracker as follows:

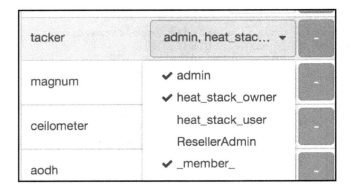

16. Additionally, the `tacker` user will trigger Heat tasks to launch NFV tasks. By default, Tacker repository files come with limited access policies that can be observed from the default `policy.json` file located under the default Tacker directory `etc/tacker/`. Make sure to add a new policy rule to allow admins and service owners to create VIM, as this will be needed in the following steps:

```
...
"create_vim": "rule:admin_or_owner or rule:shared"
}
```

 To read more about resource policies in the identity service in OpenStack, please refer to the official security guide found here at `https://docs.openstack.org/security-guide/identity/policies.html`.

17. Locate the default path of the installed run binaries of Tacker and use `tacker-server` to launch the Tacker server. To debug the running server, add the path of the destination log file as an extra argument. Optionally, use the `screen` command line to keep the server processes running if the terminal is terminated:

```
# screen /usr/bin/tacker-db-manage --config-file \
/tacker/etc/tacker/tacker.conf --log-file \
/var/log/tacker/tacker.conf
```

18. From the Tacker log file, make sure that the server is running and listening on the `9890` port as shown in the following log output:

```
INFO tacker.service [req-441c6d47-0f81-40d4-8df6-8f3ff0630eb3 - - - - -] Tacker service started, listening on 172.28.128.5:9890
INFO tacker.wsgi [-] (7503) wsgi starting up on http://172.28.128.5:9890
DEBUG tacker.common.log [-] tacker.nfvo.nfvo_plugin.NfvoPlugin method monitor_vim called with arguments ({'status': u'REACHABLE',
```

19. Now we have our Tacker server up and running, we can start by creating our VIM from the OpenStack dashboard. As mentioned previously, VIM in OpenStack will manage the NFV components, including compute, network, and storage resources. Navigate to the NFV tab in Horizon, **NFV Orchestration | VIM Management.** Register a new VIM as follows:

20. Ensure that the new VIM is registered successfully by checking the status is **REACHABLE**:

Name	Description	VIM Id	Auth URL	Regions	User	Project	Status
ExtendCloud		373b581b-b3c3-4dcf-842e-b92e48bd8a40	http://172.28.128.5:5000/v3	RegionOne	tacker	services	REACHABLE

21. The next step consists of on boarding the network function or VNF. We will need to provide a TOSCA template as an input, so that Tacker can orchestrate the described VNFs through the NFVO. The default Tacker repository comes with few TOSCA samples. For the sake of demonstration, we can use a simple TOSCA template `tosca-vnfd-hello-world.yaml`, located under `tacker/samples/tosca-templates/vnfd/`. Make sure to update the template parameters, including capabilities for compute resources and the names of properties, such as image name, availability zone, and network names. The default template by default uses `cirros-0.3.4-x86_64-uec` as the image name, `nova` as the availability zone, and `net_mgmt`, `net0`, and `net1` for networks.

Navigate to **VNF Management** | **VNF Catalog** and click on **OnBoard VNF**:

 Ensure that you update the parameters for each TOSCA template with the available resource names in your OpenStack environment. VNF on boarding might fail if resource parameters do not exist. Tacker log will throw a similar error, as follows: `tacker.api.v1.resource KeyError: 'groups'`

22. Our first VNF deployment is ready to go. Navigate to **VNF Management** | **VNF Manager** and click on **Deploy VNF**:

23. Under the hood, NFV calls Heat service to orchestrate the deployment of the instance as described in the TOSCA template:

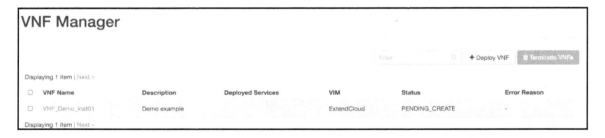

The new VNF instance can be observed from the **Instance** tab:

To read about TOSCA standard templates and specifications, refer to the official Oasis website at `http://docs.oasis-open.org/tosca/TOSCA-Simple-Profile-YAML/v1.0/csd03/TOSCA-Simple-Profile-YAML-v1.0-csd03.html`.

Summary

In this chapter, we have covered several aspects behind network extensibility in OpenStack by the means of plugins. We have explored the power of ML2 support in the latest releases of OpenStack and demonstrated how to write a custom mechanism driver as an extension to the core plugin. The topic of high network availability was left behind prior to the Havana release; later releases have empowered the Neutron project by kicking off built-in solutions in the OpenStack network service. We have covered routing redundancy using VRRP and routing distribution based on the DVR approach. While both HA network designs have drastically boosted the network architecture in an extended OpenStack environment, each solution might have its own limitations. Hence, as a cloud operator, taking architectural decisions on choosing which solution might fit depends roughly on the infrastructure network requirements and needs. Obviously, moving away from the legacy router would bring several advantages to the network layout, but might increase operational tasks and complexity. By the end of the chapter, we came across an ongoing hot topic related to network virtualization. You should have an idea of how OpenStack correlates with the SDN technology, such as the Open vSwitch plugin used in this chapter. You should also have a first impression on how moving network appliances and operational hardware to the virtual world would remove several barriers and limitations existing in a traditional network environment. We have depicted the notion of NFV and particularly in OpenStack through Tacker project. One goal of this project is to bring the NFV management platform to the new advanced form of orchestration within OpenStack ecosystem.

We are still under the umbrella of increasing the space of the OpenStack ecosystem and, in the next chapter, will be introducing another facet of innovation in the OpenStack cloud era: Containerization.

5
Containerizing in OpenStack

"I never think of the future - it comes soon enough."

–Albert Einstein

The race to the cloud paradigm has been an exciting journey, in which IT organizations have enjoyed the benefits brought by the new way of handling resources in private or public cloud environments. However, the rise of new requirements among IT service providers and the unstoppable increasing need to get on to the market put the software development process under the microscope. Besides using the cloud, *how can an enterprise takes its business agility and development to the next level?*

Nowadays, the new trend in software application development is being enforced by adopting containerization technology around the globe. Moving to containers has marked a successful experience for many IT platforms and teams in terms of automation, software delivery acceleration, and remarkable simplicity. Since 2014, the OpenStack community has shed light on the world of containers and introduced more amazing projects such as Magnum and Kolla. As they are more mature container projects, cloud operators and users have exploited the opportunity to run applications in containers on the top of OpenStack. This leverages the modular architecture of the OpenStack ecosystem and the software-defined services, including storage and network. In this chapter we will cover the following topics:

- Revisiting the container technology
- Highlighting containers in OpenStack
- Introducing the Magnum mission project in OpenStack
- Installing and running Magnum
- Revisiting and running Docker Swarm in OpenStack

- Revisiting and running Kubernetes in OpenStack
- Revisiting and running Mesos in OpenStack

Why containers?

The concept of containerization technology has existed for a few years. With Unix kernel maturity, many companies have started kicking off new paths toward the world of containers. Several projects have been created around the concept of containerization technology with slightly different architectures and purposes. Unix chroot was the earliest invention of a container implementation in Unix kernel. Based on the same concept, other projects such as FreeBSD jails, Linux-VServer, Solaris Containers, Linux containers, and OpenVZ, to name few, have emerged as new ways to adopt containers shifting through the infrastructure to a different level of flexibility.

As a result, we can observe in today's industry a worldwide interest in adopting the container concept. The necessity to switch to a containerized environment has been depicted from the years of experiencing different approaches to add a sort of flexibility to the infrastructure and increase the speed of software delivery with minimum effort.

The natural evolution of containers

Nowadays, containers are carefully considered when architecting new systems. This sudden drive to adopt them is based on natural facts of the emergence of cloud computing and virtualization technologies. Both latter concepts have drastically changed how containers run and serve in an IT infrastructure. An essential key driver responsible for the rebirth of containers nowadays is virtualization technology.

The virtualization concept has addressed several infrastructure challenges by increasing flexibility and scalability. With the adoption of a cloud computing approach, it becomes easier to scale up and down in an unlimited space of resources and gain more confidence to face increased demand resources with almost no downtime. On the other hand, modern infrastructural needs have raised new challenges that the proven virtualization concept cannot completely solve. This point must be seen from an architectural perspective. As depicted in the following illustration, virtualization adds a new abstraction layer or hypervisor that enables various VMs to run in the same host. Each VM has its own operating system and shares the underlying hardware resources. This isolation benefit allows us to run multiple applications in the same host with zero software system dependency issues.

If we take a closer look at the sole part of virtualization, we will raise the question of application portability when dealing with multiple hypervisors setup. Each piece of hypervisor vendor software exposes different requirements and types of workloads that increase the level of complexity. Applications cannot be easily portable and should stick to a specific hypervisor vendor. Additionally, the VM itself expressed more needs for storage, compute, memory, and network, as running its own operating system might result in resource overheads and influence its performance. Moreover, although virtualization adds more flexibility to the infrastructure, the management, and operation of the virtual environment, including guest hosts, network appliances, and associated storage, still presents a level of complexity.

Besides the benefits of isolation that virtualization brought, the containerization concept has enlarged a smooth environment for the application scope to run. This key difference can be observed from the following figure:

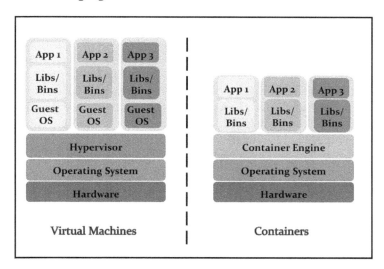

Unlike a VM, a container does not need a fully dedicated operating system to run. By sharing the same operating system, kernel, and all relevant system libraries and dependencies, it is still possible to run multiple containers and keep them completely isolated. That enlightens the concept of decoupling the application layer from hardware limitations and software dependencies. As a result, the container can be launched much faster than a traditional VM. Since they do not need a dedicated operating system to run, they can be considered a very lightweight application environment. Detached from any hypervisor nature compatibilities, containers are designed to be portable.

The emergence of cloud computing adds another amazing benefit of containers—they are cloud agnostic. From a development perspective, containers can be expressed as a rapid solution for software deployment that enhances the continuous delivery pipeline from the local test environment to production.

Game changing – microservices

The massive usage of containers has raised a new architectural flag named **microservices**. Previously, architects and developers have sought to decouple their monolithic applications into more loosely coupled and reusable modules known as **Service Oriented Architecture (SOA)**. With the advent of containers and thanks to the cloud paradigm and diversity of APIs, an application is now decomposed by placing each application entity into a small and mono-task service that scales across a fleet of servers and communicates with the rest of the other services through APIs.

The term microservices existed before the recent massive switch to containers. Although SOA existed to resolve the drawbacks of monolithic and big applications, it was quite challenging to provide the right field that scales and rolls back a service quickly enough when it is necessary. As discussed in the previous sections, VMs could not reach the deployment speed and performance characteristics that a container provides. For this reason, containers present a perfect match for the implementation and architecture of microservices. Besides their lightweight and scaling key drivers, containers are empowered by an orchestrator that composes the intended application to run into them, run faster, and scale.

Building the ship

As elucidated in the previous section, an application built in containers can be easily deployed with a minimum level of configuration and maintenance. As many containers will be running across a fleet of servers, there should be a way to manage them effectively with less effort. To form the big picture of a containerized environment, many pieces should be gathered and connected to deliver a functional application that is highly available, resilient to failures, and portable. This is where orchestration comes into the picture. The rebirth of container technology has brought the initiative to develop a complete suite of tools and engines to manage containers assembled in one software platform.

Most of the prevailing and mature container cluster management platforms are Apache Mesos, Kubernetes, Docker Swarm, Rocket, and Nomad to name few. Giant cloud providers have also joined the containerization era, by exposing self-managed containers as a service in the cloud, such as **Elastic Container Service** (**ECS**) by Amazon Web Services and **Azure Container Service** (**AKS**) by Microsoft. *What about OpenStack?* Of course, the OpenStack community did not leave this new opportunity behind. Since 2015, several projects under the umbrella of containers have been launched to leverage the OpenStack ecosystem and find the right spots for container technology. The latest OpenStack releases have officially included several incubated projects around containers, as follows:

- **Magnum**: A multi-tenant container CaaS project
- **Kolla**: A dedicated project for running OpenStack services in containers
- **Murano**: An application catalog of container-based applications for OpenStack
- **Kuryr**: A network plugin dedicated project leveraging Neutron into Docker containers
- **Fuxi**: A persistence storage access to Cinder and Manila for containers in OpenStack
- **Zun**: An OpenStack API for container runtime management in OpenStack

This amazing emergence of containers into the OpenStack ecosystem has also leveraged other core components, including:

- **Nova**: Adopting a Docker hypervisor driver
- **Heat**: Integrating a plugin template for Docker resources orchestration

In the next parts of this chapter, we will dive deeper into the Magnum project in OpenStack.

 The Murano project will be explored in more detail in `Chapter 7`, *Evolving Self-Cloud Ready Applications in OpenStack.*

Containers in OpenStack

Like Swarm, Kubernetes, or Mesos, the sole part of the Magnum project is the **Container Orchestration Engine** (**COE**) that aims, essentially, to orchestrate a collection of containers providing the application features. As shown in the following architectural diagram, the Magnum COE leverages different OpenStack services, including:

- **Keystone**: Managing multi-tenancy for different container clusters

- **Neutron**: Wiring COE nodes through multi-host networking
- **Heat**: Orchestrating the underlying COE nodes and resources
- **Cinder**: Hosting containers connected COE nodes
- **Nova**: Spawning the COE nodes to run and manage containers

 Magnum adds a great way to access containers running on Docker Swarm or Kubernetes through their native container APIs.

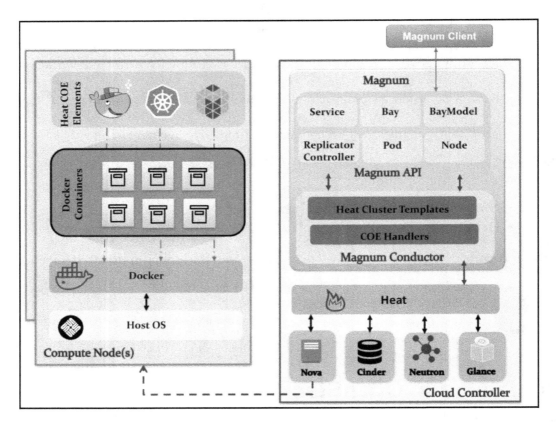

Magnum exposes an API supporting container orchestration for different engines including Mesos, Docker Swarm, and Kubernetes.

Magnum support for Kubernetes COE comes with its native multi-master configuration and includes Marathon framework for Mesos. The Pike OpenStack release supports a Kubernetes dashboard by default to manage Kubernetes clusters.

Magnum refers to each collection of COE nodes and their associated containers using the following terminologies:

- **Bay**: A collection of nodes running the COE. Magnum uses Heat to orchestrate and setup the bay farm.
- **BayModel**: A definition of the bay resources constructed in a simple template. Several bays can inherit from the same model template and use different COE types.
- **Pod**: A collection of containers running on the same COE node.
- **Replication controller**: A Magnum process for monitoring, replicating, and scaling pods across COE nodes.
- **Service**: An arrangement of pods and access policies.
- **Magnum client**: A native client to query COE that includes `docker` for Docker COE, `kubectl` for Kubernetes COE or through Marathon API for Mesos COE.

Magnum offers different bay options. Depending on which one will be used, native APIs will be invoked for each COE to manage containers. Magnum has been designed to be a multi-tenant container platform—operators keep enjoying the isolation feature for each resource layer in the OpenStack ecosystem allocated to many tenants. The Magnum architecture allows us to run containers either on Nova instances or on bare metal machines.

Magnum facilitates the deployment of the COE by passing each COE collection's attributes to the Heat engine in OpenStack through the Heat stack templates.

In the next section, we will revisit the layout of each COE that covers Docker Swarm, Kubernetes, and Mesos and deploy a cluster of each in OpenStack through Magnum.

 Make sure to have Magnum installed and running in OpenStack. If you do not have Magnum installed, refer to the OpenStack Magnum install guide at `https://docs.openstack.org/magnum/latest/install/install-guide-from-source.html`.

Docker Swarm in OpenStack

Docker Swarm is the default Docker orchestration tool. It uses the Docker command line interface and leverages compatibility with other Docker-based solutions.

 Docker Swarm has been integrated as a core tool for Docker engines since version 1.12 of Docker release.

As an OpenStack cloud operator, there will be no need to reinvent the wheel by tweaking the compute driver to include Docker Swarm to manage containers on the top of OpenStack. Magnum is featured to claim Swarm as a COE available and ready to go, further strengthening the focus on deploying cloud native and legacy applications in containers.

Running Swarm on top of OpenStack will not make a huge difference from an operation perspective, as Magnum keeps using the Docker native API. On the other hand, it is imperative to revise the Docker Swarm building blocks first.

Let's take a closer look at the Docker Swarm and how it is positioned in the OpenStack ecosystem:

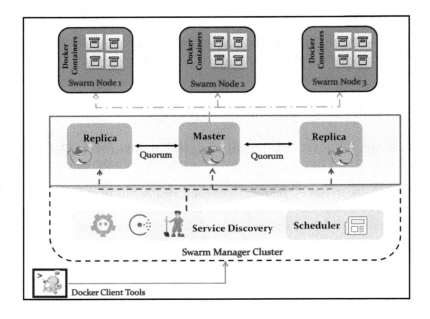

From a Magnum perspective, the collection of Swarm manager cluster nodes including master and replicas as well as the Swarm nodes hosting the Docker containers form a bay. In Magnum, defining the Swarm cluster is straightforward by the means of the bayModel. This is a simple cluster template specifying the Swarm cluster objects including the Swarm managers and nodes. Pods in Magnum can pinpoint to set of containers running on the same Nova instance or across different ones. All necessary resources for the Docker Swarm deployment will be scheduled and orchestrated by Heat, which invokes OpenStack services to get the Swarm cluster environment up and running.

From an architectural perspective, there is no need to tweak or update the OpenStack services APIs to recognise the COE Docker Swarm. Magnum provides it out of the box and makes it available through its native API. In addition, there is no need to install any service discovery tools for Swarm, as it integrates etcd by default.

etcd is a distributed key-value store. etcd handles machine failures by replicating data across multiple nodes. To read more about the etcd project, refer to the URL https://github.com/coreos/etcd/.

Example – NGINX web server

In the following example, we will setup a new Magnum bay running Docker Swarm as the COE. The Swarm cluster will deploy a simple NGINX web server running on a Docker container and listening on port 80 and 443 as follows:

1. Create a new Magnum cluster template to deploy a Swarm cluster:

```
# magnum cluster-template-create --name coe-swarm-template \
                                 --image-id fedora-latest \
                                 --keypair-id pp_key \
                               --external-network-id pub-net \
                                 --dns-nameserver 8.8.8.8 \
                                 --flavor-id m1.small \
                                 --docker-volume-size 4 \
                                 --network-driver docker \
                                 --coe swarm
```

The previous command line assumes the existence of an image fedora_atomic in the Glance image repository, a key-pair named pp_key and an external Neutron network named pub-net. Make sure to adjust your parameters with the correct command line arguments.

2. Initiate a Swarm cluster with one manager and two worker nodes by executing the following Magnum command line:

```
# magnum cluster-create --name swarm-cluster \
  --cluster-template coe-swarm-template \
    --manager-count 1 \
    --node-count 2
+---------------------+------------------------------------+
| Property            | Value                              |
+---------------------+------------------------------------+
| status              | CREATE_IN_PROGRESS                 |
| cluster_template_id | 25ed246e-56a2-4478-be2375deac75e344|
| uuid                | 33e4e34a-8799-dde3-87366e3ef187ca48|
| stack_id            | 77e3e442-8770-e3edfea176539de36ec97|
| status_reason       | -                                  |
| created_at          | 2017-12-10T17:19:09+00:00          |
| name                | swarm-cluster                      |
| updated_at          | -                                  |
| api_address         | -                                  |
| coe_version         | -                                  |
| master_addresses    | []                                 |
| create_timeout      | 60                                 |
| node_addresses      | []                                 |
| master_count        | 1                                  |
| container_version   | -                                  |
| node_count          | 2                                  |
+---------------------+------------------------------------+
```

3. Verify the creation of the new Swarm cluster:

```
# magnum cluster-show swarm-cluster
+---------------------+------------------------------------------+
| Property            | Value                                    |
+---------------------+------------------------------------------+
| status              | CREATE_COMPLETE                          |
| cluster_template_id | 25ed246e-56a2-4478-be2375deac75e344      |
| uuid                | dde35ee1-8772-7d35-9901-ba3ea53402ee     |
| stack_id            | 77e3e442-8770-e3edfea176539de36ec97      |
| status_reason       | Stack CREATE completed successfully      |
| created_at          | 2017-12-10T17:19:09+00:00                |
| name                | swarm-cluster                            |
| updated_at          | 2017-12-10T17:22:30+00:00                |
| discovery_url       | https://discovery.etcd.io/a2ef615f68d3775a|
| api_address         | tcp://192.168.47.147:2376                |
| coe_version         | 1.0.0                                    |
| master_addresses    | ['192.168.47.147']                       |
| create_timeout      | 60                                       |
```

```
| node_addresses      | ['192.168.47.148', '192.168.47.149']
| master_count        | 1
| container_version   | 1.9.1
| node_count          | 2
+---------------------+-----------------------------------------+
```

Magnum uses Heat to orchestrate the provisioning of different resources needed by the Swarm cluster. It is possible to check and monitor the process of the cluster creation by listing the Heat resources status using the command line # `heat resource-list stack_id`. Here, `stack_id` refers to the ID of the Heat stack assigned upon the creation of the Magnum bay.

4. To log in to the created Swarm cluster, we will need to generate signed client certificates. The following command line will place the necessary TLS files and key in cluster directory `swarm_cluster_dir`:

```
# magnum cluster-config swarm-cluster --dir swarm_cluster_dir
{'tls': True, 'cfg_dir': swarm_cluster_dir '.', 'docker_host':
u'tcp://192.168.47.147:2376'}
```

5. The generated certificates are in the `swarm_cluster_dir` directory:

```
# ls swarm_cluster_dir
ca.pem cert.pem key.pem
```

6. Copy the generated TLS artifacts and the key to the Swarm master node under the ~/.docker folder:

```
# rsync -r swarm_cluster_dir fedora@192.168.47.147:.docker
```

7. Access Swarm master node through SSH and populate the generated environment variables, as follows:

```
# ssh fedora@192.168.47.147
[fedora@my-7zwwd8rdi-0-qasdqq3aa3e2-swarm-master-6dssfrage8z2 ~]$
export DOCKER_HOST=tcp://192.168.88.238:2376
[fedora@my-7zwwd8rdi-0-qasdqq3aa3e2-swarm-master-6dssfrage8z2 ~]$
export DOCKER_TLS_VERIFY=1
[fedora@my-7zwwd8rdi-0-qasdqq3aa3e2-swarm-master-6dssfrage8z2 ~]$
export DOCKER_CERT_PATH= /swarm_cluster_dir
```

8. Check the Swarm node cluster list by using the native Docker CLI:

```
$ docker node ls
ID              HOSTNAME            STATUS AVAILABILITY MANAGER STATUS
ba34rwedhd * my-..-swarm-master Ready  Active       Reachable
t5ertsd6ud   my-..-swarm-node   Ready  Active
he4ds9dfde   my-..-swarm-node   Ready  Active
```

From the previous listing, MANAGER STATUS refers to the status of the Swarm manager node as primary leader. The other two nodes are set to Active with empty MANAGER STATUS fields as being worker nodes in the Swarm.

As a best practice, use more than one master or manager node per cluster. Generally, it is recommended to include an odd number or master in the Swarm to maintain quorum.

9. Now we have a Swarm cluster up and running, it is time to deploy a simple web server running NGINX and listening on port 80, exposed by the host's port 8080. We can use the native Docker service CLI to create a new service running NGINX:

```
$ docker service create -p 8080:80 --name swarm-nginx
--replicas 2 nginx dter345ghfk5k6kdroct
```

By specifying the replica factor, Swarm will create two additional containers running NGINX on two Swarm nodes. The master node will be managing the scheduling of the web server task when one of the containers becomes unreachable.

10. Verify that two NGINX services are running and scheduled on two nodes:

```
$ docker service ls
ID NAME MODE REPLICAS IMAGE
dter345ghfk5k6kdroct swarm-nginx replicated 2/2 nginx
```

11. Check if the port is exposed on the host as intended:

```
$ docker port swarm-nginx
80/tcp -> 0.0.0.0:8080
```

12. From the master node, query the web server locally on port 8080:

```
$ curl -I http://172.31.0.5:8080
<!DOCTYPE html>
```

```
<html>
<head>
<title>Welcome to nginx!</title>
<style>
```

Kubernetes in OpenStack

Kubernetes is another container deployment and management platform that aims to strengthen the Linux container orchestration tools. Kubernetes growth comes from its long experience journey, led by Google for several years and offered to the open source community as one of the fast-growing container-based application platforms with more overwhelming features that cover scaling, auto deployment, and resource management across multiple clusters of hosts.

As mentioned in the previous section, Magnum makes Kubernetes available in the OpenStack ecosystem. Like Swarm, users can use Magnum API to manage and operate Kubernetes clusters, objects, and services. Let's first summarize the major player components in the Kubernetes architecture to understand later how its backend will be managed by Magnum in OpenStack:

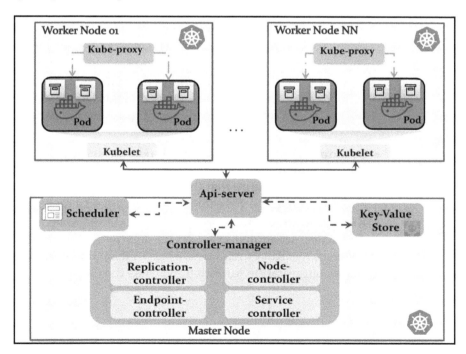

The Kubernetes architecture is modular and exposes several services that can be spread in multiple nodes. Unlike Swarm, Kubernetes uses different terminologies, as follows:

- **Pods**: A collection of containers forming the application unit and sharing networking configuration, namespaces, and storage
- **Service**: A Kubernetes abstraction layer exposing a set of pods as a service, typically, through a load balancer

From an architectural perspective, Kubernetes essentially defines the following components:

- **Master node**: This controls and orchestrates the Kubernetes cluster. A master node can run the following services:
    - **Api-server**: This provides API endpoints to process RESTful API calls to control and manage the cluster
    - **Controller manager**: This embeds several management services including:
        - **Replication controller**: This manages pods in the cluster by creating and removing failed pods.
        - **Endpoint controller**: This joins pods by providing cluster endpoints.
        - **Node controller**: This manages nodes initialization and discovery information within cloud provider.
        - **Service controller**: This maintains service back-ends in Kubernetes running behind load balancers. The service controller configures load balancers based on the service state update.
    - **Scheduler**: This decides on which pod the service deployment should happen. Based on the nodes resources capacity, the scheduler makes sure that the desired service would run onto the nodes belonging to the same pod or across different ones.
    - **Key-value store**: This stores REST API objects, such as node and pod states, scheduled jobs, service deployment information, and namespaces. Kubernetes uses `etcd` as its main key-value store to share configuration information across the cluster.

To read more about `etcd`, check the main **CoreOS** official page at `https:/ /coreos.com/etcd/docs/latest/getting-started-with-etcd.html`.

- **Worker node**: This runs Kubernetes pods and containers runtime environment. Each worker node runs the following components:
  - **Kubelet**: A primary node agent that takes care of containers running in their associated pods. The kubelet process reports periodically the health status of pods and nodes to the master node.
  - **Docker**: The default container runtime engine used by Kubernetes.
  - **Kube-proxy**: A network proxy to forward requests to the right container. Kube-proxy routes traffic across pods within the same service.

Example – application server

In the following example, we will set up a new Magnum bay running the Kubernetes cluster as COE. The Kubernetes cluster will deploy a simple application server running WordPress and listening on port 8080 as follows:

1. Create a new Magnum cluster template to deploy a Kubernetes cluster:

```
# magnum cluster-template-create  --name coe-swarm-template \
                                  --image-id fedora-latest \
                                  --keypair-id pp_key \
                                  --external-network-id pub-net\
                                  --dns-nameserver 8.8.8.8 \
                                  --flavor-id m1.small \
                                  --docker-volume-size 4 \
                                  --network-driver docker \
                                  --coe swarm
# magnum cluster-template-create  --name coe-k8s-template \
                                  --image fedora-latest \
                                  --keypair-id pp_key \
                                  --external-network-id pub-net\
                                  --dns-nameserver 8.8.8.8 \
                                  --flavor-id m1.small \
                                  --docker-volume-size 4 \
                                  --network-driver flannel \
                                  --coe kubernetes
```

The previous command line assumes the existence of an image `fedora_atomic` in the Glance image repository, a key pair named `pp_key` and an external Neutron network named `pub-net`. Make sure to adjust your parameters with your correct command line arguments.

2. Initiate a Kubernetes cluster with one master and two worker nodes by executing the following `magnum` command:

```
# magnum cluster-create --name kubernetes-cluster \
--cluster-template coe-k8s-template \
--master-count 1 \
--node-count 2
+---------------------+-------------------------------------+
| Property            | Value                               |
+---------------------+-------------------------------------+
| status              | CREATE_IN_PROGRESS                  |
| cluster_template_id | 258e44e3-fe33-8892-be3448cfe3679822 |
| uuid                | 3c3345d2-983d-ff3e-0109366e342021f4 |
| stack_id            | dd3e3020-9833-477c-cc3e012ede5f5f0a |
| status_reason       | -                                   |
| created_at          | 2017-12-11T16:20:08+01:00           |
| name                | kubernetes-cluster                  |
| updated_at          | -                                   |
| api_address         | -                                   |
| coe_version         | -                                   |
| master_addresses    | []                                  |
| create_timeout      | 60                                  |
| node_addresses      | []                                  |
| master_count        | 1                                   |
| container_version   | -                                   |
| node_count          | 2                                   |
+---------------------+-------------------------------------+
```

3. Verify the creation of the new Swarm cluster:

```
# magnum cluster-show kubernetes-cluster
+---------------------+-----------------------------------------+
| Property            | Value                                   |
+---------------------+-----------------------------------------+
| status              | CREATE_COMPLETE                         |
| cluster_template_id | 258e44e3-fe33-8892-be3448cfe3679822     |
| uuid                | 3c3345d2-983d-ff3e-0109366e342021f4     |
| stack_id            | dd3e3020-9833-477c-cc3e012ede5f5f0a     |
| status_reason       | Stack CREATE completed successfully     |
| created_at          | 2017-12-11T16:20:08+01:00               |
| name                | kubernetes-cluster                      |
```

```
| updated_at           | 2017-12-11T16:23:22+01:00                |
| discovery_url        | https://discovery.etcd.io/ed33fe3a38ff2d4a |
| api_address          | tcp://192.168.47.150:2376                |
| coe_version          | 1.0.0                                    |
| master_addresses     | ['192.168.47.150']                       |
| create_timeout       | 60                                       |
| node_addresses       | ['192.168.47.151', '192.168.47.152']     |
master_count           | 1                                        |
| container_version    | 1.9.1                                    |
| node_count           | 2                                        |
+----------------------+------------------------------------------+
```

The progress of the cluster deployment can be checked from the Horizon dashboard by pointing to the stack section that visualizes different events of each provisioned resource per stack.

4. Generate the signed client certificates to log in to the deployed Kubernetes cluster. The following command line will place the necessary TLS files and key in cluster directory kubernetes_cluster_dir:

```
# magnum cluster-config kubernetes-cluster \
--dir kubernetes_cluster_dir
{'tls': True, 'cfg_dir': kubernetes_cluster_dir '.', 'docker_host':
u'tcp://192.168.47.150:2376'}
```

5. The generated certificates are in the kubernetes_cluster_dir directory:

```
# ls kubernetes_cluster_dir
ca.pem     cert.pem     key.pem
```

6. Access the master node through SSH and check the new Kubernetes cluster info:

```
# ssh fedora@192.168.47.150
fedora@...rage8z2 ~]$ kubectl cluster-info
Kubernetes master is running at http://10.10.10.47:8080
KubeUI is running at http://
10.10.10.47:8080/api/v1/proxy/namespaces/kube-system/services/kube-
ui
```

7. To get our WordPress up and running, we will need to deploy our first pod in the Kubernetes worker nodes. For this purpose, we will use a Kubernetes package installer called **Helm**. The brilliant concept behind Helm is to provide an easy way to install, release and version packages. Make sure to install Helm in the master node by downloading the latest version, as follows:

```
$ wget https://github.com/kubernetes/helm/archive/v2.7.2.tar.gz
```

8. Unzip the Helm archive and move the executable file to the bin directory:

```
$ gunzip helm-v2.7.2-linux-amd64.tar.gz
$ mv linux-amd64/helm /usr/local/bin.
```

To read more about Helm, refer to the official project website at https://docs.helm.sh/.

9. Initialize the Helm environment and install the server component:

```
$ helm init
Creating /root/.helm
Creating /root/.helm/repository
Creating /root/.helm/repository/cache
Creating /root/.helm/repository/local
Creating /root/.helm/plugins
Creating /root/.helm/starters
Creating /root/.helm/repository/repositories.yaml
Writing to /root/.helm/repository/cache/stable-index.yaml
$HELM_HOME has been configured at /root/.helm.

Tiller (the helm server side component) has been instilled into
your Kubernetes Cluster.
Happy Helming!
```

The server portion of Helm is called Tiller; it runs within the Kubernetes cluster and manages the releases.

10. Once installed, we can enjoy installing applications and manage packages by firing simple command lines. We can start by updating the chart repository:

```
$ helm repo update
Hang tight while we grab the latest from your chart repositories...
...Skip local chart repository
Writing to /root/.helm/.helm/repository/cache/stable-index.yaml
...Successfully got an update from the "stable" chart repository
Update Complete. Happy Helming!
```

11. Installing WordPress is straightforward with Helm command line tools:

```
$ helm install stable/wordpress
...
NAME: wodd-breest
LAST DEPLOYED: Fri Dec 15 16:15:55 2017
NAMESPACE: default
STATUS: DEPLOYED
...
```

The helm install command line output shows a successful deployment of the default release. Different items that refer to the configurable resources of the WordPress chart are listed during the deployment. The application install is configurable through template files defined by the application chart. The default WordPress release can be configured by providing default parameters passed in the Helm install command line interface.

 The default templates for our deployed WordPress application can be found at https://github.com/kubernetes/charts/tree/master/stable/wordpress/templates.

Specifying a different default set of values for the WordPress install is just a matter of issuing the same command line and specifying the name of the new WordPress release and updated values as follows:

```
$ helm install --name private-wordpress \
-f values.yaml \
stable/wordpress

NAME: private-wordpress
LAST DEPLOYED: Fri Dec 15 17:17:33 2017
NAMESPACE: default
STATUS: DEPLOYED
...
```

Stable charts ready to deploy using Kubernetes Helm package manager are available at `https://github.com/kubernetes/charts/tree/master/stable`.

12. Now that we have deployed a first release of WordPress in Kubernetes in the blink of an eye, we can verify the Kubernetes pod status:

```
# kuberctl get pods
NAME                         READY STATUS    RESTARTS  AGE
my-priv-wordpress-...89501   1/1   Running   0         6m
my-priv-mariadb-.....25153   1/1   Running   0         6m
...
```

13. To provide access to the WordPress dashboard, we will need to expose it locally by forwarding default port 8080 in the master node to port 80 of the instance running the pod:

```
$ kubectl port-forward my-priv-wordpress-42345-ef89501 8080:80
```

14. The WordPress can be made accessible by pointing to the Kubernetes IP address and port 8080:

```
http://192.168.47.150:8080
```

Mesos in OpenStack

Since its early releases back to 2011, Mesos has been widely used to efficiently manage computer resources in data center environments. As a distributed data center operating system, Mesos enables sharing cluster resources between multiple applications that can scale to over dozens of thousands of nodes. The Mesos framework ensures high availability and fault tolerance for the applications sharing cluster resources. As another type of COE, Mesos provides a level of isolation for applications to run in Linux containers. Orchestrating containers in Mesos can be performed by Marathon, a featured framework to launch and manage applications running on top of Mesos.

Since the OpenStack Liberty release, the Magnum project includes the Mesos bay. This adds a third amazing option to cloud operators to leverage running containerized applications in OpenStack. The default COE integration adds Mesos and a Marathon framework that can be created from a single baymodel in Magnum. An overview o the Mesos architecture in OpenStack through Magnum can be illustrated in the next diagram:

- **Master node(s)**: This manages slave nodes and frameworks running tasks on agent daemons. It also manages resource sharing across slave daemons, based on sharing policies.
- **Slave node(s)**: This runs the executors for each framework.
- **Framework**: This composes applications that run on the Mesos cluster. A commonly used Mesos framework is Marathon that can be divided in two main components:
    - **Scheduler**: This registers with the Mesos master nodes. A scheduler manages a task life cycle and its error handling.
    - **Executor(s)**: This launches a task on slave nodes and reports its status back to the scheduler.

- **Service discovery**: This runs ZooKeeper to coordinate quorum between Mesos master nodes, elect a Mesos master leader node, and join Mesos agents to the running cluster:

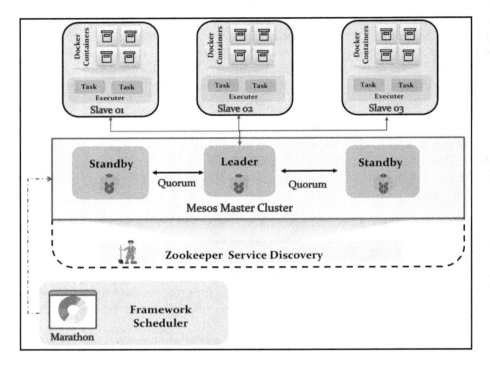

The Marathon framework offers an overwhelming amount of features and capabilities to Mesos. It ensures high availability, provides self-healing, scaling, and health checks to the applications running on top of the mesosphere cluster. Marathon also provides a web user interface to simplify operating and monitoring the running applications. To read more about Marathon, check the mesosphere web site at `http://mesosphere.github.io/marathon/`. Mesos supports other frameworks, such as Chronos and Hadoop.

Now that we have revisited the basic architecture of the Mesos jargon, let's move to the next step and deploy our Mesos application in OpenStack. Without going through a long running journey of installing Mesos, Marathon, and other different dependencies, we will take advantage of the Magnum support and automate the Mesos cluster deployment in few commands.

Example – a Python-based web server

In the following example, we will set up a new Magnum bay running Mesos as COE. The Mesos cluster will deploy a simple python web server running on a Docker container and listening on port 8080, as follows:

1. Create a new Magnum cluster template to deploy a Swarm cluster:

```
# magnum cluster-template-create --name coe-mesos-template \
                          --image-id fedora-latest \
                          --keypair-id pp_key \
                        --external-network-id pub-net\
                          --dns-nameserver 8.8.8.8 \
                          --flavor-id m1.small \
                          --docker-volume-size 4 \
                          --network-driver docker \
                          --coe mesos
```

The previous command line assumes the existence of an image fedora_atomic in the Glance image repository, a key pair named pp_key, and an external Neutron network named pub-net. Make sure to adjust your parameters with the correct command line arguments.

2. Initiate a Mesos cluster with one master and two slave nodes by executing the following Magnum command line:

```
# magnum cluster-create --name mesos-cluster \
--cluster-template coe-mesos-template \
--master-count 1 \
--node-count 2
+--------------------+------------------------------------+
| Property           | Value                              |
+--------------------+------------------------------------+
| status             | CREATE_IN_PROGRESS                 |
| cluster_template_id | 35de332e-f342-d344-d569001dc2182339 |
| uuid               | 66e36d90-8da2-f98e-01e3dacb37664209 |
| stack_id           | 1255387d-c6da-6e8c-6621ca4df6990151 |
| status_reason      | -                                  |
| created_at         | 2017-12-12T17:19:09+00:00          |
```

```
| name                | mesos-cluster
| updated_at          | -
| api_address         | -
| coe_version         | -
| master_addresses    | []
| create_timeout      | 60
| node_addresses      | []
| master_count        | 1
| container_version   | -
| node_count          | 2
+--------------------+-----------------------------------------+
```

3. Verify the creation of the new Swarm cluster:

```
+--------------------+------------------------------------------+
| Property            | Value
+--------------------+------------------------------------------+
| status              | CREATE_COMPLETE
| cluster_template_id | 35de332e-f342-d344-d569001dc2182339
| uuid                | 66e36d90-8da2-f98e-01e3dacb37664209
| stack_id            | 1255387d-c6da-6e8c-6621ca4df6990151
| status_reason       | Stack CREATE completed successfully
| created_at          | 2017-12-12T17:19:09+00:00
| name                | mesos-cluster
| updated_at          | 2017-12-12T17:24:10+10:00
| discovery_url       | -
| api_address         | tcp://192.168.88.238:2376
| coe_version         | 1.0.0
| master_addresses    | ['192.168.47.128']
| create_timeout      | 60
| node_addresses      | ['192.168.47.129', '192.168.47.130']
| master_count        | 1
| container_version   | 1.9.1
| node_count          | 2
+--------------------+------------------------------------------+
```

Make sure that the Marathon web console and Mesos user interface are accessible from the Mesos master node on ports 8080 and 5050, respectively.

4. Create a Mesos application file in which we define the image resources including CPU, memory, networking, and both host and container ports. In the following example, we will instruct Marathon to run our Python web server on container port 8080 and mapped to instance port 8888:

```
{
 "id": "python-app",
 "cmd": " python3 -m http.server 8080",
 "cpus": 0.25,
 "mem": 50,
 "networks": [ { "mode": "container/bridge" } ],
 "container": {
 "type": "DOCKER",
 "docker": {
 "image": "python:3"
 },
 "portMappings": [
 { "containerPort": 8080, "hostPort": 8888 }
 ]
 }
}
```

It is highly recommended that health checks directives are included in the Mesos application definition file to detect report application failure. To read more about Mesos and Marathon level health checks, refer to the official mesosphere documentation available at https://mesosphere. github.io/marathon/docs/health-checks.html.

5. Start the application deployment by posting the JSON application definition file to Marathon, as follows:

```
$ curl -X POST -H "Accept: application/json" \
-H "Content-Type: application/json" \
http://172.31.0.10:8080/v2/apps -d @sample_py.json

{
 "dependencies" : [],
...
 "mem" : 32,
...
 "cpus" : 0.5,
...
 "cmd" : "python3 -m http.server 8080",
...
"docker" : {
 "portMappings" : [
```

```
{
"containerPort" : 8080,
"hostPort" : 8888,
...
 "image" : "python:3",
...
 "type" : "DOCKER"
...
```

6. Make sure that the new application deployment is successful. This can be checked and monitored from the Marathon user interface:

7. Testing our Python-based web server is straightforward. We can simply use the `curl` command line pointing to the Mesos slave node on the configured port 8888:

```
$ curl http://192.168.47.129:8888
<!DOCTYPE HTML PUBLIC "-//W3C//DTD HTML 4.01//EN"
"http://www.w3.org/TR/html4/strict.dtd">
<html>
<head>
<meta http-equiv="Content-Type" content="text/html; charset=utf-8">
<title>Directory listing for /</title>
...
```

Summary

In this chapter, we have unleashed the power of containerization technology. Containers are expanding and becoming a very hot topic by helping IT organizations to make a transition towards the next application deployment trend. We have explored how OpenStack has empowered its ecosystem by providing a CaaS as a new and exciting managed service that combines the major benefits of container orchestration engines in its core. The Magnum project automates the deployment and configuration of container clusters running different models of container orchestration engines. We have reviewed each of the COEs supported by Magnum, including Docker Swarm, Kubernetes, and Mesos. We have explored the power of Magnum API that enables cloud operators to choose the COE model and manage bays simply by using their native COE command line tools. We have deployed a simple cluster for each COE using Magnum API and used the native CLI for each bay to manage the deployed application.

As the Magnum project has brought a large variety of containers to the OpenStack ecosystem, we will continue exploring them. In the next chapter, we will look at another tenting and mature project handling big data and elastic data processing in OpenStack, code named **Sahara**.

6
Managing Big Data in OpenStack

"The greater our knowledge increases the more our ignorance unfolds."

–John F. Kennedy

In the previous chapter, we looked at the benefits of using containers for application development and management life cycle. We have seen the OpenStack community's focus on the containerization concept. Integrating amazing projects such as Magnum would help us increase the agility in running and scaling containerized applications in an OpenStack environment. However, there are still other areas that we haven't looked at, concerning the needs of IT organizations. The past decade has shown an impressive increase in data usage that generates more data cycles to analyze and quantify. IT organizations have started to invest in finding the right tools to extract the most valuable results from this immense amount of data in real time. Big data has become one of the most important fields in which businesses can invest. The need to provide the right tools to save the business value of growing data within an organization has become a necessity. Thanks to the joint effort of several open source projects, a few solutions have become the first steps in starting a big data venture, such as Hadoop and Spark.

But going faster and being real time might not be sufficient, even if you have the right software. Data size cannot be easily predictable, and that raises up more questions on how to put them in a dynamic chain. The advent of cloud technology will answer questions related to scalability and elasticity. Unleashing the perfect solution will put the big data and cloud paradigm in one frame: running big data analysis in the cloud. The OpenStack community has developed a great project, code named **Sahara**, enabling users and cloud operators to rapidly access big data clusters and easily run workloads on them.

In this chapter, we will explore the following topics:

- Introducing and understanding the Sahara project in the OpenStack ecosystem
- Installing and integrating the Sahara service into the OpenStack environment
- Discovering how to build images for different Sahara plugins
- Deploying a big data cluster on top of OpenStack through the Sahara project
- Running a simple job against data input and grabbing results across the big data cluster

Big data in OpenStack

Big data analytics has recently seen a lot of hype. With the increasing amount of generated and used data, organizations today are facing new challenges to satisfy the exponential increase in data needs. Managing petabytes of records and trying to analyze the growing data in real time won't be possible without having the right tools. Fortunately, several open source solutions have come to the rescue, such as the Hadoop and Spark frameworks.

Other tools and projects have been developed around the Hadoop and Spark ecosystems to address the specific needs of different big data use cases, including HBase, Storm, MapReduce, and Avro, to name but a few. Organizations could start a less painful journey in analyzing and processing the huge amount of data by integrating Hadoop tools and others in their data science endeavors. On the other hand, this smooth start will quickly turn to a more cumbersome experience when dealing with the continuous and exponential growth of data that needs more compute and storage resources at scale.

There are two main concepts that will help you ensure a successful use of big data—**operation cost** and **time to market**. The operational team will face more challenges when dealing with big data infrastructure deployment, changes, and scaling. This will influence the business direction on the other side, where data guides the margins of the market and needs to be queried in a reasonable time. With the rise of cloud computing paradigm, processing massive amount of data becomes possible.

This comes from the cloud computing IT secret sauces—elasticity and scalability. The marriage between the cloud paradigm and the world of big data pushed the organizations to focus on the value of data and efficiently grab precious results instead of putting too much effort on managing big data in a traditional way.

But again, *what about OpenStack as private cloud computing software?* Because it has a great modular architecture, including a big data project into OpenStack's ecosystem was a very natural thing to consider. The maturity of the basic OpenStack services, including computing, networking, and storage consequently allows you to move with a high degree of confidence to tackle the world of big data. Roughly during the Havana release, the OpenStack community has started touching the sole part of big data automation and processing. The project has been code named Sahara.

The Sahara project was officially incubated in the Icehouse release. One goal of this project is to provide more agility to access and analyze structured and unstructured data in a more automated fashion. The following diagram illustrates the intersection of the big data world and the OpenStack ecosystem by reviewing Sahara's architecture:

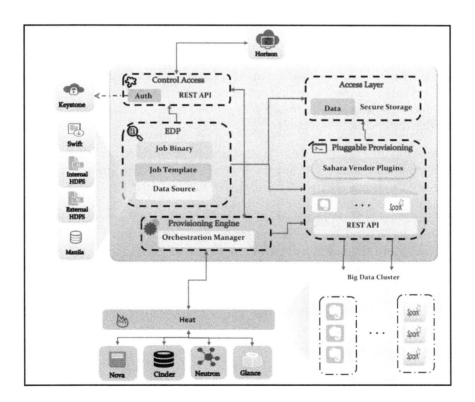

The major components shown in the preceding diagram are explained as follows:

- **Control Access**: This is formed essentially by the REST API to respond to every initiated call from the Sahara client CLI or from Horizon. The new service must be authenticated against **Keystone** through the auth module that includes the user and the service authorization.

- **Elastic Data Processing (EDP)**: EDP forms the core part of the process, the job scheduling in the Sahara project. It manages and monitors the jobs to run on Sahara clusters. The EDP component maps the input/output for each data source and its associated job.

- **Provisioning Engine**: This represents the contact point with the rest of the OpenStack components to provision and deploy cluster resources. The **Provisioning Engine** initiates the big data cluster provisioning by initiating a call to the orchestration service in OpenStack. **Heat** will use the described resources as code templates and provision the cluster components in an automated way, including compute, network, and storage.

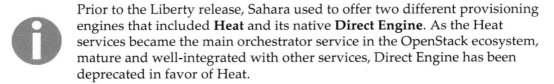 Prior to the Liberty release, Sahara used to offer two different provisioning engines that included **Heat** and its native **Direct Engine**. As the Heat services became the main orchestrator service in the OpenStack ecosystem, mature and well-integrated with other services, Direct Engine has been deprecated in favor of Heat.

- **Access Layer**: This includes the **data access layer** (**DAL**) as the persistent internal data store for Sahara. The latest versions offer a **secure storage** access layer to store and manage secure, secret data for Sahara clusters.

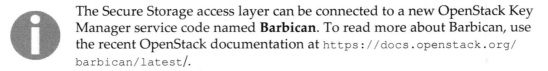 The Secure Storage access layer can be connected to a new OpenStack Key Manager service code named **Barbican**. To read more about Barbican, use the recent OpenStack documentation at `https://docs.openstack.org/barbican/latest/`.

- **Pluggable Provisioning**: This endeavors to launch frameworks of different vendors for data processing. Each vendor plugin provides a deployment implementation ready to be used for big data clusters with Sahara.

Rolling OpenStack Sahara service

In the following section, we will integrate and configure Sahara in an existing OpenStack environment:

1. Install the Sahara CLI and API services package on the cloud controller nodes:

   ```
   # yum install openstack-sahara
   ```

2. Configure the Sahara database by entering the database connection URL in the main Sahara configuration file. Make sure that you create a valid database:

   ```
   # vim /etc/sahara/sahara.conf
   ...
   [database]
   connection mysql://sahara:sahara@192.168.47.47:3306/sahara
   ...
   ```

3. Create a Sahara database schema:

   ```
   # sahara-db-manage --config-file /etc/sahara/sahara.conf \ upgrade
   head
   ```

4. The next step requires a valid identification of the Sahara service in the OpenStack environment. As with any other OpenStack service, we will need to authenticate Sahara through Keystone. Start by creating a Sahara user:

   ```
   # keystone user-create --name sahara --pass sahara_pass
   ```

5. Assign the services tenant to the new Sahara user with a role as `admin`:

   ```
   # keystone user-role-add --user sahara --role admin \
   --tenant services
   ```

6. Create the new Sahara service:

   ```
   # keystone service-create --name=sahara \
    --type=data_processing \
    --description="Elastic Data Processing"
   ```

7. Create the Keystone endpoint for the Sahara service:

   ```
   # keystone endpoint-create --service sahara \
      --publicurl "http://192.168.47.47:8386/v1.1/%(tenant_id)s" \
      --adminurl "http://192.168.47.47:8386/v1.1/%(tenant_id)s" \
      --internalurl "http://192.168.47.47:8386/v1.1/%(tenant_id)s"
   ```

8. Update the Sahara configuration file to comply with the Keystone configuration entries in the previous steps for the Sahara API authentication, including authentication host IP, authentication port, the configured tenant username, and the password, as follows:

```
# vim /etc/sahara/sahara.conf
...
[DEFAULT]
os_auth_host=192.168.47.47
os_auth_port=5000
os_admin_tenant_name=services
os_admin_username=admin
os_admin_password=5235ee593125fb762
...
```

9. Make sure that the Sahara service uses the OpenStack network service Neutron:

```
...
[DEFAULT]
use_neutron   true
...
```

10. Like many other OpenStack projects, installing and running a new service can be performed through Horizon. The Sahara dashboard comes along by installing the following package:

```
# yum install python-django-sahara
```

11. Once installed successfully, add `sahara` to the `/usr/share/openstack-dashboard/openstack_dashboard/settings.py` OpenStack dashboard Python file:

```
# vim /usr/share/openstack-
dashboard/openstack_dashboard/settings.py
...
HORIZON_CONFIG = {
    'dashboards': ('nova',...,'sahara')
...
```

12. Use the same file by adding `saharadashboard` in the `INSTALLED_APPS` configuration stanza:

```
...
INSTALLED_APPS = (
    'saharadashboard',
    ...
```

13. In the `/etc/openstack_dashboard/local_settings.py` file, make sure that Sahara is configured to use Neutron for OpenStack networking service and specify the Sahara URL endpoint as follows:

```
# vim /etc/openstack_dashboard/local_settings.py
        ...
        SAHARA_USE_NEUTRON = True
        ...
        SAHARA_URL = '192.168.47.47: 8386/v1.1'
        ...
```

14. Restart the Sahara API service and the OpenStack dashboard server:

```
# systemctl restart sahara-api
# systemctl restart httpd
```

15. Configure the cloud controller operating system to start the Sahara services upon booting:

```
# systemctl enable openstack-sahara-all
```

16. Make sure that you enable internal Sahara traffic through port `8386` within the OpenStack environment. To do so, add the following `iptables` rule and restart the `iptables` service on the cloud controller node:

```
# vim /etc/sysconfig/iptables
-A INPUT -p tcp -m multiport --dports 8386 -j ACCEPT
...
# systemctl restart iptables
```

17. Verify that the Sahara service is up and running and listening to the configured port:

```
# systemctl status openstack-sahara-api
...
Loaded: loaded (/usr/lib/systemd/system/openstack-sahara-
api.service; enabled; vendor preset: disabled)
    Active: active (running) since Sat 2017-12-30 22:11:35 ...
# systemctl status openstack-sahara-engine
...
Loaded: loaded (/usr/lib/systemd/system/openstack-sahara-
engine.service; enabled; vendor preset: disabled)
    Active: active (running) since Sat 2017-12-30 22:11:35 ...
```

18. Log in to the **Horizon** dashboard. A new **Data Processing** tab should appear in the main right-corner menu under the **Project** tab:

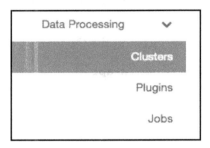

Now we have successfully installed and integrated the Sahara service in an existing OpenStack environment, we will explore how this new service can be used by deploying our first Hadoop cluster in OpenStack.

If you are using `openstack-ansible` to deploy OpenStack services in your existing environment, it is possible to deploy the Sahara service using the `os-sahara-install.yml` playbook included in the playbook repository at `https://github.com/openstack/openstack-ansible/blob/master/playbooks/os-sahara-install.yml`. Make sure that you adjust the necessary variables successfully to install the Sahara container service that includes the following variables:

- `sahara_galera_address`
- `sahara_container_mysql_password`
- `sahara_service_password`
- `sahara_rabbitmq_password`

A complete list of the OpenStack-Ansible Sahara role default variables can be found at `https://docs.openstack.org/openstack-ansible-os_sahara/latest/`.

Deploying the Hadoop cluster

The Sahara project follows the same extensibility fashion as other OpenStack projects using the plugin terminology. Depending on which data processing framework a user or cloud operator would use, Sahara offers different sets of distributions by means of provisioning plugins. At the time of writing of this book, Sahara allows the provisioning of any data processing framework supporting one of the following vendors in OpenStack:

- **Vanilla**: Vanilla Apache Hadoop
- **HDP**: Hortonworks Data Platform
- **MapR Distribution**: MapR Filesystem (**MapR-FS**)
- **Cloudera**: Cloudera Hadoop
- **Spark**: Apache Spark

It is important to keep in mind that within every new OpenStack release, there are new, updated plugin versions. For the current setup, we keep using the Ocata release, supporting the following Sahara plugin versions:

```
# openstack dataprocessing plugin list
```

```
+----------+-------------------------------+
| Name     | Versions                      |
+----------+-------------------------------+
| vanilla  | 2.7.1                         |
| spark    | 1.3.1, 1.6.0, 2.1.0           |
| cdh      | 5.11.0, 5.5.0, 5.7.0, 5.9.0   |
| ambari   | 2.3, 2.4, 2.5                 |
| storm    | 0.9.2, 1.0.1, 1.1.0           |
| mapr     | 5.1.0.mrv2, 5.2.0.mrv2        |
+----------+-------------------------------+
```

In the following example, we will be guiding you through some simple steps to deploy the first Hadoop cluster running in OpenStack using the Spark plugin:

1. Build a CentOS image with Apache Spark 1.6 preinstalled. Use the OpenStack tool out of the box to create Sahara image elements found at `https://github.com/openstack/sahara-image-elements`:

   ```
   # git clone https://github.com/openstack/sahara-image-elements
   # cd sahara-image-elements/
   # tox -e venv -- sahara-image-create -u -p spark -v 1.6 \
   -i ubuntu
   ```

```
venv installed: Babel==2.5.1,bashate==0.5.1,decorator==4.1.2,dib-utils==0.0.11,diskimage-builder==2.9.0,flake8==2.5.5,hacking==0.12.0
.3,PyYAML==3.12,-e git+https://github.com/openstack/sahara-image-elements@2a0fa0d58b0dbfe56f09355e0eb1f8caae43aa15#egg=sahara_image_e
venv runtests: PYTHONHASHSEED='2883751908'
venv runtests: commands[0] | sahara-image-create -u -p spark -v 1.6 -i ubuntu
Spark version not specified
Spark 2.2.0 will be used
package no package provides qemu-kvm is not installed
Retrieving http://dl.fedoraproject.org/pub/epel/6/x86_64/epel-release-6-8.noarch.rpm
warning: /var/tmp/rpm-tmp.MoJaIQ: Header V3 RSA/SHA256 Signature, key ID 0608b895: NOKEY
Preparing...                  ############################### [100%]
Updating / installing...
   1:epel-release-6-8          ############################### [100%]
Loaded plugins: fastestmirror
epel/x86_64/metalink
```

The `tox` command will install the necessary Python packages and execute a disk image script that allows the creation of disk images and the parameterization of operation systems, including Ubuntu, Fedora, and CentOS. The disk image creator script is by default named `diskimage-create.sh`.

The previous command will build a CentOS-based Spark image. The `tox` command will start the download of the Spark distribution and install it in the corresponding image:

```
2017-12-25 23:10:19.120 INFO diskimage_builder.block_device.blockdevic
Converting image using qemu-img convert
Image file ubuntu_sahara_spark_latest.qcow2 created...

venv: commands succeeded
congratulations :)
```

2. Once the image is built, we upload it to our OpenStack image repository using the Glance CLI or Horizon:

```
# glance image-create --name=pp-sahara-spark \
--disk-format=qcow2 \
-container=bare < ubuntu_sahara_spark_latest.qcow2
```

Property	Value
checksum	076a15b96ce95546812a8cde5b394f69
container_format	bare
created_at	2017-12-25T23:15:40Z
disk_format	qcow2
id	54ef8e7c-1526-48c1-bef3-fb56dc45dcd8
min_disk	0
min_ram	0
name	pp-sahara-spark
owner	72c9f0b3319f45dc81b9bf4beeac497e
protected	False
size	1058078720
status	active
tags	□
updated_at	2017-12-25T23:15:48Z
virtual_size	None
visibility	shared

3. Register the new uploaded image to Sahara so the new service can use it as a source image when creating the Spark cluster. Make sure that you grab the image ID of the Spark image if you are using CLI:

```
# openstack dataprocessing image register \
--username ubuntu --description "Sahara Image Spark Ubuntu PP" pp-
sahara-spark
```

```
+--------------+------------------------------------------+
| Field        | Value                                    |
+--------------+------------------------------------------+
| Description  | Sahara Image Spark Ubuntu PP             |
| Id           | 54ef8e7c-1526-48c1-bef3-fb56dc45dcd8     |
| Name         | pp-sahara-spark                          |
| Status       | ACTIVE                                   |
| Tags         |                                          |
| Username     | ubuntu                                   |
+--------------+------------------------------------------+
```

4. The Spark plugin requires a tagged image with `spark` and `spark_version` tags. From CLI, add the `spark` and `1.6` tags to the newly uploaded image:

```
# openstack dataprocessing image tags \
add pp-sahara-spark --tags spark 1.6
```

```
| Name      | pp-sahara-spark   |
| Status    | ACTIVE            |
| Tags      | 1.6, spark        |
```

Once the image is registered by Sahara, we can create the node group templates and the cluster instances configuration descriptor within the same role, which can be achieved from CLI or through Horizon. Navigate to the **Data Processing** tab in the **Horizon** dashboard and select **Node Group Templates**. Click on **Create Template** to be guided through the cluster creation wizard. The first interface requires the plugin and the corresponding version. Select the plugin name as **Apache Spark** and the version as **1.6.0**:

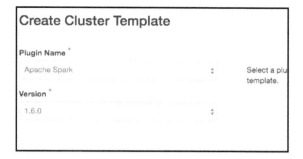

5. Create the first node group template for the Spark master node:

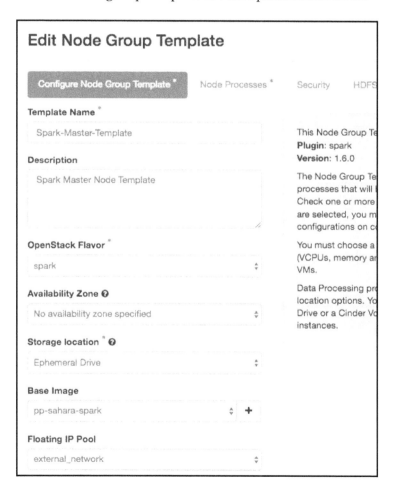

Bear in mind that tags for Sahara images are required to correctly configure the Sahara cluster. You may note that the base image won't load the list of registered images in Sahara if they have missed one of the mentioned tags.

6. Assign the **namenode** checkbox of the **HDFS processes** option and the **master** role of **Spark processes** for the master node group template:

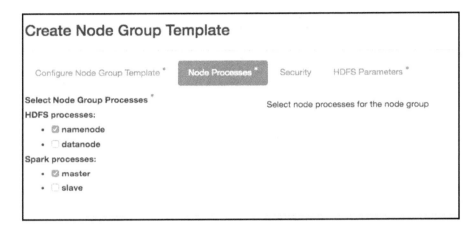

The **namenode** role is assigned to the node orchestrator in Sahara cluster.

7. It is possible to control the security groups from the Sahara cluster group templates. For the sake of simplicity, we will keep the default one:

It is recommended that you allow only the required ports within the same Sahara node cluster. Depending on the type of the big data cluster you want to launch, make sure that you select the required ports and create dedicated security groups per node group for the sake of smooth security.

8. Keep the default DFS values in the **HDFS Parameters** tab. It is possible to update the **NameNode** and **DataNodeHeap Size** if you want to, depending on the available memory resources:

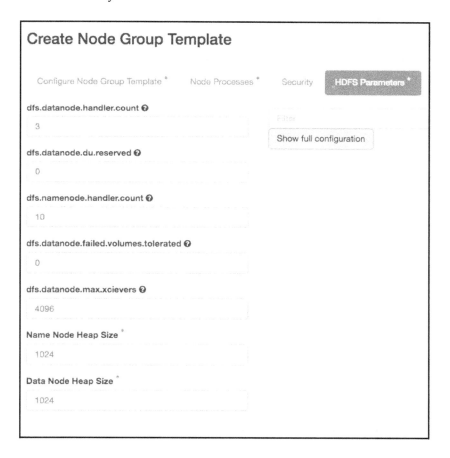

The **HDFS parametrization** wizard allows the customization of HDFS settings in the Sahara cluster. When running jobs, binaries will be streamed locally to the Hadoop filesystem. Job workloads may vary, and some may require more tuning to configure the right parameters.

9. Create the first **Node Group Template** for the Spark slave node:

10. Assign the **datanode** to HDFS process and the **slave** role to Spark process for the slave node group template:

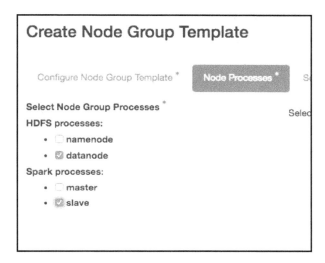

11. Set the **Security Groups** and **DFS** settings as configured in steps 7 and 8.

12. Now that we have the building blocks of the templates ready to go, let's create our Spark cluster template by associating the master and slave node group templates to it. Point to the **Cluster Template wizard** in the same **Clusters** tab and click on **Create Template**. Select the same Spark version from the drop-down menu as **1.6.0** from the drop-down menu.

13. In the next wizard tab, set the cluster template name.

14. The second tab provides a seamless way to describe how the Spark cluster would be provisioned by selecting the number of instances of each node group template previously created. For our initial deployment, we will use one master and two slave nodes for the Spark cluster:

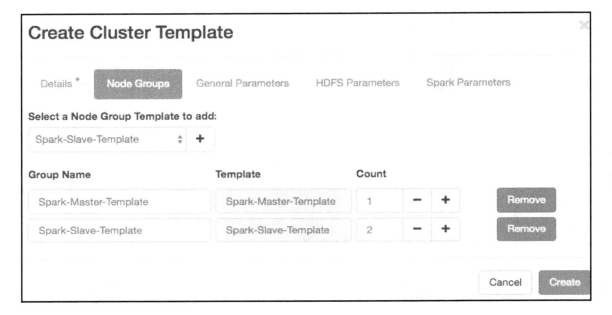

15. The next tab, **General Parameters**, shows the configurable timeout options for cluster deployment, including disk formatting, orchestration service wait condition, instances decommissioning (when scaling down the cluster node count), and data node startup timeouts:

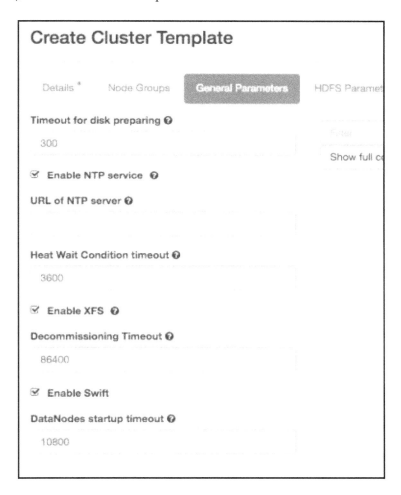

16. The next tab, **HDFS Parameters**, configures the DFS replication settings across the cluster nodes and the file size allocation for the Hadoop filesystem:

17. The last tab, **Spark Parameters**, allows you to set the access port for the Spark web console. In our example, we set ports 8080 and 8081 for the master and slave roles respectively, as shown in the following screenshot:

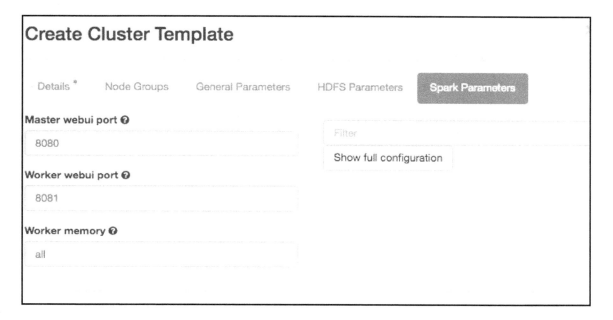

Create Cluster Template

Details *   Node Groups   General Parameters   HDFS Parameters   **Spark Parameters**

Master webui port ❷

    8080

Worker webui port ❷

    8081

Worker memory ❷

    all

Filter

Show full configuration

18. To deploy our Spark cluster, go through the last Sahara **Clusters** wizard. Click on the **Launch Cluster** button and choose the same Spark version, **1.6.0**. In the next window, specify the name of the new cluster. Make sure that you select **Spark-Cluster** from the **Cluster Template** drop-down list and set the count **1**, as we plan to deploy only one cluster. Choose the registered Spark image as a base Glance image for each instance in the Sahara cluster. It is also possible to specify the **Keypair** field to grant SSH access that will be propagated to each instance of the Spark cluster upon booting. Depending on the available network segments in the OpenStack environment, each Spark instance will be provisioned with a fixed IP if wired to a private subnet. As with any other Nova instance, it is possible to attach a floating IP for external access to any Sahara instance after cluster provisioning:

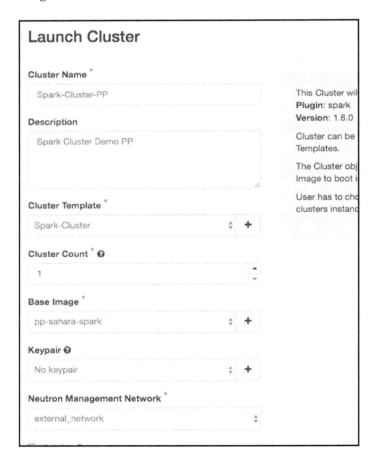

Executing jobs

Sahara facilitates the execution of jobs and bursting workloads in big data clusters running any supported EDP workload platform in OpenStack. As we have rapidly deployed a Spark cluster in the previous section, associated jobs in Sahara can be managed very easily.

Running jobs in Sahara requires the localization of the data source and destination from which the Sahara engine will fetch, analyze, and store them respectively. Sahara supports mainly three types of input/output data storage:

- **Swift**: This designates the OpenStack object storage as the main location for data input and the destination of the output result
- **HDFS**: This uses any running OpenStack instance backed by HDFS storage
- **Manila**: This uses the OpenStack network file system by exposing the data source share that is mounted among the Sahara cluster

At the time of writing this book, Sahara's EDP functionality supports numerous types of jobs that can be listed as follows:

- **MapReduce**: This splits data into different parts that can be processed and provide results in parallel using reducer and mapper.
- **MapReduce.Streaming**: This enables you to run a MapReduce task with different programming languages. The streaming of the job will be performed by both reducer and mapper by reading from STDIN and emitting the results to STDOUT.
- **Storm**: This uses a topology processes that does not stop unless killed manually.
- **Storm Pyelus**: This defines the topology of a Storm setup using Python scripts.
- **Hive**: This converts a HiveQL query against a Hadoop cluster into a MapReduce executor.
- **Spark**: This uses the Spark cluster to run multipipelined jobs on the same data.
- **Shell**: This runs script shells on Hadoop clusters.
- **Pig**: This queries data in the Hadoop setup. Pig scripts are written in the Pig Latin language and translated into chunks of MapReduce tasks.
- **Java**: This runs java-described jobs for Java in a Hadoop cluster environment.

In the following section, we will use our running Spark cluster to execute a simple job that reads from an input data source text file and counts all the unique strings. The content of the text file looks as follows:

```
OpenStack
OpenStack
Sahara
Swift
Sahara
OpenStack
Sahara
EDP
EDP
Sahara
Swift
```

The Spark job will be initiated by loading the text file stored in our Swift object storage. The WordCount application example is written in Python and looks as follows:

```
import sys
from pyspark import SparkContext, SparkConf
if __name__ == "__main__":
  # create Spark context with Spark configuration
  conf = SparkConf().setAppName("Spark Count")
  sc = SparkContext(conf=conf)
  # get threshold
  threshold = int(sys.argv[2])
  # read in text file and split each document into words
  tokenized = sc.textFile(sys.argv[1]).flatMap(lambda line: line.split("
"))
  # count the occurrence of each word
  wordCounts = tokenized.map(lambda word: (word, 1)).reduceByKey(lambda
v1,v2:v1 +v2)
  # filter out words with fewer than threshold occurrences
  filtered = wordCounts.filter(lambda pair:pair[1] >= threshold)

  # count characters
  charCounts = filtered.flatMap(lambda pair:pair[0]).map(lambda c:
c).map(lambda c: (c, 1)).reduceByKey(lambda v1,v2:v1 +v2)
  list = charCounts.collect()
  print repr(list)[1:-1]
```

The WordCount example written in Scala is available at https://git.openstack.org/cgit/openstack/sahara-tests/tree/sahara_tests/scenario/defaults/edp-examples/edp-spark/wordcountapp/src/main/scala/sahara/edp/spark/SparkWordCount.scala.

Another important factor required to run a job in Sahara is the binary objects that can be essentially JAR, scripts of credential files. During the configuration of the EDP job, a job binary file must be referenced, which can be stored internally (`sahara` database), in the Swift cluster or Manila share storage.

> A similar example for a modified version of the WorkCount Spark example can be found at `https://github.com/openstack/sahara-tests/tree/master/sahara_tests/scenario/defaults/edp-examples/edp-spark`. Make sure that you download the `spark-wordcount.jar` binary file that will be used in the next steps.

For our current example, we need to provide a Spark JAR file named `spark-wordcount.jar`. In **Horizon**, follow the next steps to execute the Spark job:

1. Create a new Swift container from the **Object Store | Containers** tab and upload the text file object as our Spark data source:

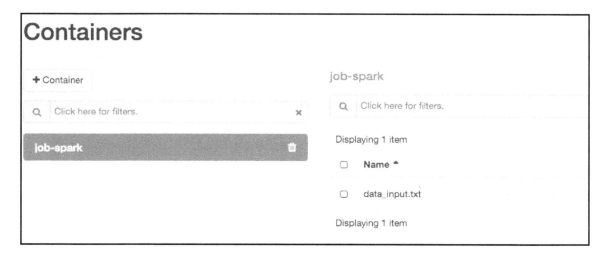

2. Go to the **Data Processing** | **Jobs** tab and select the **Data Source** section. Create a new data source pointing to the Swift text file object. Make sure to reference the correct Swift URL with the format `swift://<container_name>/<object_name>`:

It is possible to use the same username and password for the current running OpenStack project residing in the Keystone admin or project file. The Swift credentials can be updated in the Swift configuration files.

3. Create the second data source to store results of the Spark job in the same Swift container with a different object name as follows:

4. Select the **Job Binaries** tab and click on the **Create Job Binary** button to upload the `Spark-Binary` file:

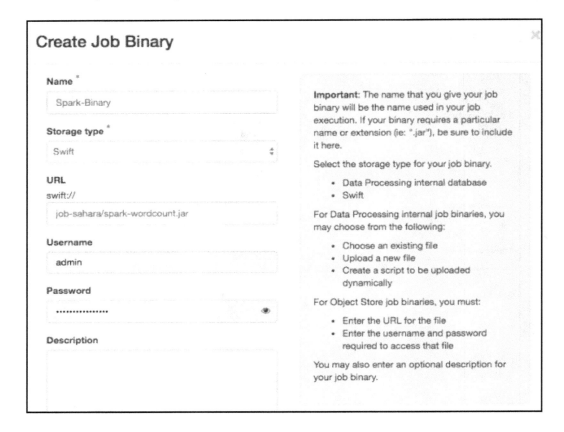

5. Now we have all the required data source input/output and Spark binary uploaded in the Sahara environment, we can create our first Spark job by selecting the **Job Template** tab, clicking on the **Create Job Template** button, and choosing **Spark** from the **Job Type** drop-down menu list:

6. Make sure that you add the uploaded `Spark-Binary` file in the second tab of the **Create Job Template** wizard as follows:

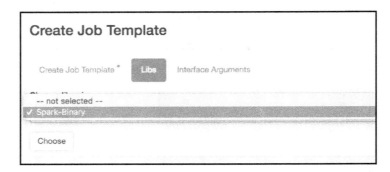

7. The newly created job can be launched on the running Spark cluster. Go to the **Jobs** tab and select the **Launch on Existing Cluster** option.
8. Specify the data input/output sources and cluster name.
9. The job execution will submit a new task to the running Spark cluster and checks the data sources availability. The job will fail if the cluster is not reachable or if the Swift container URLs do not exist:

10. When the job state changes from the **Running** to the **Succeeded** state, the result should be available on the configured output source. For our example, download and check the content of the resulting object in the spark-data-output container:

```
(OpenStack,3)
(Sahara,4)
(Swift,2)
(EDP,2)
```

Summary

In this chapter, we uncovered another concept of the OpenStack ecosystem—big data as a service. We explored most of Sahara's features that reduces all the administrators and routine tasks to deploy and provision big data clusters. This chapter has demonstrated the wide range of Sahara plugins that support the integration of many big data vendors and embrace the running of more workload types. You may have noted how simple it is to run a job in Sahara, avoiding the complexity that is usually involved in the traditional approach. This shows another success of the basic OpenStack architecture design, enabling us to orchestrate several components to expose an analytic stack to operators and users in no time.

We keep growing our OpenStack XaaS capabilities in the next chapter by extending another incubated OpenStack hot project application as a service code `Murano`.

7
Evolving Self-Cloud Ready Applications in OpenStack

"If knowledge is not put into practice, it does not benefit one."

–Muhammad Tahir-ul-Qadri

From a cloud user perspective, running a workload in an OpenStack environment can take many stages, from provisioning and allocating necessary resources and to accessing an entry point in which end users can perform their tasks. On the other hand, by looking at the maturity of the OpenStack services across all different releases, we can observe clearly that its ecosystem has been designed to facilitate, as much as possible, running any type of workload from big data to the containerization era. Undoubtedly, the orchestration engine of OpenStack has gained potential growth that has been extended to automate different sets of services and user needs in the cloud environment as we have explored in `Chapter 5`, *Containerizing in OpenStack* and `Chapter 6`, *Managing Big Data in OpenStack*. What about users with an immense application deployment appetite? Ideally, preparing the infrastructure is great, but for those who are seeking faster deployment and distribution of their application code, they still need another favor for the OpenStack ecosystem to achieve this. Without worrying too much about resource management to run a given application, OpenStack has unleashed an additional powerful project that provides an application catalog ,like App Store or Google Play, where users can easily navigate through different categorized applications and deploy them by the click of a button. The new implemented application catalog service is code named **Murano**. This is where developers and end users will gain a solid experience that allows them to deploy an entire cloud application environment through simple steps.

In this chapter, we will enjoy a great addition of the application catalog service in OpenStack by going through the following topics:

- Briefly discuss what Murano is and its evolvement in OpenStack
- Revisit the Murano architecture and understand its integration within the OpenStack ecosystem
- Integrate the application catalog service in an existing OpenStack environment
- Deploy a first containerized application in OpenStack using Murano

The evolvement of Murano

By leveraging the power of the orchestration service in OpenStack, the Murano project has unchained developers from the complexity of setting up the correct environment with all the needed resources just to deploy a simple or complex application.

No more dependency on administrator's actions to allow resource usage access for specific tenant services. Without the need to have a deep understanding of what is running under the hood, any developer can deploy and publish any type of application (if shared) without spending too much time on digging into the infrastructure details that are not visible to end users.

The Murano project was primarily targeting three different types of actors, which can be categorized as follows:

- **Cloud Operator/Administrator**: Operators/administrators can define more granular **Role-based access control** (**RBAC**) rules and choose how an application catalog will be accessed across different users and tenants. The cloud operators also check the legitimacy of the published application packages in the catalog service and meters its own billing.
- **Cloud Application Publisher**: Publishers import the applications as packages into the application catalog. Any published application exposes its own service metadata and properties as described by the publisher. Other application terms such as metrics can be defined by the publisher by declaring which edges of the application service should be monitored and billed.

- **Cloud Application Consumer**: As an application consumer, available imported applications by publishers are maintained by operators and are browsed, selected, and deployed in a created environment. In case of a more complex application environment, it might include other service dependencies that can be selected by the user and should be present in its current environment. Consumers could monitor the deployment progress of the application and should be able to verify the state of their deployment from a resources perspective, including creation of the instances and the correctness of the provided configuration during the deployment wizard.

The nirvana of the Murano addition in the OpenStack ecosystem is the ability to run applications into a virtual machine or even into containers with Heat functions such as auto-scaling capabilities. In the following section, we will briefly discuss how Murano has been integrated into the OpenStack ecosystem.

Murano supports multiple application formats that can be published in the application service by using HOT templates and **Murano Programming Language** (**MuranoPL**).

The Murano ecosystem

The Murano project has been incubated in the OpenStack Juno release. Its excessive development has yielded to a seamless and tied integration of the application catalog service in the OpenStack ecosystem. From a high-level architecture perspective, Murano uses existing core OpenStack services that include Keystone, Glance, Heat, Horizon, Ceilometer, Cinder, Docker using Nova plugins, and optionally Mistral.

Mistral is a new innovative OpenStack project providing Workflow-as-a Service. Mistral can be used to manage processes and trace their states in an asynchronous way. To read more about the latest updates of the Mistral project, please refer to the official OpenStack project page found at https://docs.openstack.org/mistral/latest/.

The Murano architecture in OpenStack can be broken down as illustrated in the following figure:

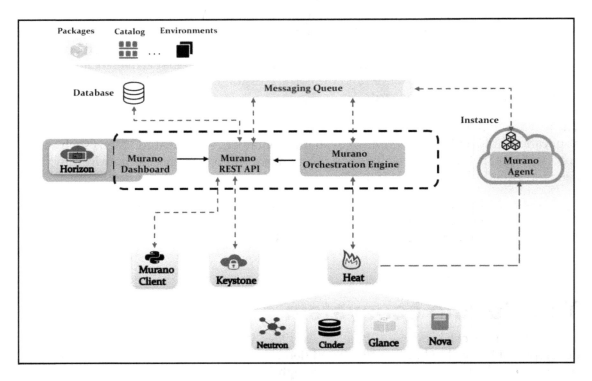

The Murano major components are detailed as follows:

- **Murano REST API**: Exposes and serves users requests to the Murano engine service through the messaging queue service. The Murano API can handle multiple requests by resource type or category.
- **Murano Orchestration Engine**: This calls the OpenStack orchestration service upon each received request from the messaging queue service. Once the required infrastructure resources for the deployment of the Murano application are provisioned, the Murano engine service initiates an agent in the created instance to start receiving tasks through the messaging queue service.
- **Murano Dashboard**: This exposes a simplified user interface in the OpenStack dashboard. As with any other OpenStack service, users can also call the Murano API by using the Python Murano client package.

- **Murano Agent**: Once created by the Murano orchestration engine service, the Murano agent service located in the instance handles all of the necessary software and packaging configuration for the application deployment. Upon every received task from the engine service, the agent gets the execution plan and executes it on the VM, and uses the messaging queue service to return results.

Integrating Murano in OpenStack

In this section, we will go through a few steps to install and configure the Application Catalog service in OpenStack. As with any other OpenStack service, we will need to make sure some prerequisites are installed. The following steps assumes the existence of an OpenStack cluster on CentOS 7 and running Ocata release:

1. On the cloud controller node, make sure that the following dependencies are satisfied:

   ```
   # yum install python-setuptools postgresql-devel libffi-devel git
   gcc
   ```

2. Before installing the Murano packages, we need to make sure to have a safe way to check the packages install by using a generic virtual environment. For this purpose, install tox on the controller node using the pip command line:

   ```
   # pip install tox
   ```

3. Create a murano database:

   ```
   # mysql -u root -p
     > CREATE DATABASE murano
   ```

4. Create a new Murano user granted with all privileges access to the created database:

   ```
   > GRANT ALL PRIVILEGES ON murano.* TO 'murano'@'localhost'
   IDENTIFIED BY 'secretpassword';
   > GRANT ALL PRIVILEGES ON murano.* TO 'murano'@'%' IDENTIFIED BY
   'secretpassword';
   ```

5. Download the Murano repository from the Ocata branch release in Git:

   ```
   # git clone -b stable/ocata
   git://git.openstack.org/openstack/murano
   ```

6. Under the `murano` directory, make sure to install the list of dependent packages found in the `requirements.txt` file:

    ```
    # pip install -r requirements.txt
    ```

7. Make sure that all necessary requirements are successfully installed or satisfied if they already exist in the operating OpenStack cloud controller node. Run the `setup.py` script to install Murano:

    ```
    # python setup.py install
    ```

    The output of the preceding code can be shown in the following screenshot:

    ```
    running install_scripts
    Installing murano-wsgi-api script to /usr/bin
    Installing murano-engine script to /usr/bin
    Installing murano-manage script to /usr/bin
    Installing murano-cfapi-db-manage script to /usr/bin
    Installing murano-cfapi script to /usr/bin
    Installing murano-api script to /usr/bin
    Installing murano-db-manage script to /usr/bin
    Installing murano-test-runner script to /usr/bin
    ```

8. Inside the same directory, use the `oslo_config_generator` script to generate a sample Murano main configuration file as follows:

    ```
    # oslo-config-generator --config-file etc/oslo-config-
    generator/murano.conf
    ```

9. Create a new `murano` directory under the `/etc` and copy the sample Murano configuration files to the new location:

    ```
    # mkdir /etc/murano && cp etc/murano/* && mv \
    /etc/murano/murano.conf.sample /etc/murano/murano.conf
    ```

10. Update the `murano.conf` file with the minimum configuration settings as follows:

    ```
    ...
    [oslo_messaging_rabbit]
    ...
    rabbit_host= 10.10.248.12
    rabbit_port=5672
    rabbit_hosts= 10.10.248.12:5672
    ```

```
rabbit_userid=guest
rabbit_password=guest
rabbit_virtual_host=/
rabbit_ha_queues=False
...
[database]
connection = mysql://murano:password@10.10.248.12 /murano
...
[keystone_authtoken]
auth_uri=http:// 10.10.248.12:5000/v3.0
identity_uri=http:// 10.10.248.12:35357
admin_user=murano
admin_password=password_murano
admin_tenant_name=services
   ...
[murano]
url = http://10.10.248.12:8082
...
[rabbitmq]
host=10.10.248.12
login=guest
password=guest
virtual_host=/
...
```

11. Create a new OpenStack user named `murano`:

    ```
    # openstack user create --password password_murano murano
    ```

    The output of the preceding code can be shown in the following screenshot:

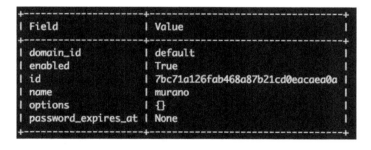

12. Assign the services tenant to the created `murano` user as `admin`:

```
# openstack role add --project services --user murano admin
```

13. Create a Murano service in OpenStack:

```
# openstack service create --name murano --description "Murano
APpaaS" application-catalog
```

The output of the preceding code can be shown in the following screenshot:

14. Create new OpenStack endpoints associated to the new Murano service for the following interfaces:
    - `admin`:

    ```
    # openstack endpoint create --region RegionOne
    6df88fa1889e467abab3476b61d0dfbb admin
    'http://10.10.248.12:8082/'
    ```

    The output for the preceding command can be seen in the following screenshot:

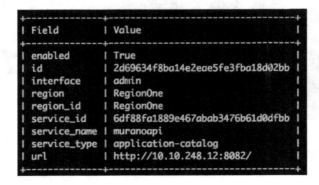

- `internal`:

```
# openstack endpoint create --region RegionOne
6df88fa1889e467abab3476b61d0dfbb internal
'http://10.10.248.12:8082/'
```

The output for the preceding command can be seen in the following screenshot:

```
+--------------+-------------------------------------------+
| Field        | Value                                     |
+--------------+-------------------------------------------+
| enabled      | True                                      |
| id           | c6fb9f5ae76345f3a39f5b14aa25949f          |
| interface    | internal                                  |
| region       | RegionOne                                 |
| region_id    | RegionOne                                 |
| service_id   | 6df88fa1889e467abab3476b61d0dfbb          |
| service_name | muranoapi                                 |
| service_type | application-catalog                       |
| url          | http://10.10.248.12:8082/                 |
+--------------+-------------------------------------------+
```

- `public`:

```
# openstack endpoint create --region RegionOne
6df88fa1889e467abab3476b61d0dfbb public
'http://10.10.248.12:8082/'
```

The output for the preceding command can be seen in the following screenshot:

```
+--------------+-------------------------------------------+
| Field        | Value                                     |
+--------------+-------------------------------------------+
| enabled      | True                                      |
| id           | a1b650a5c18f439488ffcc2e16aa59ab          |
| interface    | public                                    |
| region       | RegionOne                                 |
| region_id    | RegionOne                                 |
| service_id   | 6df88fa1889e467abab3476b61d0dfbb          |
| service_name | muranoapi                                 |
| service_type | application-catalog                       |
| url          | http://10.10.248.12:8082/                 |
+--------------+-------------------------------------------+
```

15. Initialize a database synchronization with the database connection set in the new Murano configuration file:

```
# murano-db-manage --config-file /etc/murano/murano.conf upgrade
```

16. Start the Murano `api` and `engine` services:

```
# screen murano-api --config-file /etc/murano/murano.conf
# screen murano-engine --config-file /etc/murano/murano.conf
```

Murano services can be added to `systemd` for better services handling management.

17. Now, the Murano services are up and running in the controller node. That enables the users to start creating and deploying applications using the Murano CLI. The Murano dashboard module is developed entirely in a separate repository. To add it to Horizon, download the Murano dashboard module from Git by pointing to the Ocata branch release:

```
# git clone -b stable/ocata
git://git.openstack.org/openstack/murano-dashboard
```

18. Install the rest of the Murano dashboard module dependencies by running the following command lines:

```
# cd ~/murano-dashboard
# pip install -r requirements.txt
```

19. Once all requirements are satisfied with the required packages installed, we will need to enable the new Murano Horizon module. This can be achieved by copying the module files in `muranodashboard/local/enabled/` to the default OpenStack dashboard installation directory:

```
# cp muranodashboard/local/enabled/_* /usr/share/openstack-
dashboard/openstack_dashboard/enabled/
```

The output for the preceding command can be seen in the following screenshot:

```
_50_admin_add_panel.py.example
_50_dashboard_catalog.py
_51_muranodashboard.py
_60_admin_remove_panel.py.example
_60_panel_group_browse.py
_63_panel_murano_catalog.py
_70_admin_default_panel.py.example
_70_panel_group_manage.py
_71_panel_murano_packages.py
_72_panel_murano_images.py
_73_panel_murano_categories.py
_80_admin_add_panel_group.py.example
_80_panel_group_applications.py
_81_panel_applications_environments.py
_90_admin_add_panel_to_group.py.example
```

20. Restart the OpenStack web server to load the enabled modules:

    ```
    # systemctl restart httpd
    ```

21. By navigating to the OpenStack dashboard, we can observe the newly added **App Catalog** tab in Horizon:

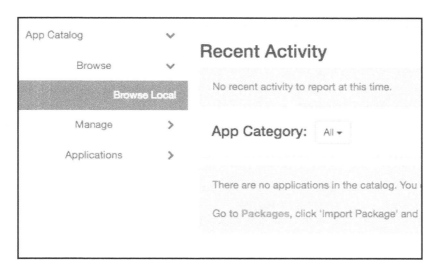

The basic integration of the Application Catalog service in OpenStack is completed. As a user, administrator, or application publisher, we will walk-through the added Murano dashboard in the next section to deploy and run our first cloud-ready application.

Deploying a self-contained application

Before we dive into deploying a simple application in OpenStack using the Murano dashboard, let's briefly discuss the Murano glossary and key concepts to understand the deployment workflow for each step. From the dashboard, we can reveal a few concepts that include the following Murano naming conventions:

- **Environment**: Defines a group of applications owned per single tenant. Applications living in different environments are independent.
- **Package**: Forms the basic ingredients units for the deployment of an application that contains different installation, classes, scripts, and dynamic UI definition files. An application package is zipped and uploaded to the application catalog by the user.

 During the upload of the application package, Murano makes sure that a pre-defined application entry-point file with the fixed name `manifest.yaml` exists.

- **Bundle**: These are grouped sets of packages. A bundle can be used to organize different types of packages in collections. Application packages in a bundle are sorted by usage. Importing a bundle will automatically import all the declared applications in the bundle to the application catalog in Murano.
- **Category**: Organizes applications by category based on the application type.
- **Deployment**: Defines the process of the installation of an application. During the deployment, different resources will be provisioned by the orchestration engine and information will be updated during the deployment, which includes the status of the deployment.

By introducing the notion of the previous Murano concept naming conventions, we will consequently move forward to explore how Murano would help users to orchestrate cloud applications in OpenStack in a very automated and easy way.

We will stay in the era of containerization and we will now walk-through the deployment of an ElasticSearch application running in Docker. To run Docker applications in the application catalog service in OpenStack, we will need to use the Docker support for Murano packages, which can be found at https://github.com/openstack/k8s-docker-suite-app-murano. The project repository exposes the following packages that need to be added to the application catalog in Murano to deploy applications in containers:

- **Docker Interface Library**: Defines a set of libraries to interact with hosts running Docker engine.
- **Docker Standalone Host**: Defines a dedicated host that will run the Docker engine software.
- **Kubernetes**: Provides an installed container cluster management with Kubernetes to run Docker containers in single or multiple cluster nodes.
- **Application**: Contains a bunch of predefined dockerized applications that includes the ElasticSearch application. It can be deployed and run using the Docker Standalone Host or the Kubernetes application one.

Let's walk-through the following steps to get our Dockerized Elasticsearch application deployed using the App Catalog panel in Horizon:

1. Download the k8s-docker-suite-app-murano repository and create a ZIP file for each of the following folders:

```
# git clone
https://github.com/openstack/k8s-docker-suite-app-murano
# cd ~/k8s-docker-suite-app-murano/DockerInterfaceLibrary/package
# zip -r DockerInterfaceLibrary.zip .
# cd ~/k8s-docker-suite-app-murano/DockerStandaloneHost/package
# zip -r DockerStandaloneHost.zip .
# cd ~/k8s-docker-suite-app-murano/Kubernetes/package
# zip -r Kubernetes.zip .
# cd cd ~/k8s-docker-suite-app-
murano/Applications/Elasticsearch/package
# zip -r ElasticSearch.zip .
```

2. In the **App Catalog** panel, point to the **Manage** and then **Packages** tab and click on **Import Package** to import each of the zipped files created in step 1:

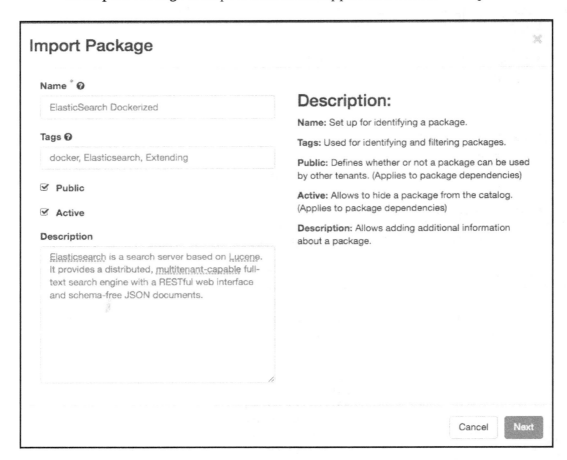

3. Once all of the zipped packages have been imported successfully, navigate to the **Browse** | **Browse Local** tabs to view all of the available applications from the imported packages in step 2:

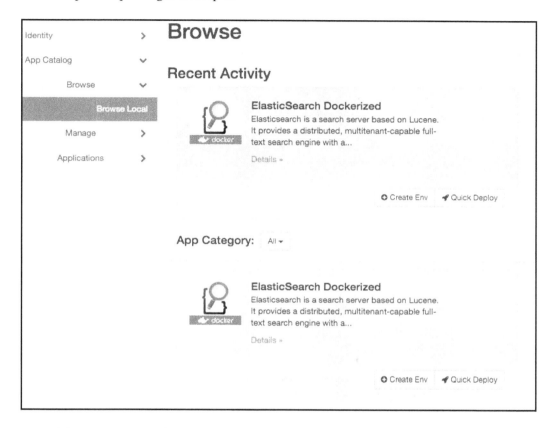

4. The next essential step is to prepare the basic ingredients of the application deployment by building the instance image where the application container will be placed. The Docker Standalone Host application in Murano requires the presence of a Docker image in input. To achieve this, we will need to install a few tools to build the image. Start by installing the diskimage-builder, kpartx, and qemu-utils tools in the cloud controller node:

```
# pip install diskimage-builder
# yum install kpartx  qemu-utils
```

5. Build an Ubuntu image by referring to the elements items in the `DockerStandaloneHost` directory:

```
# ELEMENTS_PATH=murano-agent/contrib/elements:k8s-docker-suite-app-
murano/DockerStandaloneHost/elements disk-image-create vm ubuntu
murano-agent docker -o ubuntu14.04-x64-docker
```

The output for the preceding command can be seen in the following screenshot:

```
2018-02-16 18:15:17.030 | INFO diskimage_builder.block_device.level0.localloop [
2018-02-16 18:15:17.079 | INFO diskimage_builder.block_device.level0.localloop [
2018-02-16 18:15:20.145 | INFO diskimage_builder.block_device.utils [-] Calling
2018-02-16 18:15:20.308 | INFO diskimage_builder.block_device.blockdevice [-] Re
2018-02-16 18:15:20.637 | Converting image using qemu-img convert
2018-02-16 18:17:06.894 | Image file ubuntu14.04-x64-docker.qcow2 created...
```

The previous command will build an Ubuntu image with a pre-installed Murano agent. Make sure to instruct the command line to point to the `diskimage-builder` elements that contain the Murano agent installation. To download the Murano agent use the command line `# git clone https://git.openstack.org/openstack/murano-agent.git`. To get more details about building an image with a pre-installed Murano agent, check out the URL `https://github.com/openstack/murano-agent`.

6. Once the image is built successfully, import the Ubuntu disk image to the OpenStack image service:

```
# openstack image create ubuntu-app --disk-format qcow2 --
container-format bare --file ubuntu14.04-x64-docker.qcow2 --
property murano_image_info='{"title": "Murano Ubuntu", "type":
"linux"}'
```

Note that `murano_image_info` is added to the image property argument that can be recognized as an available image for application deployment by Murano:

```
+-------------------+--------------------------------------------------------------+
| Field             | Value                                                        |
+-------------------+--------------------------------------------------------------+
| checksum          | b9556a392c81b1b031dce45c3eb7c31c                             |
| container_format  | bare                                                         |
| created_at        | 2018-02-16T18:20:21Z                                         |
| disk_format       | qcow2                                                        |
| file              | /v2/images/a7b61083-fe98-4e81-863b-849254f58f2e/file         |
| id                | a7b61083-fe98-4e81-863b-849254f58f2e                         |
| min_disk          | 0                                                            |
| min_ram           | 0                                                            |
| name              | ubuntu-app                                                   |
| owner             | bb2e456704724548a08371a83f0d7479                             |
| properties        | murano_image_info='{"title": "Murano Ubuntu", "type": "linux"}' |
| protected         | False                                                        |
| schema            | /v2/schemas/image                                            |
| size              | 648871936                                                    |
| status            | active                                                       |
| tags              |                                                              |
| updated_at        | 2018-02-16T18:20:25Z                                         |
| virtual_size      | None                                                         |
| visibility        | shared                                                       |
+-------------------+--------------------------------------------------------------+
```

7. By browsing to the **Manage | Images** tab, the uploaded image will appear automatically on the **Marked Images** page:

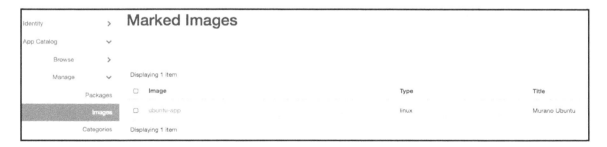

8. The uploaded image metadata can be customized further by clicking on the **Mark Image** button to add specific Murano metadata:

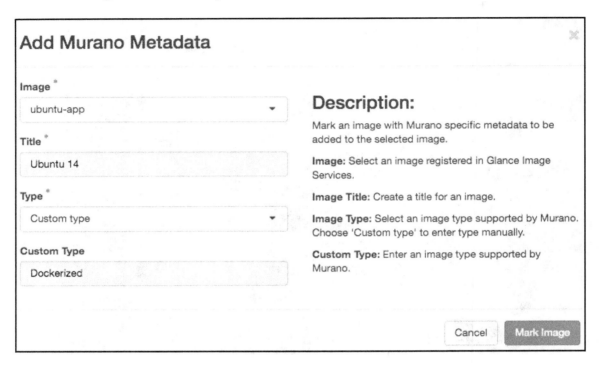

9. Our deployment preparation stage should be accomplished. Next, we will move on to deploy the application by browsing the **App Catalog | Browser | Browse Local** tab. We can be fast without creating a custom Environment and click on the **Quick Deploy** button on the ElasticSearch application section.

10. The next wizard will guide us in configuring our intended ElasticSearch application. That includes the application name, ElasticSearch credentials, and on which type of host the container will run. Note that in step 2 we have imported both Docker and Kubernetes hosts requirement packages that will be listed during each application deployment configuration step:

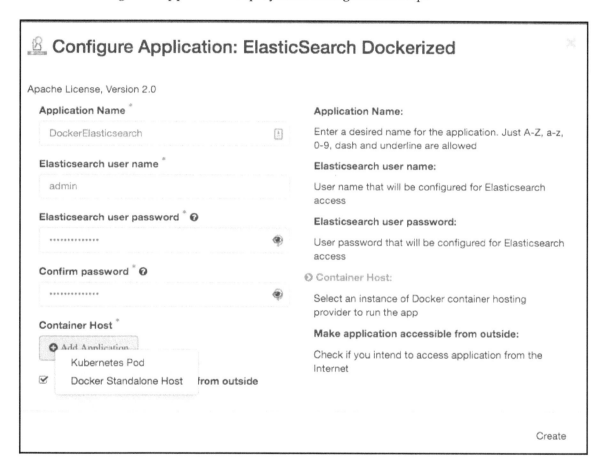

11. Click on **Create** and proceed by providing a custom name for the Dockerized application that will be used by the Docker engine running on the **Docker Standalone Host**:

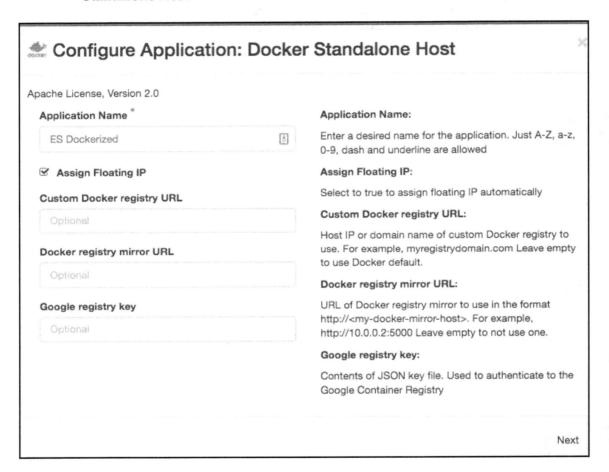

12. Click on **Next** and provide the imported image for the drop-down list and the instance flavor. It is also possible to provide the **Key Pair** value if any exists to access the instance once an application is deployed:

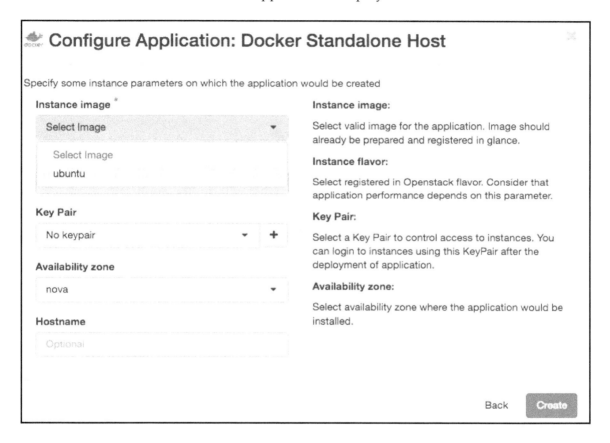

13. The deployment configuration stage is accomplished. By clicking on the **Create** button, Murano validates the correctness of the deployment configuration wizard by creating a deployment draft for the current environment:

14. By browsing to the **Applications | Environment** tab in the **App Catalog** panel, we can notice that Murano automatically creates a named environment **quick-env-1** that assembles two application components—Docker Standalone Host to run the Docker engine and ElasticSearch that will run the application in a container. A simple click on **Deploy Environment** will initiate the deployment of the application and orchestrates the provisioning of the needed OpenStack services:

15. The **Environments** tab provides direct access to get more insight about the progress of the deployment that can be checked through the **Last Deployment Log** and **Deployment History**, without the need to jump into command line and tail logs in the cloud controller node. Additionally, the Murano dashboard has been inspired by the Neutron and Heat ones by projecting the deployed application components for a given environment:

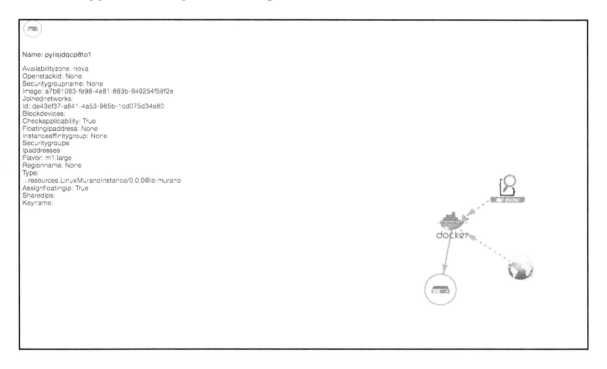

Name: pyiisjdqcp8to1

Availabilityzone: nova
Openstackid: None
Securitygroupname: None
Image: a7b61083-fe98-4e81-863b-849254f58f2e
Joinednetworks:
Id: de43ef37-a841-4a53-985b-1cd075d34e80
Blockdevices:
Checkapplicability: True
Floatingipaddress: None
Instanceaffinitygroup: None
Securitygroups:
Ipaddresses:
Flavor: m1.large
Regionname: None
Type:
...resources.LinuxMuranoInstance/0.0.0@io.murano
Assignfloatingip: True
Sharedips:
Keyname:

Summary

The application catalog service has revolutionized the way applications are deployed into the cloud by cutting the burden of infrastructure details complexity. Murano has brought an abstraction layer between the OpenStack infrastructure and third-party services. This is like a PaaS and IaaS marriage in OpenStack that has boosted the development of applications in the cloud to the next era and simplified the process of deploying, managing, and browsing a ready-state release of an application. Consequently, the Murano project has rapidly changed the gears by bringing containers onto the stage. As we have explored in this chapter, an amazing work has been done around Murano Docker support. Through simple steps, we have deployed a fully containerized simple application without worrying about all the manual steps, such as installing and configuring the environment dependencies. We have let Murano do that for us by just importing our packages and in a few steps configuring how our application will look when it is deployed. By now, you should have a better overview of how Murano works and a good understanding of the application life cycle within the application catalog service in OpenStack. Although we have deployed a ready-to-go application in Murano from a developer or consumer perspective, we will dig deeper in the next chapter and act as a Cloud Application Publisher and build an application using the available and supported Murano formats.

8
Extending the Applications Catalog Service

"It is not enough to have a good mind; the main thing is to use it well."

–René Descartes

In the previous chapter, we explored the application catalog service in OpenStack, which has proven a very simplistic and effortless way to deploy applications in the OpenStack environment. As demonstrated in the previous chapter, Cloud Application Publishers could easily import an application in Murano, so Cloud Application Consumers can browse it and use it in no time. As we used a cloud-ready application example in the previous chapter, we will change the spot in the current one and break the application into pieces by developing a cloud-native application and publishing it into the cloud.

In this chapter, we will discuss the following points:

- Exploring the structure of a Murano application
- Creating and developing the first Murano application and publishing it into the cloud
- Discovering different ways to customize an application package
- Unleashing the novelty of the Murano-supported application formats

Murano application under the hood

The Murano project defines a specific structure that should be used to develop and successfully publish an application in the catalog container. As we have explored in the previous chapter, a Murano application is simply a deployable package that includes a set of files in a ZIP format. Once uploaded to the catalog service, Murano unzips the package and runs a series of checks on the structure and presence of predefined files that we would expect to be present at different levels.

A Murano application package should be organized as illustrated in the following hierarchical file tree:

```
Application.zip
        |
        |------------- manifest.yaml
        |------------- logo.png
        |------------- Classes\
        |              |--------- application.yaml
        |------------- Resources\
        |              |--------- scripts
        |                         |------- script.sh
        |                         |------- ....
        |              |--------- application_plan.template
        |------------- UI\
                       |--------- UserInterface.yaml
```

Let's break down the file tree and briefly parse the definition of each folder and file that Murano expects when uploading the .zip file:

- manifest.yaml: This is a fixed file name that Murano expects as the first application entry point. The manifest file can be expressed as a main file that exposes general application information.
- logo.png: This is an optional preview image that will be shown in the application catalog when importing the package to the application catalog service.
- Classes: This folder encapsulates the different class definitions of the application written in YAML format. Murano classes define the deployment of the application workflow.

- `Resources`: Murano fetches different script files that are used to install the applications with different custom configuration setups into the `Resources` directory. The same directory may contain an execution plan template that inform the Murano agent running on the destined VM of the different steps to deploy the application.
- `UI`: The `UI` directory contains all sets of forms that will be exposed to the end user to configure the application by entering the installation options defined by the publisher.

Developing application publisher perspective

Now that we have an overview of each piece of the application package, let's dig deeper into the content of each file in the presented hierarchy. One essential aspect of the Murano project is to give more flexibility to the developers in defining how the deployment of an application should be based on their specific needs and requirements. The secret sauce of achieving this goal is by programming the application deployment itself.

Murano provides its own programming language, MuranoPL, to develop deployable applications written in YAML and **Yet Another Query Language** (**YAQL**) languages.

YAQL is an extensible query language written in Python that addresses complex queries against large arbitrary data and objects. YAQL code can be integrated easily in any code and can be extended by defining custom functions. More information about the YAQL language can be found at the YAQL official documentation

at `https://yaql.readthedocs.io/en/latest/`.

As shown in the previous file structure, Murano makes an extensive usage of MuranoPL language. Each MuranoPL file is written in combination with YAML and embedded YAQL language.

Check the MuranoPL official reference documentation
`http://murano.readthedocs.io/en/latest/draft/appdev-guide/murano _pl.html#murano-pl` to develop more customized applications and learn more about the MuranoPL core libraries and classes.

To have a basic understating of how the MuranoPL code works, we will develop a Murano application package to deploy a custom webserver for packtpub website as follows:

1. Create an empty package repository skeleton as presented in the previous package files hierarchy. The root application directory can be named `PacktPub_WebServer`.

2. Starting with the `manifest.yaml` file, we will provide custom information about the application with the following content:

```
Format: 1.3
Type: Application
FullName: com.example.apache.packtpub.WebServer
Version: 1.0.0
Name: PacktPub_WebServer
Description: |
 A custom Httpd Server with accelerated caching capabilities for
 the     PacktPub domain name
Author: 'PacktPub Cloud Application Publisher'
Tags: [Apache, WebSite, HTTP, WebServer, PacktPub, Publisher]
Classes:
 com.example.apache.packtpub.WebServer: HttpWebSite.yaml
```

The different main directives can be listed as follows:

- `Format`: This version attribute refers to the YAQL and Murano versions used. Format versions might change between OpenStack releases, and the compatibility of the versions should be checked between different releases and formats.
- `Type`: This describes the type of package, and requires a naming convention that starts with a capital letter.
- `FullName`: This defines a fully qualified name of the application. It refers to a unique application namespace that can be addressed by an other application using the `FullName` string.
- `Name`: This is the name of the application that will be visible in the application catalog user interface.
- `Description`: This short description of the application will be presented in the description section in the application catalog user interface.
- `Author`: This is the publisher/developer's name.
- `Tags`: These are additional tags defined in an array format that could be useful when searching an application using its tags and organizing them by category.

- Classes: This points to the application class file located in the Classes directory named as HttpWebSite.yaml.

3. Let's move on and chain the HttpWebSite.yaml MuranoPL class in the Classes directory as specified in the manifest.yaml file. We are assuming the usage of a VM image based on CentOS:

```
Namespaces:
=: com.example.apache.packtpub
std: io.murano
res: io.murano.resources
sys: io.murano.system
conf: io.murano.configuration
Name: WebServer
Extends: std:Application
Properties:
  enablePHP:
    Contract: $.bool()
    Default: false
  instance:
    Contract: $.class(res:Instance).notNull()
Methods:
  .init:
    Body:
      - $._environment: $.find(std:Environment).require()
  deploy:
    Body:
      - If: not $.getAttr(deployed, false)
        Then:
          - $._environment.reporter.report($this, 'Creating VM for
Httpd Server.')
          - $securityGroupIngress:
            - ToPort: 80
              FromPort: 80
              IpProtocol: tcp
              External: true
            - ToPort: 443
              FromPort: 443
              IpProtocol: tcp
              External: true
            - ToPort: 22
              FromPort: 22
              IpProtocol: tcp
              External: false
          -
$._environment.securityGroupManager.addGroupIngress($securityGroupI
```

```
ngress)
            - $.instance.deploy()
            - $._environment.reporter.report($this, 'Instance is
created. Deploying Httpd.')
            - $file: sys:Resources.string('deployHttpd.sh')
            - conf:Linux.runCommand($.instance.agent, $file)

            - If: $.enablePHP
              Then:
                - $._environment.reporter.report($this, 'Installing
PHP.')
                - conf:Linux.runCommand($.instance.agent, "sudo yum
install -y php5")
            - $._environment.reporter.report($this, HttpD is
installed.')
            - If: $.instance.assignFloatingIp
              Then:
                - $host: $.instance.floatingIpAddress
              Else:
                - $host: $.instance.ipAddresses.first()
            - $._environment.reporter.report($this, format('WebServer
is available at http://{0}', $host))
            - $.setAttr(deployed, true)
```

Let's decompose the main directives of the class file as follows:

- Namespaces: These are the different namespaces as predefined in the manifest file and Murano core library.
- Name: This is the class name defined in the manifest file corresponding to com.example.apache.packtpub.WebServer.
- Extends: Like object-oriented programming, classes in MuranoPL can inherit from others through the Extends directive. The application's Murano class represents the parent class that all applications inherit from.
- Properties: This directive attributes the application properties. In our example, each of the enablePHP and instance properties has a Contract field. Note that enablePHP is not required by setting Default to false, while the Contract option for the instance property is required, which is defined in the Murano resources core class io.murano.resources.Instance.

- `Methods`: This presents two methods, as follows:
  - `init`: This initializes the running environment by instructing the application deployment state to send progress reports at each stage.
  - `deploy`: This provisions and configures instances through different sets of tasks. In our example, we instruct the `deploy` method to send notification report messages for the instance provisioning stages. Security groups can also be defined in the `deploy` method. In our example, we allow ingress traffic from the external network for HTTP and HTTPS, and SSH only from the internal network. It is also possible to define the location of the deployment script of the web server application, specified by the `$file` parameter, so that the Murano agent can run once the instance is up and running. Note that it is possible to nest the `-if-else-` condition in the `Methods` stanza code for example, if the `enablePHP` property is enabled, the Murano agent will install the PHP binary package in the instance. The same condition is interpreted if the instance has assigned a floating IP address; otherwise, it will use the first address in the fixed pool of IP addresses.

The `deploy` method can be extended based on the application file structure to load an execution plan template if defined. User input parameters should be part of the `deploy` method to update the plan.

4. Create a script file named `deployHttpd.sh` under the `Resources` directory as defined in the `deploy` method to instruct the Murano agent to install the `httpd` web server with the `mod_file_cache` module to speed up file access. In doing this, serving static files will be accelerated on slow file systems using the file map cache technique. In addition, as specified in the `deploy` method, the Murano agent should open HTTP and HTTPS ports for the external network and the SSH port only for the VM internal network:

```
sudo yum update
sudo yum install httpd httpd-devel -y
echo "LoadModule file_cache_module modules/mod_file_cache.so" >>
/etc/httpd/conf.modules.d/00-cache.conf
```

```
echo "CacheFile /var/www/html/index.html
/var/www/html/somefile.index" >> /etc/httpd/conf/httpd.conf
echo "MMapFile /var/www/html/index.html
/var/www/html/somefile.index >> /etc/httpd/conf/httpd.conf"
systemctl restart httpd
sudo iptables -I INPUT 1 -p tcp -m tcp --dport 80 -j ACCEPT -m
comment --comment "PacktPub WebServer HTTP Access - Public"
sudo iptables -I INPUT 2 -p tcp -m tcp --dport 443 -j ACCEPT -m
comment --comment "PacktPub WebServer HTTPS Access - Public"
sudo iptables -I INPUT 3 -p tcp -m tcp --dport 22 -s 10.1.0.0/16 -j
ACCEPT -m comment --comment "PacktPub WebServer SSH Access -
Private"
```

5. The last piece of our website application is the dynamic UI forms. Create a new `ui.yaml` file under a `UI` directory of the package with the following content:

```
Version: 2.2
Application:
  ?:
    type: com.example.apache.packtpub.WebServer
  enablePHP: $.appConfiguration.enablePHP
  instance:
    ?:
      type: io.murano.resources.LinuxMuranoInstance
    name:
generateHostname($.instanceConfiguration.unitNamingPattern, 1)
    flavor: $.instanceConfiguration.flavor
    image: $.instanceConfiguration.osImage
    keyname: $.instanceConfiguration.keyPair
    assignFloatingIp: $.appConfiguration.assignFloatingIP

Forms:
  - appConfiguration:
      fields:
        - name: license
          type: string
          description: Apache License, Version 2.0
          hidden: true
          required: false
        - name: enablePHP
          label: Enable PHP
          type: boolean
          description: >-
            Add php support to the Httpd WebServer
          initial: false
          required: false
        - name: assignFloatingIP
```

```
type: boolean
label: Assign Floating IP
description: >-
    True to assign floating IP to the instance
initial: false
required: false
- instanceConfiguration:
    fields:
    - name: title
    type: string
    required: false
    hidden: true
    description: Specify some instance parameters on which
the application would be              created
    - name: flavor
    type: flavor
    label: Instance flavor
    description: >-
        Select registered in Openstack flavor. Consider that
application performance
        depends on this parameter.
    required: false
    - name: osImage
    type: image
    imageType: linux
    label: Instance image
    description: >-
        Select valid image for the application. Image should
already be prepared and
        registered in glance.
    - name: keyPair
    type: keypair
    label: Key Pair
    description: >-
        Select the Key Pair to control access to instances. You
can login to
        instances using this KeyPair after the deployment of
application.
    required: false
    - name: unitNamingPattern
    type: string
    label: Instance Naming Pattern
    required: false
    maxLength: 64
    regexpValidator: '^[a-zA-z][-_w]*$'
    errorMessages:
        invalid: Just letters, numbers, underscores and hyphens
are allowed.
```

```
            helpText: Just letters, numbers, underscores and hyphens
are allowed.
            description: >-
              Specify a string, that will be used in instance
hostname.
              Just A-Z, a-z, 0-9, dash and underline are allowed.
```

The dynamic UI form YAML file contains the following sections:

- `Version`: This is an optional directive that specifies the UI definition format version. By default, it uses the latest version supported by MuranoPL.
- `Application`: This refers to the defined object model that refers to the `com.example.apache.packtpub.WebServer` class mentioned in the `manifest` file. Note that for each `Application` section, a `?` is included to trace a piece of system information. The next line `enablePHP` associated with `appConfiguration` form gives the user the choice to enable PHP or not. The following `instance` section defines a MuranoPL object with the `io.murano.resources.LinuxMuranoInstance` type. That generates an application object module with instance parameters that will be filled by the user, including the name, flavor, image, keyname, and floating IP.
- `Forms`: This defines the following two different UI forms:
  - `appConfiguration`: This places the parameters of the web server including the PHP installation (`enablePHP`) and floating IP assigment (`assignFloatingIP`). The parameters will be invoked by the Murano agent during the deployment. Note that each of the `appConfiguration` parameters can be marked as required or not with a default initial value.

- `instanceConfiguration`: This places the parameters related to the provisioning of the instance that includes the name, flavor, image, and key-pair of the instance. It is also possible to extend the parameters to set a hardware limit as a requirement of the deployment. `unitNamingPattern` is another important parameter that defines naming convention conditions when a user is filling the UI forms. The MuranoPL engine will load the `regexpValidator` parameter value as declared and throws an error message when the naming pattern is not respected.

More information about the Dynamic UI MuranoPL development reference can be found at
`http://murano.readthedocs.io/en/latest/draft/appdev-guide/murano packages/dynamic_ui.html#dynamicuispec`.

6. Once all files are committed, assemble the package by creating a `.zip` archive:

```
# zip -r webserver_packtpub.zip *
```

7. Upload the composed package to Murano:

```
# murano package-import webserver_packtpub.zip
```

Deploying application consumer perspective

As a Cloud Application Publisher, we have successfully imported a custom web server that will be used by developers to develop and run tests for the packtpub website. Let's check how our developed application will be deployed from the consumer's perspective:

1. Log in to the OpenStack dashboard and navigate to **App Catalog** | **Browse** | **Browse Local**; we can see that the new package has been added to the **App Catalog**:

2. By clicking on the **Quick Deploy** button, we will be faced with the first UI form to select, asking whether the user wishes to enable PHP and assign a floating IP address to the instance as configured in the appConfiguration section in the ui.yaml file:

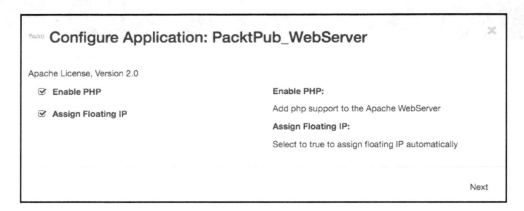

3. The next UI will prompt you to fill in the instance parameters as described in the `instanceConfiguration` section in the `ui.yaml` file:

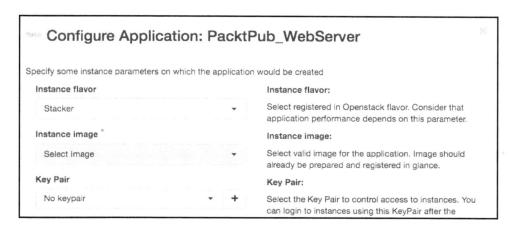

4. The next form will ask you to fill the applications name. Note that the naming convention discussed in the `unitNamingPattern` will be visible for consumers when parameterizing the application:

5. A few clicks, and our website deployment is ready to go live:

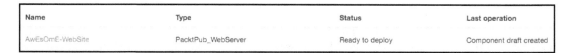

6. To go fast, click on **Deploy This Environment** and Murano will automatically create a new environment where the application will and run:

Displaying 1 item			
Name	**Type**	**Status**	**Last operation**
AwEsOmE-WebSite	PacktPub_WebServer	Deploying	Component draft created
Displaying 1 item			

Summary

In this chapter, you learned how to develop a Murano package by going through the structure of an application package, and acquired a basic understating of its workflow. You should feel more confident in driving more customized applications and bringing them to the cloud through the application catalog service, thanks to the Murano programming language. As mentioned in the previous chapter, Cloud Application Publishers can use Heat orchestration templates to create and import them into the application catalog service. However, introducing the MuranoPL programming language has ultimately yielded a richer user experience in terms of flexibility and customization of the package layout. In addition, to drive a great Murano application development experience, it is recommended that you include a continuous integration pipeline that gathers cloud application developers and administrators together and keeps them in the same wavelength. That could go beyond the defining stages for each application deployment that goes from checking YAQL and YAML syntax and system integration tests to security checks, through different stages.

The latest releases of OpenStack have included several intuitive projects for cloud-based applications and containers that make deployment easy and straightforward, such as Murano and Magnum. Those great innovative steps introduced in the OpenStack ecosystem are not limited only to the incubated projects, but also the core components. In gaining greater popularity around the globe, the OpenStack setup has introduced more extended architectural layouts touching on internal enterprise software integration and the public and hybrid cloud design patterns. The first thing to revisit to enable such enormous extension is the authentication service in OpenStack. The community has brought Keystone to the next level by making it think bigger, which will be the topic of the next chapter.

9
Consolidating the OpenStack Authentication

"The more you know, the more you know you don't know."

–Aristotle

In this chapter, we will tackle the identification service in OpenStack from a different angle. Firstly, we will revisit the key concepts forming the Keystone service. In a second iteration, we will bring under the scope an extended identification setup in OpenStack by adopting the identity federation layout. Since the Icehouse release, the OpenStack community has greatly increased the number of ways in which users can authenticate against the Keystone service. That includes identity federation support, which delegates authentication tasks to a central trusted identifying entity defined as **Identity Providers** (**IdP**). At the time of writing, Keystone supports various federation protocols, such as **Security Assertion Markup Language** (**SAML**) and **OpenID Connect**, based on OAuth protocol. We will discover how to redesign the identity service in OpenStack and enable more profitable and secure user management access to resources across different enterprise's endpoints. In this chapter, we will go through the following points:

- Briefly parsing the basic components of the identity service in OpenStack
- Projecting the identity federation architecture in OpenStack
- Implementing an identity federation layout in OpenStack using SAML
- Adapting an additional federation setup in Keystone using OpenID Connect

Recapping the Keystone blocks

Before diving into relooking the identity service in OpenStack, let's get to grips with the basic concepts of Keystone in a nutshell:

- **Project**: In the OpenStack's early releases, the project concept was referred to as a **tenant**. A project in OpenStack is a container of a number of resources for specific users or groups that abstracts their isolation.
- **Domain**: Another abstraction layer added to the identity service, a **domain** assembles projects, users, and groups in an OpenStack environment. The new domain structure enables the definition of organizational cloud setup by isolating projects and groups for each organization.
- **Role**: A user in OpenStack can be a member of one or many projects. This can be achieved by defining a new role that can be assigned to the project(s) and the OpenStack user. In this way, roles in OpenStack determine the user or user group authorization layout.
- **Catalog**: As an endpoint registry of the OpenStack services, Keystone exposes the catalog provider to users and services to use a specific OpenStack service endpoint.
- **Token**: To access any OpenStack service, a user or a service must obtain a validated token that contains different information about the user, expiration date, associated projects, and authorized endpoints. The concept of a token in OpenStack has been excessively developed through the OpenStack releases, and today, we can find many token types offered by Keystone, which will be discovered in the next section.
- **IdP**: The IdP validates the legitimacy of users accessing OpenStack resources. A group user's credentials are stored in the Keystone's database. In other extended cloud setups, the IdP backend can be external and the latest Keystone design supports the integration of SQL, **Lightweight Directory Access Protocol (LDAP)**, and Federated IdP. From the third version of Keystone, it is possible to use multiple IdP backends for different cases. Different IdP setups will be discussed in the following parts of the chapter.

 To read more about the identity concepts and relative updates for the latest OpenStack release, please refer to the link: `https://docs.openstack.org/keystone/pike/admin/identity-concepts.html`.

Now that we have revisited the building blocks of authentication and authorization mechanisms in Keystone, let's uncover how an OpenStack cloud designer would leverage the latest supported features of Keystone in an existing OpenStack environment.

The multitude faces of the token

This section will be dedicated to briefly analyzing the evolution of the Keystone token and the different formats it can support. This might be important to bear in mind before starting to evaluate the most suitable solution to consolidate an authentication and authorization system management tool in the cloud environment:

- **Universally Unique IDentifier (UUID) token**: As far as back as the Folsom release, Keystone used the UUID format. For each API call, the UUID token will be passed along the request to the service endpoint and therefore, to Keystone. It will be then validated against the Keystone backend. UUID tokens are a 32-character length string.

- **Public Key Infrastructure (PKI) tokens**: Starting from Grizzly release, the Keystone team has implemented a new token format by passing the validation response in it referred to as PKI format. Keystone generates a private key and **Certificate To Sign (CTS)** that will be stored locally. When dealing with the first API endpoint call, the service will cache the CTS to be used for the future calls. Thus, the service itself will not need to contact Keystone for each user's token validation any more. The PKI token is quite large and holds much information in its payload. To work around this issue, the PKI has been enhanced by compressing the token payload, which is called **PKIZ**.

- **Fernet tokens**: A fernet token consists of serialized authorization and authentication metadata encapsulated into a message packed payload. Fernet tokens use a smaller payload size containing the required information for the token validation. The fernet format does not interact with any persistent token database. This decreases the token validation time for Keystone and increases performance. Fernet tokens use a symmetric key to get signed. Each key needs to be rotated in configurable intervals of time.

 Fernet has been developed by Heroku as a secure messaging format. It was originally designed to generate tokens for APIs requests between servers.

Looking to the token evolution in Keystone, it can be very interesting to formulate a brief comparison overview between existing token formats. This can be illustrated in a nutshell in the following table:

	Pros	Cons
UUID	• Small payload size • Simple to use through curl	• Keystone performance degradation when validating tokens for each request
PKI/PKIZ	• Enhancement of Keystone service performance by token validation caching • Improvement of data payload validation by compression	• Large payload size • Lack of token encryption • Need to flush Keystone database
Fernet	• Smaller payload size • Faster on creation and manipulation • Persistence database not required	• Keys rotation required

Multiple identity actors

Another Keystone active area that has been developed during the latest OpenStack releases is the implementation of the IdP and supported backends.

As mentioned in the beginning of this section, Keystone may come with various IdPs using a variety of store backends, as follows:

- **LDAP**: Keystone authentication requests will be delegated to an LDAP server. This requires minimal permissions for Keystone to read and write data.
- **SQL**: User information can be stored in an SQL database. In this case, the identity service will be presented as an IdP.
- **Federated IdP**: The identity service in OpenStack will consume a centralized authentication exposed by an existing third party IdP. In this case, the OpenStack acts as **Service Provider** (**SP**) while Keystone does not store any users and groups but relies on trusted IdPs. A federated IdP can be backed by multiple backends that includes—LDAP, **Active Directory** (**AD**), SQL, MongoDB, and even social login-enabled platforms, such as Google and Facebook.

- **Hybrid model**: The latest version of Keystone supports the integration of different backends within the same OpenStack environment. It is possible to have more than one backend type such LDAP and SQL in an existing enterprise. For example, most enterprises dictate a policy to split users for each department, so it may have more than one LDAP server in place. By leveraging the domain concept in OpenStack, this logical split can be maintained and reflected for the same enterprise.

Various identity options are represented for the OpenStack audience within the latest releases to accommodate the most suitable solution. A list of advantages and disadvantages for each enumerated option is illustrated in the following table:

	Pros	Cons
LDAP	• Move IdP role from Keystone	• Service accounts in LDAP
SQL	• Fastest way to setup an identity back-end	• Keystone as IdP
Federated IdP	• Move IdP role from Keystone • Use existing authentication tools in the infrastructure • Flexible way to federate user roles in a different cloud layout	• More complex setup
Hybrid model	• Use existing authentication tools in the infrastructure (LDAP)	• Requires domain configuration

In the next sections, we will change the color of our default identity service and develop, in more detail, how to extend its power by leveraging the federated IdP mechanism.

All in one authentication hub

The concept of the federation offers a way of bringing different parties under one centralized umbrella. Most enterprises prefer to expose a unified platform to internal users within different service providers. One of the most common federation use cases are identity and authentication federation systems. An organization might have different services around its IT infrastructure that require authentication and authorization for each privileged user.

Implementing many database back-ends for each service would potentially increase a security risk to map several accounts for each user service. That can easily result in losing track of each individual account for each service when off-boarding a user. Additionally, managing identity separately for each service by a different system can be very confusing for users as well as it presents an administrative nightmare task.

 Identity federation is becoming a common way for many organizations to grow their cloud services to a hybrid extension. That presents a smooth way to provide access across multi-cloud setup and environments.

The identity federation mechanism allows users to keep using their authentication credentials against the existing identity setup. Administrators won't worry about adding a new, separate authentication logic and increasing the system's complexity level. This can be achieved just by leveraging an existing IdP that holds user accounts and maps their access level to different services across the organizations referred as SP. In this way, users will be able to access different services as configured by the administrator, who will have better experience with more control over credentials management.

Before we tackle federation support with Keystone, let's revisit some essential terms around the federation identity mechanism, as follows:

- **IdP**: A trusted identity store holding users and group informations and managing which identity has permissions to consume which services in each account. An IdP can be backed by an LDAP, an AD, or an SQL database.
- **SP**: An IdP consumer service that uses the identity information to manage only access to specific services.
- **Assertion**: A representation identity document generated by IdP to establish trust with the SP. An assertion can be represented using two different methods:
  - **SAML**: An XML-based document containing user attributes used to exchange authentication and authorization data between different federated actors.
  - **OpenID Connect**: A JSON-based document containing user's information referred as a **Claim**. OpenID Connect is based on OAuth 2.0.

In the following sections, we will configure the Keystone service as SP, so it will outsource the authentication steps to an external IdP. We will set up assertions for both SAML and OpenID.

Keystone as SP – SAML

The next federated identity layout outsources the management of users and service authentication to an external IdP by using SAML. This federation setup can be briefly described with the following steps, as illustrated in the following diagram:

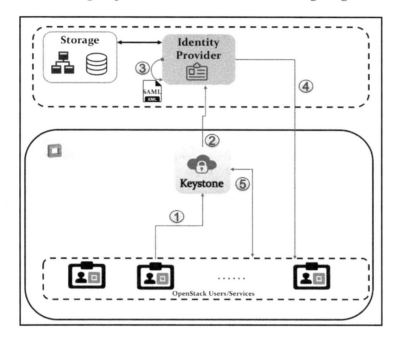

Consider the steps as follows:

1. An OpenStack user or a service requests a resource.
2. As the SP, the Keystone service captures the request and redirects it to the **Single Sign-On** (**SSO**) service.
3. The external IdP (with user/service request SSO request) generates a SAML document response.
4. The external IdP returns the SAML assertion to the requesting user/service.
5. The user/service requests the Keystone service and the assertion resource (obtaining the identity assertion) redirects it (user/service) to the target resource.

In the next section, we will use Shibboleth SSO as an IdP. Make sure that Keystone is using Apache web server (default `mod_wsgi` enabled). This will help us to leverage the web and identity servers through the Apache modules; that includes the Shibboleth one.

Shibboleth is a free, open source project widely used for providing identity federation and SSO capabilities. The Shibboleth IdP uses SAMLv1 and SAMLv2 for SSO and identification. To learn more about Shibboleth, visit the official documentation website found at `https://docs.shib.ncsu.edu/docs/shibworks.html`.

1. Install the Shibboleth IdP in a new server located in the same administrative network segment, so it can reach the cloud controller running the Keystone service. The following installation is based on CentOS 7 Linux OS:

```
# curl -o /etc/yum.repos.d/security:shibboleth.repo
http://download.opensuse.org/repositories/security://shibboleth/Cen
tOS_7/security:shibboleth.repo
# yum install shibboleth
```

2. Once installed, edit the Apache configuration server under the `/etc/httpd/conf.d` directory. A new file `shib.conf` will be located in the same directory as a `httpd` server configuration extension:

```
<Location /v3/auth/OS-FEDERATION/websso/saml2>
  ShibRequestSetting requireSession 1
  AuthType shibboleth
  ShibRequireSession On
  ShibExportAssertion Off
  Require valid-user
</Location>
<Location /Shibboleth.sso>
 SetHandler shib
</Location>
```

Make sure that the new Shibboleth is enabled and loaded by listing the supported modules in the current Apache server setup, using the `apachectl -M` command line tool.

3. Optionally, update the main `/etc/httpd/conf/httpd.conf` file to use server names when handling requests by enabling the `UseCanonicalName` directive:

```
...
UseCanonicalName On
...
```

4. Uncomment the `methods` directive in the main `/etc/keystone/keystone.conf` file by adding the `saml2` option to the `methods` list and the `saml2` plugin:

```
[auth]
...
methods = external,password,token,oauth1,saml2
...
[saml2]
saml2 = keystone.auth.plugins.mapped.Mapped
```

5. To map the Shibboleth entity ID and the Keystone one, assign the `remote_id_attribute` directive the `Shib-Identity-Provider` value in the `federation` section, as follows:

```
[federation]
...
remote_id_attribute = Shib-Identity-Provider
...
```

6. In the same section, make sure to enable the `websso` redirection to the Horizon dashboard:

```
...
trusted_dashboard = http://cc01.pp.com/dashboard/auth/websso/
...
```

7. Locate the Horizon's configuration file and enable the Shibboleth federation protocol by editing the `WEBSSO_CHOICES` directive. The `OPENSTACK_KEYSTONE_URL` option must point to the Keystone authentication URL. Make sure to specify version 3 of the identity API set by the `OPENSTACK_API_VERSIONS` option. Set `WEBSSO_ENABLED` to `True` as the main SSO option in the OpenStack. The `WEBSSO_INITIAL_CHOICE` can be left with default value `credentials`:

```
# vim /etc/openstack_dashboard/local/local_settings.py
...
```

```
OPENSTACK_KEYSTONE_URL = "http://cc01.pp.com:5000/v3"
OPENSTACK_API_VERSIONS = {
    "identity": 3
}
WEBSSO_ENABLED = True
WEBSSO_CHOICES = (
  ("credentials", _("Keystone Credentials")),
  ("saml2", _("Security Assertion Markup Language"))
)
WEBSSO_INITIAL_CHOICE = "credentials"
...
```

8. Edit the default `shibboleth2.xml` file located in the `/etc/shibboleth` directory, by defining access control rules for the SP:

```
<ApplicationDefaults entityID="http://localhost:5000/">
...
    <SSO entityID="http://idp.openstack.pp:8080/idp/shibboleth">
        SAML2 SAML1
    </SSO>
    ...
    <MetadataProvider type="XML"
uri="http://idp.openstack.pp:8080/idp/shibboleth"/>
```

The TestShib website provides a great configuration generator, which is available at `https://www.testshib.org/configure.html`. This will allow us to have a new provider metadata configuration that might need more adjustments.

9. Restart the `shibd` and `httpd` services:

```
# systemctl restart httpd
# systemctl restart shibd
```

10. The last step requires assigning groups and roles in the OpenStack environment. We will need to instruct Keystone to map federated users locally by creating a new federated group and assign it a role-based resource access control. Let's start by creating a new federated domain in OpenStack:

```
# openstack domain create federated_dom
```

11. Create a new user group for the federated users (for role assignment in OpenStack later):

```
# openstack group create federated_grp
```

12. Assign an existing OpenStack role to the new created group within the new `federated` domain. We will assign the `admin` role for this exercise:

```
# openstack role add --group federated_grp --domain federated_dom
admin
```

13. Create a new IdP object in Keystone that will map users into local user group objects:

```
# openstack identity provider create --remote-id http://
idp.openstack.pp:8080/idp/shibboleth fed_idp
```

Make sure to use the exact unique identifier of the IdP in the `--remote-id` argument. It is configured in the XML directive node `<SSO entityID = ...>` in the `shibboleth2.xml` file updated at step 7.

14. The next step requires us to provide a way to refer the federated users and groups in Keystone. This is called mapping and defines a set of rules to map/project external federation attributes to the internal users/groups in Keystone. Let's create a simple mapping rule that uses the `REMOTE_USER` attribute key:

```
# cat > map_rule.json <<EOF
    {
        "local": [
            {
                "user": {
                    "name": "{0}"
                },
                "group": {
                    "domain": {
                        "name": "Default"
                    },
                    "name": "federated_grp"
                }
            }
        ],
        "remote": [
            {
                "type": REMOTE_USER
            }
        ]
    }
    EOF
```

The mapping rules describe the authenticated user attributes to the local Keystone user. The mapping protocol uses the JSON format to present the list of possible rules. In the previous example, the REMOTE_USER key represents the asserted data returned to Keystone. To read more about the mapping engine and the rules in Keystone, please refer to the official OpenStack documentation found at `https://docs.openstack.org/keystone/pike/advanced-topics/federation/federated_identity.html#mapping-combinations`.

15. Create a new mapping object in Keystone using the previous JSON mapping file:

```
# openstack mapping create --rules rule.json idp_map
```

16. The SP Keystone will need specific information to assign the mapping rule which will be used upon each authentication request initiated from the IdP (Shibboleth). This piece of information is encapsulated in protocol that links both IdP and the mapping objects:

```
# openstack federation protocol create mapped --mapping idp_map --identity-provider fed_idp
```

17. Test the new federated Keystone setup by pointing to the Horizon dashboard:

18. Select the **Security Assertion Markup Language** option that will be redirecting to the Shibboleth login web page:

19. By providing a valid pair credentials, the Shibboleth IdP validates them through its store backend (for example, using OpenLDAP). If the credentials are correct, it communicates the SAML assertion with Keystone, creates an ephemeral user, and returns a token to access resources based on the assigned role.

Keystone as SP – OpenID Connect

A second method to support SSO access in OpenStack is using OpenID Connect as IdP. The federation flow pretty much resembles to the SAML setup elaborated on in the previous section. The only difference is that, when using OpenID Connect, the assertion represents a set of claims.

The OpenID Connect federation setup in OpenStack can be briefly described with the following steps, as illustrated in the following diagram:

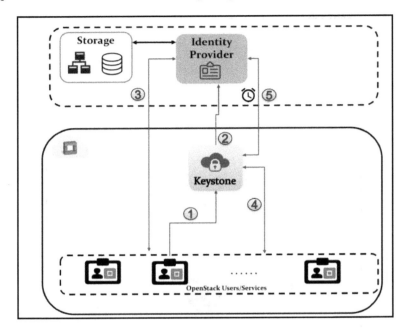

1. An OpenStack user or a service requests a resource.
2. As SP, the Keystone service captures the request and redirects it to the OAuth authentication system.
3. The external IdP requests credentials from the user that will be redirected to the SP once they are validated with an authorization token.
4. The user/service requests access to the resources from Keystone with credentials.
5. The external IdP and SP exchange user information based on the generated authorization token to determine which resources can be accessed.

In the next exercise, we will keep the same running configuration of Keystone by using the Apache web server.

OpenID Connect is an extension implementation of the OAuth authorization and authentication protocol. OAuth uses a tokens concept that provides mechanisms to obtain user profile information to grant access to protected resources. OpenID Connect has become a common authentication protocol and is widely used by several IdPs and applications, such as Google, Facebook, Yahoo and more. It simply leverages an application to contact an IdP and receive information about authenticated users. To read more about OpenID Connect, please refer to the official project website found at `http://openid.net/connect/`.

In this part, we will use Google OAuth APIs as an IdP for OpenID Connect:

1. Our Keystone will be using the Google OAuth authentication system; we will need to create a new project in the Google API console at `https://console.developers.google.com/`:

2. Before generating new credentials, we will need to create a subsequent product. On the left panel, select **Credentials | OAuth consent screen**, choose a product name, and click on **Save**:

3. In the same panel menu, select the **Credentials** tab and click on **Create Credentials**. Select the **OAuth client ID** option from the drop-down menu list:

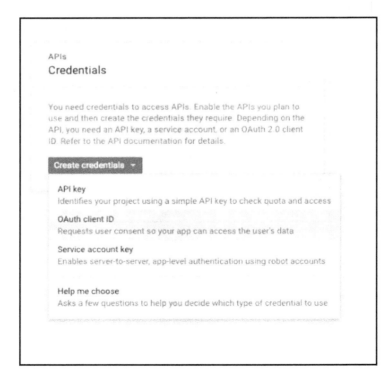

4. Select the **Web Application** option and give it a name:

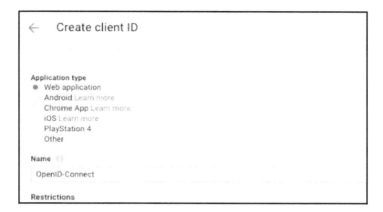

5. We will also need to specify the URI of the Keystone service (client application) and the redirected URI path once users are authenticated against Google. This can be adjusted by configuring the **Authorized JavaScript origins** and **Authorized redirect URIs** options, respectively:

6. By clicking on the **Save** button, a client ID and secret will be generated. We will need to include them in the Keystone configuration afterwards:

Client ID	1016489529489-rc99n5rkc2cfepfdbjh9lvgqdp29g86g.apps.googleusercontent.com
Client secret	NFVoWl_XXdNap9Cypf0BhNMC
Creation date	Jan 17, 2018, 9:27:31 PM

7. Let's move to the OpenStack environment and make sure that the `mod_auth_openidc` module is loaded and enabled by the Apache web server. If not, it can be downloaded and installed as the following:

```
# yum install mod_auth_openidc
```

The current setup is based on CentOS 7. Make sure to enable the EPEL repository. The module can be downloaded and installed from `https://github.com/zmartzone/mod_auth_openidc/releases`. Additionally, verify that the module is present by checking under the `httpd/modules` directory for the presence of the `mod_auth_openidc.so` file.

8. Once downloaded, edit the Keystone virtual host configuration file to load the new module and set the OpenID Connect settings, that include client ID (`OIDCClientID`) and client secret (`OIDCClientSecret`) properties generated by Google OAuth APIs console:

```
...
LoadModule auth_openidc_module
/usr/lib/httpd/modules/mod_auth_openidc.so

<VirtualHost *:5000>
    OIDCClaimPrefix "OIDC-"
    OIDCResponseType "id_token"
    OIDCScope "openid email profile"
    OIDCClientID " 1016489529489-
rc99n5rkc2cfepfdbjh9lvgqdp29g86g.apps.googleusercontent.com "
    OIDCClientSecret NFVoWl_XXdNap9Cypf0BhNMC
    OIDCCryptoPassphrase password
    OIDCRedirectURI "
http://cc01.pp.com:5000/v3/auth/OS-FEDERATION/websso/oidc/redirect
"
    <Location ~ "/v3/auth/OS-FEDERATION/websso/oidc">
```

```
      AuthType openid-connect
      Require valid-user
      LogLevel debug
   </Location>
</VirtualHost>
...
```

 Make sure that the new OpenID Connect module is enabled and loaded by listing the supported modules in the current Apache server setup using the `apachectl -M` command line tool.

9. Update the `methods` directive in the main `/etc/keystone/keystone.conf` file by adding the `oidc` option to the `methods` list and the `oidc` plugin in a new `oidc` section:

    ```
    [auth]
    ...
    methods = external,password,token,oauth1,saml2,oidc
    ...
    [oidc]
    oidc = keystone.auth.plugins.mapped.Mapped
    ```

10. To map the OpenID Connect entity and the Keystone one, set the `remote_id_attribute` directive to an `HTTP_OIDC_ISS` value in the `federation` section, as follows:

    ```
    [federation]
    ...
    remote_id_attribute = HTTP_OIDC_ISS
    ```

11. In the same section, make sure that the `websso` redirects to the Horizon dashboard:

    ```
    ...
    trusted_dashboard = http://cc01.pp.com/dashboard/auth/websso/
    ```

12. Locate the Horizon's configuration file and enable the OpenID Connect federation protocol by editing the WEBSSO_CHOICES directive. Make sure the OPENSTACK_KEYSTONE_URL is pointing to the Keystone authentication URL. We will use the version 3 of the Identity API set by the OPENSTACK_API_VERSIONS setting. The WEBSSO_ENABLED must be set to True to enable SSO in OpenStack. Optionally, the WEBSSO_INITIAL_CHOICE can be left with default value credentials:

```
# vim /etc/openstack_dashboard/local/local_settings.py
...
OPENSTACK_KEYSTONE_URL = "http://cc01.pp.com:5000/v3"
OPENSTACK_API_VERSIONS = {
    "identity": 3
}
WEBSSO_ENABLED = True
WEBSSO_CHOICES = (
  ("credentials", _("Keystone Credentials")),
  ("oidc", _("OpenID Connect"))
)
WEBSSO_INITIAL_CHOICE = "credentials"
...
```

13. Restart the httpd service:

```
# systemctl restart httpd
```

14. Create a new federated domain in OpenStack for OpenID:

```
# openstack domain create fed_dom_open
```

15. Create a local Keystone user group for the federated users:

```
# openstack group create fed_open_grp
```

16. Assign an existing OpenStack role to the newly created group within the new federated domain. We will assign a _member_ role for this exercise:

```
# openstack role add --group fed_open_grp --domain fed_dom_open
_member_
```

17. Create a new IdP object in Keystone that will map the users into the newly
    created local group objects:

    ```
    # openstack identity provider create --remote-id
    https://accounts.google.com google_idp
    ```

18. Create a simple mapping rule that uses the `any_one_of` attribute key. This will
    instruct our mapping to set any coming authenticated user to the `fed_open_grp`
    Keystone local group through Google:

    ```
    # cat > map_rule.json &lt;<EOF
    [
      {
        "local": [
          {
            "group": {
              "id": " e4ee29d32298eaba2109a9a1bea1268a"
              }
            }
          ],
        "remote": [
            {
              "type": "HTTP_OIDC_ISS",
              "any_one_of": [
                "https://accounts.google.com"
                ]
            }
          ]
      }
    ] EOF
    ```

19. Create a new mapping object in Keystone using the previous JSON mapping file:

    ```
    # openstack mapping create --rules rule.json open_map
    ```

20. Create the last Keystone federation resource protocol for the `google_idp` IdP
    object that we recently created:

    ```
    # openstack federation protocol create map_oidc --mapping open_map
    --identity-provider google_idp
    ```

21. Test the new federated Keystone setup by pointing to the Horizon dashboard:

22. Select the **OpenID Connect** option that will be redirecting to the Google sign in the web page:

23. By signing into Google, the web server will set the user attributes based on the initiated OpenID Connect claims as headers. If the credentials are correct, the Keystone service returns a token to access resources based on the assigned role after triggering the mapping engine rule.

Summary

In this chapter, we have revisited the identity service in OpenStack by implementing a federated setup. This new authentication design will allow cloud administrators and operators to decrease the complexity of user management across different enterprise entities and leverage a simple, efficient, and centralized authentication system. We have walked-through different terminologies that have co-existed since the rise of the federation of identity mechanism including the identity and service provider, protocols, and the mapping engine. We have explored its use case with Keystone and configured it as an SP that uses SAML and OpenID Connect protocols. Thanks to the usage of the Apache modules with Keystone, we could manage a full integration of the identity service in an existing authentication environment that includes both Shibboleth and Google authentication API. It is important to remember that users authenticating in both federated layouts are ephemeral. Keystone is getting more empowered with other additional options. Although, in this chapter, we have covered the interaction of Keystone only as a SP, the OpenStack identity service can be used as an IdP which stills under excessive development. This represents a great push towards a cloud identity federation setup that allows centralizing user authentication and increases collaborations across different OpenStack cloud environments.

Consolidating user authentication in OpenStack using identity federation mechanisms can be one of many requirements towards an extended OpenStack cloud environment. As cloud user and resource environments keep increasing, the cloud operator should keep updating the design layout and think about potential strategies to enlarge the OpenStack environment seamlessly. Before taking more extensible steps and join more new services and projects, we will need to measure the capacity of our cloud environment and identify possible bottlenecks when facing different workloads. That adds another critical requirement that addresses the performance of the private cloud which wil be the topic of the next and last chapter.

10
Boosting the Extended Cloud Universe

"By failing to prepare, you are preparing to fail."

–Benjamin Franklin

What would be the most efficient way to deliver a stable, private cloud environment that is ready for production workload at any point in time? The answer to this question could be elaborate and may even take an entire book, tackling different aspects of the cloud environment's availability and flexibility. From a performance perspective, cloud operators should ensure that the underlying infrastructure is not limiting end users access to resources at any moment. Despite the envisaged term *cloud*, resources cannot be limitless unless some metrics and a baseline for an SLA are being defined. This can be seen from several angles—*How can cloud administrators go further with more efficiency regarding management? Can the cloud environment be expanded, with more resources and services to handle more workload with less disturbance of the user experience?* If yes, *how many of them will be needed? What about configuration details? What about new services, do we still need to recalculate resources with the new workload?* To find answers to the preceding questions, cloud operators and architects should monitor the different assets of the running private cloud from day one. Based on the extracted data from the monitoring system around the OpenStack setup, operators can understand the trend usage of the cloud environment. However, unlocking the window limits of the running OpenStack setup won't be easily possible without taking a few precautionary steps, such as conducting benchmarking and performance load tests. That will define the limits of the installed OpenStack environment, and provide quick feedback on how services are behaving in some circumstances.

In this chapter, we will unlock the limits of the running OpenStack cloud environment by understanding the following topics:

- Understanding how benchmarking could help to learn the limits of the cloud
- Conducting load testing using an OpenStack project named **Rally**
- Extending the Rally benchmarking tasks by writing our own plugins

Benchmarking as a Service (BaaS)

As a cloud administrator, monitoring resource usage while running the cloud infrastructure is necessary, but not sufficient. Monitoring helps to identify the possible reasons for a resource's congestion that would trigger a custom alert so that the issues can be immediately resolved. However, that won't be the end of the process. Monitoring data from certain events should be kept as a reference to help you to understand the trend of the cloud's performance. Gathering performance measurements before going to production does not seem a simple exercise, since workloads cannot be predictable at the first run. For this matter, we will need to adopt an approach that ensures an accurate performance measurement. Before tackling this topic, we will first need to identify the required performance areas. Availability, response time, latency, and throughput can be considered as the most essential key indicators for a benchmarking exercise. The latter indicators can be evaluated based on well-defined load and stress tests. Traditionally, deploying a simple application in a production environment requires in the first place the development of additional benchmarking tools dedicated to this application. By putting more load, operators and developers will be able to identify the cause of bottlenecks and performance degradation, if it exists. But *what about the cloud environment landscape?* That would require benchmarking the whole infrastructure, including the control, storage, network, and compute planes. Moreover, we would need to drive test the project's system behavioral feedbacks to ensure that this won't break it. In the OpenStack world, several tools for this exist. In the next section, we will go through them and demonstrate their importance in the OpenStack cloud environment life cycle.

Automating OpenStack profiling with Rally

Rally has been developed as a benchmarking suite dedicated to OpenStack. Obviously, the OpenStack community has anticipated the complexity of driving machine capacity tests initiated by an OpenStack integration test suite, called **Tempest**. The Rally project leverages the capabilities of Tempest by providing ready-to-go or customized scenarios. The hallmark of Rally is the simplicity with which it drives different sets of tests serially or in parallel. It exposes different modules for each OpenStack service that can be extended to a run a specific workload against it. Results can be stored in a local Rally database and visualized in a web page.

Tempest was created as the official integration test suite for OpenStack. Rally was introduced to fill a few gaps by providing a way to store test results for future analysis, which is not present in Tempest. Rally also does not stick to one OpenStack installation. Simply by using the same instance, it is possible to run several tests from the same Rally installation, unlike Tempest tests that need to run against each of your OpenStack setups.

More advanced practices, such as benchmarking data, can be aggregated to illustrate comparisons between subsequent tests and scenarios. Before diving into running our Rally example, let's briefly look at Rally's basic components from a high-level perspective as shown in the following figure:

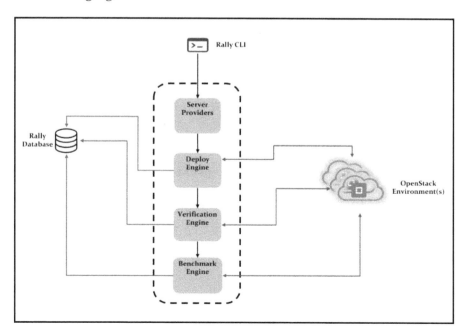

As shown in the previous figure, Rally's basic components are as follows:

- **CLI**: A Rally command-line interface to submit benchmarking tasks
- **Server Providers** (**SPs**): Exposing an SSH-accessible server(s) that can be used as a bare metal machine, a virtual server, or a container
- **Deploy Engine**: Deploying an OpenStack environment on servers generated by the SPs
- **Verification Engine**: Running a suite of tests against the cloud environment (Tempest, by default), collecting, storing, and exposing results
- **Benchmark Engine**: Running customized benchmark scenarios that can be parameterized
- **Database**: Storing benchmark tests and verification results to generate reports using MySQL, SQLite, or PostgreSQL

Installing Rally

Many options are available for installing and starting to play around with Rally in an OpenStack environment. Rally can be installed on any dedicated server, virtual machine, or even containerized environment. Essentially, it only needs to access the OpenStack API endpoint.

In the following section, we will be installing and running Rally on a container. Using Docker enables the automation tests and Rally deployments. Rally tasks will be executed and, once finished, the container will exit. Additionally, it will be very beneficial to have an immutable test environment that can be portable so that the cloud team will be in the same test suite version.

Let's start by Dockerizing the Rally environment:

1. Set up the Docker environment by installing the following packages:

   ```
   # yum install -y device-mapper-persistent-data lvm2 yum-utils
   ```

2. Install Docker by setting the yum configuration manager to the Docker Community Edition:

   ```
   # yum-config-manager --add-repo
   https://download.docker.com/linux/centos/docker-ce.repo
   # yum install docker-ce
   # systemctl start docker
   ```

3. Create a new Docker file to install Rally and OpenStack CLI Pike release:

```
FROM centos:7
MAINTAINER OpenStacker
RUN yum install -y
https://repos.fedorapeople.org/repos/openstack/openstack-pike/rdo-r
elease-pike-1.noarch.rpm
RUN yum update -y
RUN yum -y install \
        openstack-rally \
        gcc \
        libffi-devel \
        python-devel \
        openssl-devel \
        gmp-devel \
        libxml2-devel \
        libxslt-devel \
        postgresql-devel \
        redhat-rpm-config \
        wget \
        openstack-selinux \
        openstack-utils && \
        yum clean all
RUN rally-manage --config-file /etc/rally/rally.conf db recreate
```

4. Build the Rally image and tag it as `latest`:

```
# docker build -t rally/latest .
```

```
Step 6/6 : RUN rally-manage --config-file /etc/rally/rally.conf db recreate
 ---> Running in e61bff71ed64
Removing intermediate container e61bff71ed64
 ---> 9d82099bf324
Successfully built 9d82099bf324
Successfully tagged rally/latest:latest
```

5. Run the created image to start using Rally:

```
# docker run -dit rally/latest
```

6. Run `bash` inside the container to start using Rally CLI:

```
# docker ps -a
```

```
CONTAINER ID    IMAGE                 COMMAND      CREATED          STATUS          PORTS    NAMES
849957108b27    rally/latest:latest   "/bin/bash"  11 seconds ago   Up 10 seconds            objective_jackson
```

```
# docker exec -it 849957108b27 bash
[root@849957108b27 /]#
```

7. To enable Rally to run tests against the OpenStack environment, we will need to register the existing cloud by passing the `admin` authentication information. This can be set either by sourcing the admin environment variables or by using a deployment file, such as the following:

```
# vim deploy_os.json
{
    "type": "mycloud",
    "auth_url": "http://10.11.242.11:5000/v2.0",
    "region_name": "RegionOne",
    "admin": {
        "username": "admin",
        "password": "54c789f34d374468",
        "tenant_name": "admin"
    }
}
```

8. Run the Rally deployment by specifying the `deploy` file, as follows:

```
# rally deployment create --file=deploy_os.json --name mycloud
```

```
2018-01-30 22:05:35.172 28 INFO rally.deployment.engines.existing [-] Save deployment 'mycloud' (uuid
+--------------------------------------+----------------------+---------+------------------+--------+
| uuid                                 | created_at           | name    | status           | active |
+--------------------------------------+----------------------+---------+------------------+--------+
| e63b2334-51f3-4600-8c86-4db25179e24e | 2018-01-30T22:05:35  | mycloud | deploy->finished |        |
+--------------------------------------+----------------------+---------+------------------+--------+
Using deployment: e63b2334-51f3-4600-8c86-4db25179e24e
```

> The Rally deployment command line can use environment variables
> instead of a JSON file by replacing the `--file` flag with `--fromenv`.

9. The Rally deployment will generate an `openrc` file, located by default under
   `~/.rally`. To create resources in the OpenStack environment, we will need to
   source the `openrc` file:

```
# source ~/.rally/openrc
```

10. The last step should grant Rally access to the OpenStack services. This can be
    verified by checking the different authenticated OpenStack endpoints for the
    Rally container using the following command:

```
# rally deployment check
```

```
Available services:
+---------------+------------------+-----------+
| Service       | Service Type     | Status    |
+---------------+------------------+-----------+
| __unknown__   | alarming         | Available |
| __unknown__   | placement        | Available |
| __unknown__   | volumev2         | Available |
| __unknown__   | volumev3         | Available |
| ceilometer    | metering         | Available |
| cinder        | volume           | Available |
| cloud         | cloudformation   | Available |
| glance        | image            | Available |
| gnocchi       | metric           | Available |
| heat          | orchestration    | Available |
| keystone      | identity         | Available |
| magnum        | container-infra  | Available |
| neutron       | network          | Available |
| nova          | compute          | Available |
| sahara        | data-processing  | Available |
| swift         | object-store     | Available |
+---------------+------------------+-----------+
```

Benchmarking with Rally

Now that we have a fully Dockerized Rally environment up and running, we can go further by setting up a first scenario. We will start by tackling the performance of the container orchestration engine in OpenStack, called Magnum. The benchmark aims to measure the duration of creating and listing Pods based on Kubernetes under a specific load. The scenario can be described as follows:

```
# vim create_and_list_kube.json
{
    "MagnumClusters.create_and_list_clusters": [
      {
        "runner": {
          "type": "constant",
          "concurrency": 1,
          "times": 1
        },
        "args": {
          "node_count": 1
        },
        "context": {
          "cluster_templates": {
            "dns_nameserver": "8.8.8.8",
            "external_network_id": "external_network",
            "flavor_id": "m1.small",
            "docker_volume_size": 5,
            "coe": "kubernetes",
            "image_id": "fedora_atomic",
            "network_driver": "flannel"
          },
          "users": {
            "users_per_tenant": 1,
            "tenants": 1
          }
        },
        "sla": {
          "failure_rate": {
            "max": 0
          }
        }
      }
    ]
}
```

The benchmarking test scenario invoked a predefined method, MagnumClusters.create_and_list_clusters, with the following parameters:

- runner: This specifies the occurrence of the workload run. This can be defined using four different fields:
    - constant: Run the test for a fixed number of times.
    - constant_for_duration: Run the test several times until a set time.
    - serial: Run the test for a fixed number of times in one benchmark thread.
    - periodic: Run the test for a predefined interval of time.
- args: This uses customized values that can be passed to the method at run-time.
- context: This describes the main benchmarking environment by defining attributes for each context type. A context could define the number of tenants and associated users in the OpenStack project.
- sla: This shows the average success rate of the running benchmark test.

In our example, we are creating a load based on a constant value of a one-time run for one iteration of the create_and_list_clusters method. Note that the concurrency value is set to 1; the task will be executed only in one iteration. The context stanza highlights the definition of the cluster template to be created in the cluster_templates section. The create_and_list_clusters method requires the definition of template attributes so Rally can create the cluster within existing resources. This includes the name of the image, the instance flavor name to run the cluster, and an existing public network. The sla stanza marks a condition to have a total of a 100% success rate with 0 cluster creation failure attempts.

Running the `create_and_list_clusters` scenario method can be performed by using the following `rally` command:

```
# rally task start create_and_list_kube.json
```

```
-----------------------------------------------------------------
Preparing input task
-----------------------------------------------------------------

Task is:
{
    "MagnumClusters.create_and_list_clusters": [
        {
            "runner": {
                "type": "constant",
                "concurrency": 1,
```

```
2018-02-05 22:07:06.864 1630 INFO rally.task.context [-] Task 978ce786-dca7-426a-93c9-aacc28a96acb | Context cluster_templates@openstack setup() finished in 5.48 sec
2018-02-05 22:07:06.865 1630 INFO rally.task.context [-] Task 978ce786-dca7-426a-93c9-aacc28a96acb | Context cleanup@openstack setup() started
2018-02-05 22:07:06.865 1630 INFO rally.task.context [-] Task 978ce786-dca7-426a-93c9-aacc28a96acb | Context cleanup@openstack setup() finished in 0.23 msec
2018-02-05 22:07:06.896 1763 INFO rally.task.runner [-] Task 978ce786-dca7-426a-93c9-aacc28a96acb | ITER: 1 START
```

Extending benchmarking with plugins

The Rally code has been developed to be extendable and enables users to customize their benchmarking tests by writing their own plugins and task definitions. A complete reference of the plugins suite in Rally can be found at
`http://docs.xrally.xyz/projects/openstack/en/latest/plugins/plugin_reference.html#plugin-reference`. This is not limited to task scenarios, but also leverages writing runners, contexts, charts, SLAs, and deployments as plugins.

To list the available plugins referenced in a Rally environment, run the following command:

```
# rally plugin list
```

```
2018-02-04 14:33:33.374 3982 INFO rally.common.plugin.discover [-] Loading plugins from directories /usr/share/openstack-rally/samples/plugins/*
2018-02-04 14:33:33.440 3982 INFO rally.common.plugin.discover [-]        Loaded module with plugins: /usr/share/openstack-rally/samples/plugins/list_flavors.py
+-------------+------------+-----------+----------------------------------------------------------------------------+
| Plugin base | Name       | Platform  | Title                                                                      |
+-------------+------------+-----------+----------------------------------------------------------------------------+
| Chart       | Lines      | default   | Display results as generic chart with lines.                               |
| Chart       | Pie        | default   | Display results as pie, calculate average values for additive data.        |
| Chart       | StackedArea| default   | Display results as stacked area.                                           |
| Chart       | StatsTable | default   | Calculate statistics for additive data and display it as table.            |
| Chart       | Table      | default   | Display complete output as table, can not be used for additive data.       |
| Chart       | TextArea   | default   | Arbitrary text                                                             |
| Context     | allow_ssh  | openstack | Sets up security groups for all users to access VM via SSH.                |
| Context     | api_versions | openstack | Context for specifying OpenStack clients versions and service types.     |
```

The next command describes in detail
the MagnumClusters.create_and_list_clusters plugin:

```
# rally plugin show MagnumClusters.create_and_list_clusters
```

The output of the preceding command can be shown as follows:

```
create cluster and then list all clusters.

NAME
        MagnumClusters.create_and_list_clusters
PLATFORM
        openstack
MODULE
        rally.plugins.openstack.scenarios.magnum.clusters
PARAMETERS
+------------------------+-------------------------------------------+
| name                   | description                               |
+------------------------+-------------------------------------------+
| node_count             | the cluster node count.                   |
|                        |                                           |
| cluster_template_uuid  | optional, if user want to use an existing |
|                        | cluster_template                          |
|                        |                                           |
| kwargs                 | optional additional arguments for cluster creation |
+------------------------+-------------------------------------------+
```

As illustrated in the previous screenshot, the plugin supports several parameters that can be specified in the args section of the scenario file.

Let's create a sample scenario plugin that creates and then deletes Magnum clusters. The scenario will drive a benchmarking test to create and delete clusters in Kubernetes as the selected COE target. For this matter, we will need to hook a simple Python script and save it under the Rally plugins directory:

1. Source the default plugins path of the rally directory by exporting the following variable environment:

   ```
   # export RALLY_PLUGIN_PATHS=/usr/share/openstack-
   rally/samples/plugins/
   ```

2. Make sure that Rally can successfully load existing plugins under the specified directory in the previous step:

```
# rally plugin list
```

```
2018-02-13 20:55:36.432 108 INFO rally.common.plugin.discover [-] Loading plugins from directories /usr/share/openstack-rally/samples/plugins/*
```

3. Create a new Python module under the `plugins` directory by importing the necessary Rally classes and subclasses:

```
from rally import consts
from rally.plugins.openstack import scenario
from rally.plugins.openstack.scenarios.magnum import utils
from rally.plugins.openstack.scenarios.nova import utils as
nova_utils
from rally.task import validation
```

4. Add validation and scenario decorators to use Magnum services within the OpenStack platform. Note that the name of the scenario plugin is being added in the scenario decorator:

```
@validation.add("required_services",
services=[consts.Service.MAGNUM])
@validation.add("required_platform", platform="openstack",
users=True)
@scenario.configure(
    context={"cleanup@openstack": ["magnum.clusters",
"nova.keypairs"]},
    name="ScenarioPlugin.create_and_delete_magnum_clusters",
    platform="openstack")
```

5. Create a class named `CreateAndDeleteClusters` that inherits from the base `MagnumScenario` class:

```
class CreateAndDeleteClusters(utils.MagnumScenario):

    def run(self, node_count, **kwargs):
        """create cluster and then delete.
        :param node_count: the cluster node count.
        :param cluster_template_uuid: optional, if user want to use an
existing cluster_template
        :param force_delete: force delete cluster if set to True
        :param kwargs: optional additional arguments for cluster
creation
        """
        cluster_template_uuid = kwargs.get("cluster_template_uuid",
```

```
None)
        if cluster_template_uuid is None:
            cluster_template_uuid =
self.context["tenant"]["cluster_template"]
        else:
            del kwargs["cluster_template_uuid"]

        nova_scenario = nova_utils.NovaScenario({
            "user": self.context["user"],
            "task": self.context["task"],
            "config": {"api_versions": self.context["config"].get(
                "api_versions", [])}
        })
        keypair = nova_scenario._create_keypair()
```

6. Extend the Python module by declaring the Magnum cluster creation method,
   followed by the exception line code:

```
new_cluster = self._create_cluster(cluster_template_uuid,
node_count, keypair=keypair,
**kwargs)
            self.assertTrue(new_cluster, "Failed to create new
cluster")
```

7. Declare the Magnum cluster deletion method, followed by the exception line
   code:

```
self.delete_cluster(new_cluster, force=force_delete)
        self.assertIn(new_cluster.uuid, "Cluster cannot be found
and deleted")
```

8. Save the Python module file and make sure that Rally can load it successfully by
   listing the existing plugins:

   ```
   # rally plugin list
   ```

```
2018-02-13 21:36:53.494 144 INFO rally.common.plugin.discover [-]        Loaded module with plugins: /usr/share/openstack-rally/samples/plugins/create_delete_magnum.py

| Scenario   | ScenarioGroupTemplates.create_delete_node_group_templates   | openstack | create and delete Sahara Node Group Templates.
| Scenario   | ScenarioPlugin.create_and_delete_magnum_clusters            | openstack | create cluster and then delete.
| Scenario   | ScenarioPlugin.list_clusters_kube                           | openstack | list kube clusters.
```

9. Use the Rally show sub command to check out the new plugin details as, coded in the Python module:

```
create cluster and then delete.
-------------------------------------------------------------------------

NAME
        ScenarioPlugin.create_and_delete_magnum_clusters
PLATFORM
        openstack
MODULE
        create_delete_magnum
PARAMETERS
+----------------------------+------------------------------------------+
| name                       | description                              |
+----------------------------+------------------------------------------+
| node_count                 | the cluster node count.                  |
|                            |                                          |
| cluster_template_uuid      | optional, if user want to use an existing|
|                            | cluster_template                         |
|                            |                                          |
| force_delete               | force delete cluster if set to True      |
|                            |                                          |
| kwargs                     | optional additional arguments for cluster creation |
+----------------------------+------------------------------------------+
```

10. Create a simple scenario pointing to the created Python plugin `ScenarioPlugin.create_and_delete_magnum_clusters`. The following task will instruct Rally to run a load in a constant mode 50 times. The load will create a Kubernetes cluster of two nodes by creating five tenants with five users in each. To simulate multiple cluster creation and deletion executions at the same time, the scenario will be running concurrently by running four tasks for each iteration. If one creation and deletion cluster attempt fails, the Rally task will exit, noting a success rate of 0%, which is defined in the `sla` section:

```
{
    "ScenarioPlugin.create_and_delete_magnum_clusters": [
        {
            "runner": {
                "type": "constant",
                "concurrency": 4,
                "times": 50
            },
            "args": {
                "node_count": 2,
                "force_delete": "True"
```

```
      },
      "context": {
        "cluster_templates": {
          "dns_nameserver": "8.8.8.8",
          "external_network_id": "public",
          "flavor_id": "m1.small",
          "docker_volume_size": 5,
          "coe": "kubernetes",
          "image_id": "fedora-latest",
          "network_driver": "flannel"
        },
        "users": {
          "users_per_tenant": 5,
          "tenants": 5
        }
      },
      "sla": {
        "failure_rate": {
          "max": 0
        }
      }
    }
  ]
}
```

11. Run the new Rally task to gather more customized benchmarking data for the
    OpenStack performance based on the previous extended scenario. As described
    in the previous step, the generated workload might be heavy for a running
    OpenStack setup in a production environment. This can lead to performance
    issues while OpenStack cluster is fully operating and serving production user
    requests. Rally provides a useful way to abort generating more load once the
    defined SLA requirements are met by adding the `abort-on-sla-failure` flag:

    ```
    # rally task start --abort-on-sla-failure create-and-delete-magnum-
    clusters.json
    ```

The output of the preceding command can be shown in the following screenshot:

```
        "image_id": "fedora-latest",
        "network_driver": "flannel"
    },
    "users": {
        "users_per_tenant": 5,
        "tenants": 1
    }
  },
  "sla": {
    "failure_rate": {
      "max": 0
    }
  }
  ]
}

Task syntax is correct :)
Running Rally version 0.10.0
----------------------------------------------------------------
Task  758ffbbc-2770-4f71-b9cc-97b66cafacb0: started
----------------------------------------------------------------

Running Task... This can take a while...
```

12. The extended example scenario might lead to a success rate of 0%, due to the restricted SLA value:

```
                          Response Times (sec)
+-----------+--------------+-------------+-------------+-----------+-----------+---------+
| Min (sec) | Median (sec) | 90%ile (sec)| 95%ile (sec)| Max (sec) | Avg (sec) | Success |
+-----------+--------------+-------------+-------------+-----------+-----------+---------+
| 3.866     | 10.256       | 19.705      | 19.71       | 19.714    | 10.806    | 0.0%    |
| 3.866     | 10.256       | 19.706      | 19.71       | 19.714    | 10.806    | 0.0%    |
| 2.866     | 9.256        | 18.706      | 18.71       | 18.714    | 9.806     | 0.0%    |
| 1.0       | 1.0          | 1.0         | 1.0         | 1.0       | 1.0       | 0.0%    |
+-----------+--------------+-------------+-------------+-----------+-----------+---------+
```

13. The first diagnosis of the extended scenario can be conducted from Rally debug output, which can be the first guideline for performance investigation in the current OpenStack deployment:

```
ceErrorStatus: Resource <Server: s_rally_8d021c19_ajlMm2cB> has ERROR status.
  Fault: {u'message': u'No valid host was found. ', u'code': 500, u'created': u'2018-02-01T23:10:11Z'}
2018-02-01 23:10:12.614 318 INFO rally.task.runner [-] Task 22e6c6c3-c346-48e2-be25-5a86bf20a46f | ITER:
2018-02-01 23:10:14.139 319 INFO rally.task.runner [-] Task 22e6c6c3-c346-48e2-be25-5a86bf20a46f | ITER:
```

Summary

In this chapter, we have looked at performance analysis in an existing and operating OpenStack environment. The chapter puts an additional requirement under the scope that must exist in the life cycle of a private cloud environment. We have uncovered a straightforward way to exercise benchmarking and load tests using Rally. As this is becoming one of the OpenStack incubated projects, you should understand the capabilities of this tool by performing reproducible test suite cases and scenarios. Rally has become an official solution for OpenStack cloud operators to trace scalability and detect performance anomalies at an early stage. Although the OpenStack community has developed hundreds of scenarios and tasks included in Rally out of the box, this chapter has demonstrated another hallmark of Rally as a pluggable platform. We have created our own sample plugin using Python modules and automatically loaded by Rally. This should help operators to extend the capabilities of the Rally platform based on the profile match of the existing OpenStack private cloud environment. At this point, you should be able to successfully operate your existing OpenStack setup while meeting the agreed SLA requirements and increasing user experience satisfaction.

You should be now able to bring the OpenStack journey to the next stage by selecting the excessive developed features from the latest releases of OpenStack.

Our great hope is that you take the opportunities that were presented in this book and leverage your featured operating OpenStack private cloud to achieve whatever goals you want.

Other Books You May Enjoy

If you enjoyed this book, you may be interested in these other books by Packt:

OpenStack Bootcamp
Vinoth Kumar Selvaraj

ISBN: 978-1-78829-330-3

- Understand the functions and features of each core component of OpenStack and a real-world comparison
- Develop an understanding of the components of IaaS and PaaS clouds built with OpenStack
- Get a high-level understanding of architectural design in OpenStack
- Discover how you can use OpenStack Horizon with all of the OpenStack core components
- Understand network traffic flow with Neutron
- Build an OpenStack private cloud from scratch
- Get hands-on training with the OpenStack command line, administration, and deployment

OpenStack Cloud Computing Cookbook - Fourth Edition

Kevin Jackson, Cody Bunch, Egle Sigler, James Denton

ISBN: 978-1-78839-876-3

- Understand, install, configure, and manage a complete OpenStack Cloud platform using OpenStack-Ansible
- Configure networks, routers, load balancers, and more with Neutron
- Use Keystone to setup domains, roles, groups and user access
- Learn how to use Swift and setup container access control lists
- Gain hands-on experience and familiarity with Horizon, the OpenStack Dashboard user interface
- Automate complete solutions with our recipes on Heat, the OpenStack Orchestration service as well as using Ansible to orchestrate application workloads
- Follow practical advice and examples to run OpenStack in production

Leave a review - let other readers know what you think

Please share your thoughts on this book with others by leaving a review on the site that you bought it from. If you purchased the book from Amazon, please leave us an honest review on this book's Amazon page. This is vital so that other potential readers can see and use your unbiased opinion to make purchasing decisions, we can understand what our customers think about our products, and our authors can see your feedback on the title that they have worked with Packt to create. It will only take a few minutes of your time, but is valuable to other potential customers, our authors, and Packt. Thank you!

Index

www.ingramcontent.com/pod-product-compliance
Lightning Source LLC
Chambersburg PA
CBHW080628060326
40690CB00021B/4848